GROWING UP LATINX

CRITICAL PERSPECTIVES ON YOUTH
General Editors: Amy L. Best, Lorena Garcia, and Jessica K. Taft

Fast-Food Kids: French Fries, Lunch Lines, and Social Ties
Amy L. Best

White Kids: Growing Up with Privilege in a Racially Divided America
Margaret A. Hagerman

Growing Up Queer: Kids and the Remaking of LGBTQ Identity
Mary Robertson

The Kids Are in Charge: Activism and Power in Peru's Movement of Working Children
Jessica K. Taft

Coming of Age in Iran: Poverty and the Struggle for Dignity
Manata Hashemi

The World Is Our Classroom: Extreme Parenting and the Rise of Worldschooling
Jennie Germann Molz

The Homeschool Choice: Parents and the Privatization of Education
Kate Henley Averett

Growing Up Latinx: Coming of Age in a Time of Contested Citizenship
Jesica Siham Fernández

Growing Up Latinx

Coming of Age in a Time of Contested Citizenship

Jesica Siham Fernández

NEW YORK UNIVERSITY PRESS
New York

NEW YORK UNIVERSITY PRESS
New York
www.nyupress.org

© 2021 by New York University
All rights reserved

References to Internet websites (URLs) were accurate at the time of writing. Neither the author nor New York University Press is responsible for URLs that may have expired or changed since the manuscript was prepared.

Library of Congress Cataloging-in-Publication Data
Names: Fernández, Jesica Siham, author.
Title: Growing up Latinx : coming of age in a time of contested citizenship / Jesica Siham Fernández.
Description: New York : New York University Press, [2021] | Series: Critical perspectives on youth | Includes bibliographical references and index.
Identifiers: LCCN 2021003109 | ISBN 9781479801213 (hardback) | ISBN 9781479801220 (paperback) | ISBN 9781479801237 (ebook) | ISBN 9781479801244 (ebook other)
Subjects: LCSH: Hispanic American youth—Social conditions. | Hispanic American youth—Ethnic identity. | Children of immigrants—United States—Ethnic identity. | Children of immigrants—United States—Social conditions. | Group identity—United States. | Citizenship—United States.
Classification: LCC E184.S75 F475 2021 | DDC 305.23089/68073—dc23
LC record available at https://lccn.loc.gov/2021003109

New York University Press books are printed on acid-free paper, and their binding materials are chosen for strength and durability. We strive to use environmentally responsible suppliers and materials to the greatest extent possible in publishing our books.

Manufactured in the United States of America

10 9 8 7 6 5 4 3 2 1

Also available as an ebook

For Hossein Talebi. May we continue embracing life together.

CONTENTS

Preface	ix
Introduction: Latinx Youth Growing Up in the United States	1
PART I. MAKING MEANING OF CITIZENSHIP	29
1. Legality as Having *Papeles*	34
2. Socializing Future Citizens	55
3. Rights as a Privilege	79
PART II. EMBODYING CITIZENSHIP	107
4. Citizenship as a Sociopolitical Process	112
5. Claiming Rights beyond State Relations	147
Conclusion: Reimagining Citizenship, Legality, and Rights	169
Acknowledgments	183
Appendix	187
Notes	189
Bibliography	203
Index	219
About the Author	225

PREFACE

Every now and then, at family gatherings or when asked to give an update on *el libro* (the book, this book), as my parents have come to call it, my mother shares a story—to whoever will listen—about the time an immigration border patrol agent interrogated me at the El Paso-Ciudad Juárez immigration checkpoint. I was six years old. My parents could not provide the required documentation or proof that I could "legally" enter the United States. I had no US "green card" (i.e., legal permanent residence, LPR), visa, or passport, only a birth certificate with Huandacareo (Michoacán, México) indicating my place of birth. I was born in Morelia, but my parents had registered me in their hometown for convenience. As the immigration border patrol agent questioned my parents' status, requiring proof of their "documented" status, they showed their green cards and Mexican *matrículas* (identification cards).

Uncertain about my status, however, the immigration border patrol agent quizzed me about seemingly every aspect of my life. Who were these people? Where was I coming from? Where was I going? Where did I go to school, and what were the names of my teachers and friends? But with my quasi-articulate broken English, and an overemphasis on rolling my *r*'s and sounding my *s*'s, I answered all that he asked: My parents. From my *abuelitas en ONE-da-KA-rreO*. To our home in Tracy. I go to Southwest Park Elementary School. My teacher is Miss Soto and my friends, Jennylin, Maritza, and Yolanda. The responses must have appeased the immigration border patrol agent because we then crossed to *el norte* (the north, the United States).

According to my mother, that was the last time, out of many before, that I crossed the border *sin papeles* (without papers, legal documentation). On account of that experience, and the fear of my being "taken," my parents vowed never to risk the journey back to Huandacareo without the proper documentation. A few years later, at the age of eight, I received my green card. Twelve years after, as I approached my undergraduate college graduation, I filed for naturalization and in less than a year I became a naturalized citizen of the United States.

As a Latinx youth in a mixed-status family, growing up among other transmigrant families in the Central Valley of California, I never questioned the legality of my border-crossing experiences or those of my parents.[1] Most of the families and youth I knew and grew up with moved across the México-United States border season by season for agricultural work. As I recall, we never spoke explicitly or expressed our fears about the risks of "crossing," deportation, or family separations.

My early childhood experience of contending with questions of citizenship, legality, and rights, as well as belonging in school, family, and community contexts, resurfaced during my time as a program coordinator and researcher in the Change 4 Good afterschool program while I pursued my graduate studies in the social psychology program at the University of California, Santa Cruz. Through my experiences, interactions, and relationship building with the young people in Change 4 Good, I learned of their school, family, and community experiences, and how questions of home and belonging were often tethered to their fears and concerns over their families' safety and well-being amidst the anti-immigration discourses and policies that circulated throughout their lives. To a degree, my mother's fears of having me taken when I was interrogated as a child paralleled the concerns that some Latinx youth were describing in our conversations and activities in Change 4 Good. The questions and conversations we engaged in unearthed repressed memories of my experiences growing up Latinx between México and the United States. This became the starting point for my research interests and scholarship.

From a very young age, questions of citizenship and belonging perplexed me because I witnessed my own family grapple with the racist nativism that still informs dominant US-based constructions of citizenship. In bearing witness to personal family experiences of deportation, as well as Change 4 Good Latinx youth's similarly expressed concerns, I was reminded of my relationship to *papeles* (legal documentation) and the racist discourses of "illegality"—including the expression *no eres de aquí* (you are not from here [United States])—that intersect with age and other social categories. I grew up learning how to live and move across borders—physical, cultural, political, and imagined. Among Latinx youth in Change 4 Good, I observed similar social and political subjectivities.

Latinx youth growing up in the United States—spanning immigrant and mixed-status families—often experience and make meaning of citizenship, legality, and rights in unique ways that differ from those of non-Latinx immigrant youth.[2] In *Growing Up Latinx*, I feature some of the stories, reflections, and experiences associated with citizenship shared by thirteen preadolescent Latinx youth between the ages of nine and twelve in the Change 4 Good afterschool program. I describe how their lived experiences in school, family, and community contexts shaped their subjectivities and meaning-making about citizenship as a status of legality, a practice beholden to certain rights, and a sociopolitical embodiment of agency and belonging. The experiences Latinx youth shared frequently resurfaced my questions about the meaning of citizenship. What does it *mean* to be a citizen? How does it *feel* to be a citizen? Who is *seen*, or treated, as a citizen? And why are young people excluded from these conversations when their lives are often shaped by hegemonic discourses associated with US-based constructions of citizenship—such as documented, legal citizen, good student citizen, and future citizen? As a scholar, I find that the border-crossing experiences that shaped my childhood now inform and guide my intellectual curiosities to render visible people's stories, agency, and actions that are seldom noticed and affirmed.

Interweaving and reflecting upon the stories of Latinx youth, who like me grew up unsettled by the ageism[3] and racist nativism[4] that surrounded their lives, I describe how Latinx youth confronted and reimagined US-based constructions of citizenship, legality, and rights. Informed by my relationships, experiences, and interactions with Change 4 Good Latinx youth, I describe how they critically, socially, and politically drew from their lived experiences to engage their agency and make claims to citizenship and rights. By examining how Latinx youth defined and challenged constructions of citizenship, legality, and rights, as well as their poignant intersections, this book describes the social and political subjectivities of Latinx youth who are citizens in their own right—embodying and enacting agency in their school, family, and community contexts.

Social subjectivities are the meanings attached to the social and cultural aspects, experiences, and conditions of life that inform an understanding of reality.[5] Political subjectivities account for the critical awareness of institutional systems of power that shape social experiences, and how through this understanding, actions, often political, are embodied and enacted.[6] Thus, social and political subjectivities reflect an expression of agency through a person's understandings of themselves as being embedded in structures of power that shape their contexts and inform their worldviews. *Growing Up Latinx* centers Latinx youth voices to describe the development of what I conceptualize as sociopolitical citizenship.

Through an ethnography of Change 4 Good, I demonstrate and describe Latinx youth constructions of citizenship, particularly how these meanings were deployed to shape their lived experiences and agency as sociopolitical citizens. The intent is to demonstrate how Latinx youth made meaning at the same time as they grappled with and resisted the hegemony of citizenship discourses, as well as legality and rights, that surfaced in their lives.[7] Scholarship examining the intersections of racism, nativism, and ageism that imbue Latinx youth lives is imperative in a US political context that continues to dehumanize and compromise the quality of life, well-being, and dignity of Latinx immigrant families and their children. It is of critical importance that we understand the contexts in which Latinx youth grow up in the United States to develop, engage, and make meaning of their positionalities as citizens, rights bearers, active participants, and in some cases advocates for their families. This effort to comprehend is especially necessary for the democratic thriving of Latinx immigrant communities living in the US nation-state.

Growing Up Latinx features the stories, reflections, and lived experiences of Latinx youth and their meaning-making about citizenship, legality, and rights in the United States, with the intention of expanding and challenging society's views about who these young people are. The book invites readers, scholars, educators, students, parents, youth advocates, and anyone interested in understanding the lives of Latinx youth to reconsider meanings of citizenship that exclude young people. I encourage you to engage in three actions as you read. First, we can acknowledge and recognize that Latinx youth have agency. If provided with the resources, conditions, and opportunities to make their voices heard, they will speak up! And we must listen. Second, it is imperative that we support and encourage the sociopolitical citizenship of Latinx youth by cultivating their agency in the development of their social identities, critical consciousness, socioemotional awareness, and political participation to create change in their communities. Third, each of us needs to challenge deficit views of Latinx youth that do not attend to the complexities of their lived experiences as young people who are embedded in social structures that view them as noncitizens, or future citizens at best. Centering the voices and experiences of Latinx youth can contribute to the reimagining and transformation of US-based constructions of citizenship, legality, and rights.

Introduction

Latinx Youth Growing Up in the United States

On an early afternoon in November, Lina and I sat on the bleachers of the multipurpose room of her elementary school watching students rehearse for the talent show performance. Lina is an outspoken, vibrant, and cheerful fourth-grader. However, on this day Lina appeared unusually quiet. I perceived that something was unsettling her, as she seemed deep in thought. I sat next to her, as she squatted hugging her hands over her knees in a cannonball-like shape. Slowly she adjusted her seat on the bleachers. Seated next to her, I leaned in to ask, "¿Estás bien?" (Are you okay?), to which she replied with a headshake, indicating *no*. I noticed her red eyes and sad expression as her face flooded with tears. I asked if she needed a hug, and as she leaned in she began to sob. I cried too. The reason for her pain was unknown to me, but I felt her pain. I held her as I asked again if she was okay, and she shared that she was afraid of the thought of having her father taken away. As she gasped for air and contained her tears, she began to explain how in recent weeks she had learned of the raids happening in the community, of deported family acquaintances, and of the fears and concerns her family was experiencing. I then understood the cause of her tears and pensiveness. Wanting to offer words of comfort but unable to find any, I listened to Lina share that her father "no tiene papeles" (has no papers, legal documentation), and "no es de aquí, como yo" (is not from here [United States], like me), and that she feared he'd be deported. She cried, "¡No quiero que se lo lleven!" (I don't want him to be taken).[1]

Lina, a second-generation Mexican American elementary schoolaged student in a mixed-status family, was a vibrant, sociable, and outspoken youth. I met Lina during my time in the Change 4 Good youth participatory action research (YPAR) afterschool program located in a predominantly Latinx immigrant, low-income unincorporated community in the Central Coast of California. From the summer of 2009 through the summer of 2013, I helped coordinate Change 4 Good, and during this time I learned about Latinx youth lived experiences, like Lina's, and how these informed their thoughts on citizenship, legality, and rights. Lina's fears were heightened by the racist nativism and anti-immigrant sentiments that surrounded the political climate of an election year, hegemonic discourses that have become commonplace and amplified in the current context. Lina's concerns, like those of many other Latinx youth in mixed-status families, reflected her experiences as a youth coming of age in the United States.

Lina's story remains most vivid in my memory because it pained me to be reminded that there was very little that I could do to protect her family and prevent her from experiencing such anguish and possible loss. All I could do was comfort her, share with her my own immigration experiences, and offer a sense of hope that all would be well. Yet what I shared with Lina could not guarantee her father's safety. I could not guarantee the rights, dignity, and respect that all Latinx and undocumented immigrants deserve. I also could not assure her a sense of belonging or a supportive environment that she and all Latinx youth are entitled to, regardless of their own or their parents' immigrant status.[2] To a degree, Lina's fears of having her father "taken" paralleled some of the experiences my own family often endured because of our mixed status, fears that continue to be experienced by youth today.

Growing up in the United States, I, too, was seen as "not from here," like Lina's father. As trespassers, border crossers, and immigrants, Latinx hold differing positionalities and lived experiences in the United States. Yet regardless of the specificities of their immigrant status, Latinx are entangled in a citizenship regime characterized by the "institutionalized systems of formal and informal norms that define access to membership, as well as rights and duties associated with membership, within a polity."[3] The experiences and fears Lina expressed highlight aspects of her relationship to and meaning-making about the citizenship regime.

Like Lina, I, too, was attuned to the immigrant status of my family. Consequently, her concerns echoed my past insecurities and lack of belonging given my experiences in a Latinx mixed-status and transmigrant family.[4] Latinx youth from immigrant and mixed-status families experience a unique, qualitatively different childhood than non-immigrant, non-Latinx youth in the United States.⁵ Socially constructed and legally informed meanings of citizenship, as well as legality and rights, inform Latinx youth understandings of their families as existing in a state of deportability, uncertainty, and fear.⁶ Latinx youth experience disparate social, cultural, and political contexts. Yet some Latinx youth are provided with or able to gain access to resources and networks of support that facilitate their critical literacy to engage their agency in efforts to create social change. How Latinx youth understand, engage with, and trouble meanings of citizenship, legality, and rights at the intersections of the ageism and racist nativism they experience in their school, family, and community contexts is featured in *Growing Up Latinx*.

Latinx Communities in the United States

Latinx account for approximately 18 percent of the total US population.⁷ Approximately one-fourth of the population under the age of eighteen is of Latinx heritage. Estimates suggest that 59.9 million people in the United States are of Latin American descent. From this population group, one-third are Latinx youth under the age of eighteen.⁸ The demographics of Latinx as a pan-ethnic group are projected to increase to 29 percent by the year 2050. The demographic trends that characterize Latinx communities will have a profound impact on the social, cultural, economic, and political structures of the US nation-state.

Across multiple industries, Latinx communities are innovating new forms of music, food, fashion, and entertainment, as well as entrepreneurialism. In 2015 Latinx contributed approximately $2.13 billion to the nation's GDP.⁹ Relatedly, Latinx businesses and entrepreneurs accounted for 70 percent of the increased workforce over the past five years. In the area of politics, during the 2017 to 2018 term, forty-six members serving in the US Congress identified as Latinx or Hispanic.¹⁰ Relatedly, that same year, there were 6,100 Latinx elected officials, and 27.3 million Latinx were eligible to vote.¹¹ The cumulative contributions by Latinx communities and their vast representations of *Latinidad* are significant and worth noting.¹² Yet the reality is that in the United States, many Latinx continue to be perceived as perpetual foreigners, a key concept described in Raymond Rocco's book *Transforming Citizenship*.¹³ The racist nativism that informs Latinx's positionality as "not from here" has justified the historical and contemporary hegemonic discourses about Latinx communities, as well as the anti-immigration legislation and deportation campaigns that have targeted Latinx and immigrant communities.

During the last year of Barack Obama's presidency, 65,332 individuals were detained and deported by Immigration and Customs Enforcement (ICE), under the Department of Homeland Security. In 2017 Human Rights Watch estimated that more than ten thousand parents of US citizens are detained in California annually, and nearly half of those detained have no criminal record.[14] These rates amount to an appalling number of approximately two million deportations during the Obama presidency. Furthermore, heightened criminalization, detention, and deportations have taken place under the Secure Communities initiative that began during the George W. Bush presidency and escalated under the Trump administration. As a deportation campaign, Secure Communities relies on federal, state, and local law enforcement agencies collaborating with ICE to carry forward targeted deportation campaigns.[15] Although this program was halted from 2014 to 2016, Secure Communities was reinstated in full force under the Trump administration.[16]

Approximately four million US-born youth of Latin American descent live in mixed-status families, in low-income and working-class communities.[17] Latinx youth born in the United States to immigrant parents hold rights as citizens of the nation-state and equal protections under US constitutional law.[18] Despite these rights, however, Latinx youth are not immune from harm and disenfranchisement. Families, including parents and youth, are subject to various forms of discrimination and criminalization that ultimately have implications for their well-being.[19] In particular, Latinx youth in mixed-status families suffer from their parents' precarious legal standing, as they are at a greater risk of family separation due to arrests, detention, and deportation.[20] The unnerving fear of having a parent detained and/or deported poses a significant threat to a young person's overall thriving and healthy development.[21]

I opened this chapter with Lina's story because it made palpable the consequences of Secure Communities, among other anti-immigrant legislation and deportation campaign programs, all of which underscore the racist nativism of past administrations that has continued in the current US political climate. Santa Cruz County, the community where this study took place and Lina lived, experienced massive ICE raids between 2007 and 2013. Raids in work settings and public places have continued because of the community's unincorporated status, its growing immigrant and Latinx presence, and its proximity to one of the most generative agricultural regions in the nation. Furthermore, the economic thriving of Santa Cruz County's agricultural industry is at the expense of the predominantly Latinx migrant farmworkers, whose bodies are exploited by the underpaid and dehumanizing labor they endure. Lina's concerns, fears, and anger were valid expressions in response to the political climate that predated the Trump administration. Across the United States, moreover, these fears have been further amplified by the rise in white supremacy, racist nativism, and structural violence toward immigrants, people of color, and other institutionally marginalized groups, among them Latinx communities.

Latinx, Citizenship, and Racialized Exclusions

In the United States, citizenship, like race, gender, social class, and other categories, has been used as a marker of status that affords or denies people certain rights and privileges.[22] Citizenship operates as a regime because it structures a set of cultural, social, legal, and political practices that enfranchise or marginalize certain individuals and communities. Conventional meanings of citizenship are constituted, reinforced, and learned through institutionalized practices that ultimately serve to socialize, categorize, and label people apart from one another—for example, as citizens, noncitizens, good or bad citizens, and citizens in the making. The mechanisms of legitimizing a person's existence as either a citizen or noncitizen become especially salient for those whose mere presence in the nation-state is questionable by virtue of their positionalities along social categories or markers of difference and power.[23]

Age, in addition to race, ethnicity, gender, and immigrant status, figures prominently in US-based constructions of citizenship. Historically, citizenship was accorded on the basis of reaching adulthood at the age of twenty-one. According to women, gender, and sexuality studies historian Corinne T. Field, the sociocultural construction of maturity as the precondition for the achievement of citizenship was largely a function of associating adulthood with masculinity and whiteness; in turn, women and people of color were denied full citizenship and rights.[24] To a degree, this condition of disenfranchisement has remained in place, relegating those with intersecting marginalized positionalities to a second-class citizenship status.

Latinx have a complicated history with citizenship and, more broadly, immigration and enfranchisement in the United States. Emigrants from Latin America, Mexicans and Central Americans in particular, have experienced extreme systemic disenfranchisement, informed by persistent racist and nativist ideologies. The racism that characterizes US immigration policies stems from a history of US colonialism, as well as past and ongoing economic and political interventions in Latin America.[25] These conditions are amplified by the imposed segregation and forced assimilation of Latinx immigrants in the United States.

From a historical perspective, México-United States relations have long been contentious. In 1848, when the Mexican-American War ended with the signing of the Treaty of Guadalupe Hidalgo, one-third of México's northern territory, amounting to 525,000 square miles, was annexed by the United States as part of a resolution to end the war. México's northern territories became part of the US Southwest, and with that some people of Mexican heritage residing on the newly acquired soil were claimed as new members of the nation-state, while others were displaced farther south of the border into Mexican territory. As neither immigrants nor full citizens, Mexicanos, or people of Mexican descent, grappled with the dilemma of citizenship, nationality, and belonging produced by a new border that literally crossed over their lives. The few Mexicanos who were granted US citizenship were those who owned land or property and had European white phenotypic features that did not make salient their Indigenous *mestizo* or *mulato* heritage.[26] On both sides of the border, Mexicanos struggled to rebuild their lives, identities, and communities. Central Americans have also encountered similar experiences of struggle as they have sought asylum, humane living conditions, and better opportunities in the United States amidst various forms of civil, political, and economic unrest in their countries of origin, largely rooted in foreign economic, political, and military interventions. To this day, many immigrants still undergo these struggles and experience these displacements as they strive to reconcile their sense of belonging, legal status, and rights with their hopes and dreams, in an anti-immigrant US context of reception.

The differential avenues for legality or lawful immigrant documentation provided to Latinx from various countries, such as México, El Salvador, and Guatemala, reflect the unique histories and tensions between the United States and Latin American countries. The exclusionary inclusion[27] and tolerated "illegality"[28] of Mexicans and Central Americans have been largely informed by the differing contexts of reception that communities encounter upon arriving in the United States. Immigrants from México have a longer history of migration and border crossing to the United States, rooted in a history of annexation and economic instability that foreclosed avenues to lawfully pursue more permanent status. On the other hand, Central Americans, particularly Salvadoreans, have been granted to a modest degree temporary protected status (TPS), which is a special designated category that offers temporary legal status to immigrants who, because of extreme conditions of unrest, violence, or natural disaster, are not able to return to their country of origin.

Unequivocally, Latin America-United States relations have shaped contemporary patterns of migration, as well as Latinx communities' experiences following the process of emigrating. The historical yet enduring forms of racist nativism that have shaped the struggles of Latinx communities in the United States position them, among other racialized immigrant groups, as perpetual foreigners.[29] The disenfranchisement of Latinx-heritage people, while rooted in colonial histories of violent displacement and foreign intervention, still persists; it is an enduring perpetual form of exclusionary inclusion. In large part, this is due to US policies and discourses that continue to marginalize Latinx communities, specifically those whose phenotypic characteristics are not racialized as white or white-passing, and relegate them to a status of second-class citizenship.

Citizenship is a contested status because discourses on rights, freedom, and enfranchisement in the United States have been constructed in relation to race. As a master category, race influences implicitly or explicitly how people are judged and positioned along hierarchies of power and status. As critical race studies historian Natalia Molina writes in *How Race Is Made in America*, for Mexican Americans, like other Latinx groups, citizenship and race are intertwined to enforce their deportability.[30] Citizenship is the social and legal mechanism that legitimates forms of categorization. For racial and ethnic minority groups, the attaining of citizenship is an uphill battle, requiring resistance to marginalization in the struggle to belong. The positioning of Latinx in relation to citizenship is particularly complex because of histories of Latinx racialized exclusion and disenfranchisement. Considered amidst a political climate that supports restrictive, exclusionary, and violent anti-immigrant legislation, these factors have consequences for Latinx immigrant families and communities where youth grow up and live.

The discourses that US institutions have produced and reified about Latinx communities have positioned their voices and experiences at the margins. Yet Latinx communities are participating in and contributing to the US economy, political landscape, and sociocultural industries in significant ways that are reshaping the image of what it means to be an "American." The fact that Spanish, a language spoken by most people of Latin American descent, is the second-most commonly spoken language in the United States, yet there are hegemonic discourses and accounts of people and institutions still promoting "English-only" policies, underscores the tenuous position of Latinx in the United States. Despite these experiences, Latinx continue to claim a stake in US democracy and its social, economic, and political institutions. Latinx affirm their agency and recognition as human beings deserving of inclusion, dignity and respect, and a right to belong as full citizens with rights.[31] Young people of Latinx descent are making similar claims.

Sociocultural Constructions of Youth Citizenship

Latinx youth, because of their likelihood of growing up in immigrant and/or mixed-status families racialized as foreigners in the US nation-state, are uniquely positioned to reframe discourses and understandings of citizenship for Latinx communities and young people. Sociocultural theories on youth citizenship development have approached the topic from a future-oriented perspective that describes and views young people, especially preadolescents, as *citizens to be*.[32] The implication of such theorizing is that youth are not citizens, but will *become* citizens once they transition into adulthood. In the United States, reaching adulthood means turning eighteen and taking on rights and responsibilities associated with being an adult, a legitimate citizen in the eyes of the nation-state. Sociopolitical citizenship, a conceptual standpoint I develop further in this book to characterize the unique and quotidian meanings and embodiments of Latinx youth citizenship, is useful for describing how young people in Latinx immigrant families enact and claim their citizenship. As sociopolitical citizens, they often trouble US-based constructions of citizenship as a status, practice, and rights-bearing construct that is predicated on certain qualities: white, male, adult, and US-born.

Sociopolitical citizenship challenges the theoretical and applied limitations of US-based constructions of citizenship and sociocultural perspectives on youthhood. The failure to recognize young people as full citizens is problematic because it assumes that youth are deficient and incapable of agency, self- and collective determination, and political action. Furthermore, it situates young people as subjects to be formed or molded into adulthood. Additionally, the perspective of youth as future citizens positions them as the responsibility of adults. Critical feminist scholars argue that the positioning of youth as *becoming*—becoming adults and thus becoming citizens—parallels the structural positioning as well as objectification of women and enslaved people, who were considered subordinate and the property of white adult men.[33] The historical positioning of nonwhite people and women—categories that intersect with age—renders youth as second-class citizens. The institutional marginalization of youth as second-class citizens denies them their rights as well as claims to citizenship, and this has implications for their rights and belonging in the US nation-state. Together, these perspectives render youth as noncitizens or future citizens with limited responsibilities.[34] Yet, as Emir Estrada argues in her book *Kids at Work*, the phenomenon of Latinx youth street vending with their families challenges the invisibility of youth everyday multiple roles and responsibilities. In fact, it constitutes them as contributing members and participants in their families and communities, allowing them to be recognized as active citizens.

Among other roles and responsibilities that youth might take are the following: helping their families around the home,[35] generating income from work to contribute to the family,[36] and engaging in political movements or grassroots activism.[37] As everyday modes of engagement in the social, cultural, economic, and political lives of their families and communities, these roles and responsibilities constitute youth as citizens. As active participants, Latinx youth are citizens with agency and the capacity to effect change in their community. Yet the theorizing on citizenship often positions young people as citizens in the making, a perspective rooted in Western Eurocentric frameworks of childhood that reify discourses of youth as developing citizens. Instead of changing the power structures that reproduce adults' authority over youth agency and rights, the citizen of the future approach views youth as noncitizens because they are dependent on adults and presumed incapable of critical, political, and self-determined action.[38]

Unlike the future citizen approach, the present citizen framework purports that young people have a right to full participation. A present citizen perspective offers a difference-centered approach to the theorizing of youth citizenship, which acknowledges youth differences in relation to adults, yet explicitly emphasizes their citizen status irrespective of such positionalities.[39] Rather than arguing for an extension of adults' citizenship and rights to young people, the present citizen perspective recognizes youth as citizens with rights regardless of their age. By conceptualizing citizenship from the ground up, the present citizen framework argues that youth embody practices and acts of citizenship in their everyday experiences. Furthermore, it positions youth as sociopolitical citizens with agency, actively and civically engaged outside the norms of conventional citizen and youth participation frameworks.[40] Recognizing youth as citizens in the present does not necessarily imply a change in the structures and institutions that have relegated young people to a second-class citizenship status, however. In effect, what is needed, and what the present citizen framework provides, is a paradigm shift away from the deficit views and hegemonic discourses that disenfranchise young people.

Consistent with the goal of recognizing young people as active citizens is the acknowledgment of their full rights and enfranchisement. The United Nations Convention on the Rights of the Child (UN-CRC) was created to advocate for, protect, and address youth needs.[41] The UN-CRC is comprised of a list of fifty-four articles, with the last thirteen articles specifically focusing on how international organizations, governments, and their institutions will ensure and oversee that the rights of all young people are protected and upheld. Most of the articles included in the 1989 UN-CRC fall into two broad categories: nurturance rights and self-determination rights. Rights to nurturance ensure that youth are safe, cared for, and legally protected, whereas self-determination rights emphasize their active role or capacity for exercising agency in addressing social conditions that affect their lives.

In the creation of the UN-CRC, young people were seemingly involved; yet while these statuses guarantee their rights, protections, and well-being, they are not unique to the specific cultural, social, and political contexts wherein youth are located. Most institutions, including those that uphold the UN-CRC, are not necessarily structured to include the voices and subjectivities of young people, nor are they amenable to fully involving them in decision-making processes that directly affect them.[42] It is important to note that the United States is one of two countries, and the only democratic industrialized nation, that has not ratified the UN-CRC. Supporters of the UN-CRC argue that this poses a challenge to the well-being, inclusion, enfranchisement, and overall thriving of young people.

On the other hand, critical scholars purport that youth perspectives endorsed by the UN-CRC are heavily informed by Western Eurocentric frameworks of youth development that do not align with decolonial perspectives of youth, family, and community dynamics. Furthermore, the UN-CRC places high value on traditional family structures and norms that may not reflect decolonial, queer, and feminist family formations. Recognizing these complex perspectives, we can see that the UN-CRC has its limitations. Yet the United States' disavowal of the UN-CRC has significant implications for the well-being of youth as it limits opportunities and resources to support their positive development, agency, and rights as citizens, thereby furthering their marginalization in society. Troubling meanings of citizenship through the social and political subjectivities of Latinx youth is therefore imperative. The unique societal positioning of Latinx youth can help inform social, cultural, political, and scholarly perspectives on youth citizenship, rights, and belonging, specifically in the United States.

Latinx Youth and the Paradox of Citizenship

The parallels of structural and institutional exclusion that Latinx communities and young people experience in cultural, social, and political contexts require critically examining how meanings of citizenship are reproduced, troubled, and deconstructed by Latinx youth. Documenting how Latinx youth learn to engage with and challenge notions of citizenship, legality, and rights, especially as experienced in their lives, is important. Understanding Latinx youth meaning-making of citizenship in a US context can help us add nuance to and deepen the theorizing on youth citizenship, rights, and sociopolitical development.

Constructions of citizenship rooted in hegemonic discourses, reflected and maintained by the nation-state, combined with Western Eurocentric frameworks of young people, position youth as citizens in the making and future citizens. Together, these produce deficit views of youthhood that characterize them as powerless, acritical, and apolitical. These constructions maintain the hegemonic discourses inherent in institutions like schools that subsequently marginalize youth agency and participation. For youth from low-income and working-class communities, this seems to be particularly the case.[43] One explanation for this is that they are often socialized to conform to the status quo, instead of engaging their agency and autonomy as critical thinkers and change agents in school, for example.[44] Cumulatively, these conditions reify disempowering and deficit views of Latinx youth.

Troubling the paradoxes of Latinx youth citizenship through a sociohistorical analysis of Latinx in the United States requires a youth-centered perspective.[45] For Latinx, race is a salient social marker that shapes their relationship to citizenship. Similarly, for young people of Latinx descent, race and ethnicity, like age, gender, and immigrant status, intersect to reify their disenfranchisement. Although the positioning of youth in relation to citizenship is distinct from that of Latinx adults in the United States, the structures and systems of power that delegitimize their rights, belonging, and participation are quite similar. For Latinx youth, age, race, ethnicity, and immigrant status determine the parameters of their participation, sense of belonging, and rights as citizens.

Latinx youth citizenship cannot be theorized without a youth-centered intersectional framework that challenges the racist nativism along with the ageism that shapes power structures that constrain youth agency.[46] Drawing parallels between the disenfranchisement and second-class citizenship experiences of Latinx adults and those of young people is important to help us elucidate the intersections of age, race, ethnicity, and immigrant status in the lives of Latinx youth—and how these, in turn, inform their agency, participation, and belonging as sociopolitical citizens. Moreover, documenting how Latinx youth engage with and resist US-based constructions of citizenship, legality, and rights can help us deconstruct deficit views about Latinx and young people more broadly. Indeed, power structures operate to maintain the status quo, which serves the interests of adults who determine the boundaries of youth participation, and consequently their agency and rights. Thus, it is within certain structures and institutions, like schools, where Latinx youth learn to reproduce hegemonic discourses of citizenship. At the same time, however, Latinx youth have the capacity and will to challenge, trouble, and articulate counter-hegemonic stories that reject and resist the ageism and racist nativism associated with citizenship. When a youth-centered intersectional framework is used that includes Latinx youth stories, lived experiences, and agency, a nuanced theorizing of citizenship is possible.

Young People as Agents of Change

When confronted with conditions of institutional marginalization, young people often learn to develop skills in critical literacy, leadership, and social and emotional learning, which are necessary to engage in social justice–oriented actions to amplify their voices and meet their needs.[47] Young people of color growing up in social conditions of injustice and inequity, when provided with supportive environments to reflect, interrogate, and engage in actions toward social change, can develop a critical consciousness, or what community psychologist Roderick J. Watts describes as sociopolitical development.[48] Unlike other forms of consciousness, a critical consciousness is rooted in youth experiences of oppression and resistance, their understandings of the root causes of these injustices, and what actions or structural and systemic-level changes need to happen to redress and transform their situation. As a psychological process, sociopolitical development involves a critical structural analysis of social issues and the exercising of political agency to address systemic issues.[49] Sociopolitical development theory describes the processes and practices that allow for a critical social analysis and political consciousness to develop among young people, together with the attitudes and behaviors that are formed and leveraged to engage in social change.[50]

Scholars of sociopolitical development theory document how youth within and outside education institutions reimagine and claim the terms and conditions of their civic and political participation.[51] Young people from communities of color, for example, are civically engaged in ways that differ from, yet are no less powerful and meaningful than, conventional forms of civic engagement like volunteerism and community service.[52] Sociopolitical development theory accounts for the individual and social factors that shape political efficacy, agency, self-determination, and collective action among youth.[53] These processes have been well documented in contexts that support and foster a young person's social identities, critical consciousness, socioemotional awareness, and political participation. Among these contexts are youth community organizing settings,[54] positive youth development programs,[55] and youth participatory action research projects, often taking place after school.[56] Contexts that center a young person's subjectivities while making space for reflection, dialogue, and action are most conducive to cultivating their sociopolitical development in ways that align with social justice values.

As a form of critical consciousness rooted in the social and political subjectivities of youth lives, sociopolitical development is an important domain of citizenship. Yet opportunities for sociopolitical development in education institutions, particularly schools, are often inadequate or insufficiently supported to help cultivate expressions of agency and political participation among youth. The sociopolitical development that I describe as a form of citizenship among Latinx youth is characterized by their quotidian expressions and understandings of belonging in the United States. By naming sociopolitical development as a form of embodied and enacted citizenship, I posit that Latinx youth meaning-making about citizenship was characterized by a critical consciousness. This allowed them to make meaning, but also trouble the hegemonic discourses that negatively impacted their lives, families, and communities. Latinx youth subjectivities were largely formed and informed by the ageism and racist nativism that surrounded them as youth growing up in Latinx immigrant families in the United States.

Building on the literature on sociopolitical development theory, I introduce the concept of sociopolitical citizenship to describe the social and political subjectivities of Latinx youth. Grounded in notions of agency, sociopolitical citizenship is characterized by Latinx youth forging opportunities to be seen, to be heard, and to belong. Latinx youth troubling, deconstructing, and reimagining citizenship meanings—making their voices, experiences, and rights visible and heard—characterizes sociopolitical citizenship. Through a youth-centered intersectional framework I document Latinx youth sociopolitical citizenship, specifically their agency, in the context of one afterschool program called Change 4 Good.

Latinx youth sociopolitical citizenship is characterized by four interconnected domains: social identities, critical consciousness, socioemotional awareness, and political engagement. These domains are mutually constitutive, yet some might be more salient than others. Critical consciousness consists of having a sociohistorical analysis of power, and how power operates to sustain systems of oppression. Latinx youth were aware of racism and how it manifested in their lives, often in relation to other categories, like age. Latinx youth understood their experiences of being othered not only as individual acts, but as an outcome of broader hegemonic discourses. Understanding these experiences as embedded in a larger social context, Latinx youth often reflected on their own experiences, a process of critical self-awareness, to help them develop a critical consciousness about their situation along with an understanding of the significance of these experiences as tied to their social identities and emotions. Socioemotional awareness, critical consciousness, and an understanding of social identities were vital for supporting their political engagement, and thus their sociopolitical citizenship.

Together, social identity development, critical consciousness, socioemotional awareness, and political engagement illustrate the elements of sociopolitical citizenship embodied by Latinx youth. Sociopolitical citizenship is a response to calls for more humane conceptualizations of citizenship, notions that reflect and are grounded in Latinx youth lived experiences, quotidian citizen embodiments, and agency. Understanding how Latinx youth engage with, trouble, and resist US-based constructions of citizenship has implications for the significance and value attached to citizenship—and the possibilities for transforming its meaning into more humanizing constructs that better reflect Latinx and youth agency and belonging. Through the lived experiences of thirteen Latinx youth, this book explores concepts of citizenship, legality, and rights, as there is much to learn from young people living at the intersections of age, race, ethnicity, and immigrant status.

Study Background and Research Context
The Maplewood Community

Growing Up Latinx draws from an ethnography of Latinx youth in the Change 4 Good afterschool program at a local elementary school in the Maplewood community, located along the Central Coast of California. As a growing unincorporated region, Maplewood lacks infrastructure and many necessary community resources, such as a health center, post office, library, and public parks and recreation areas. The community's lack of resources is typical of unincorporated areas, which are generally administered by the county as part of a larger territorial division. During the time that I conducted this ethnography, five council members served on the Santa Cruz County Board of Supervisors, but only one represented Maplewood along with a second unincorporated area. Because the centralized county manages Maplewood, community members' concerns were often overlooked, and resources and services were frequently restricted. These conditions limited the community's democratic representation and decision-making power in matters that concerned its residents.[57] Its growing population and demographics were further exacerbated by the local challenges that surrounded Maplewood.

Consistent with other areas in Santa Cruz County, Maplewood expanded to become a receiving community for Latinx immigrant families working in the nearby agricultural labor and service economies. According to local community reports, Maplewood was one of the most populated areas in the county at the time of this study.[58] Over the years, Maplewood grew to northern regions bordering other unincorporated areas. At the time of this study, Maplewood had a population of approximately 17,000; however, some of its immigrant and undocumented residents were unaccounted for due to their legal status and the anti-immigrant political climate. According to the 2010 US census, 73 percent of the total population identified as white, 28 percent as Hispanic or Latinx, 14 percent as Pacific Islander, and 4 percent as African American. Given these demographics, Maplewood was classified as having one of the largest Latinx communities in the county.

Over the past decade, Oaxacan and Salvadorean communities have constituted a growing demographic in the United States, especially in California.[59] Maplewood, for example, includes a growing Oaxacan community, reflecting recent demographic shifts specific to emigrants from the southwestern states of México. Several residents of Maplewood organize the annual Guelaguetza festival, which is a popular Oaxacan traditional celebration. Similarly, Central American emigrants, particularly Salvadorean families who have settled in the area, have forged community spaces that reflect their traditions and cultural practices. For example, Salvadoreans often organized *colectivas* (fundraising events) and *kermeses* (food festivals) to build support for their community needs. These events functioned as informal gatherings for families to build community and make additional income, given the limited resources in Maplewood. In fact, communities often mobilized support for themselves by selling traditional foods, like *pupusas* (traditional Salvadorean dish consisting of round, thick corn flatbreads stuffed with different fillings, from beans and cheese to spinach and pork), as well as helping raise funds for individual or family aid, including but not limited to students' school supplies and field trips to science camp. The presence of Oaxacan and Salvadorean families demonstrates the diversity of communities in Maplewood.

Although it is located in proximity to relatively economically prosperous cities, the unemployment rate in Maplewood is among the highest in the county (34 percent).[60] The median household income for people who are employed is approximately $60,000. Just over half of Maplewood's residents are homeowners (56 percent), whereas the remaining are renters or living in low-income housing (44 percent). Most families in the area consist of two-parent households with children under the age of eighteen (32 percent). These demographics characterize the community of Maplewood, in the heart of tourist sites known for their beaches and surfing culture.

Maplewood Elementary School

Founded in the late nineteenth century, Maplewood Elementary School (MES) is one of the oldest public schools in the area and a California Distinguished School. In its mission statement, MES claims values of diversity, equity, and a sense of community, as well as a commitment to providing a learning environment of academic excellence and support for its students. Through these values, MES aims to understand the strengths and challenges of each student in order to foster opportunities for their academic thriving and success. Over the past several years, Latinx student demographics at MES have continued to increase. Between 2011 and 2013 the demographics at MES were comprised predominantly of Latinx (75 percent) students, followed by white (15 percent), African American (2 percent), and Asian/Asian American (0.5 percent) students.

Many Latinx students at MES are from first- and second-generation immigrant families from México, with a few from Central America, particularly El Salvador. Some students lived in mixed-status families. Mixed-status families are characterized by differences in legal status among family members, where one or both parents and/or other family members are undocumented. As one of two elementary schools in the area, MES is more centrally located and more populated. At the time of this study, approximately 355 students were enrolled in transitional kindergarten through the fifth grade. In a fourth- and fifth-grade class, the student-to-teacher ratio averaged twenty-seven to one. Some fifth-grade teachers had as many as thirty students per class, with no teaching assistant. Furthermore, the lack of support and resources in the school was representative of broader structural issues and limited resources in Maplewood.

As in many schools in California, most of the teachers and administrators at MES were white, while the students were predominantly Latinx.[61] According to Latinx students at MES, teachers demonstrated relatively little knowledge of Latinx culture, and limited to no Spanish-language proficiency. The majority of the students identified English as their second language; according to standardized measures, 86 percent of the students were identified as "English Learners." As per the California School Accountability Report Card, between 2011 and 2012 approximately 50 percent, 62 percent, and 65 percent of the students reached proficiency in subject areas of English language arts, math, and science, respectively. Moreover, according to the California Department of Education, 86 percent of the students were identified as "socioeconomically disadvantaged," thereby qualifying for free and reduced-price lunch. MES's demographics describe the context of Latinx youth interactions with teachers and students.

Change 4 Good Afterschool Program

Informed by a youth empowerment framework that is social justice–oriented, the Change 4 Good afterschool program is the context for this ethnography on Latinx youth citizenship. Change 4 Good follows a youth participatory action research (YPAR) process. Youth participatory action research is a research paradigm that strives to build collaborations with institutionally marginalized groups whose members are well-situated to determine and address social problems affecting their lives. Change 4 Good began as a university-community collaboration between the Community Psychology Research and Action Team (CPRAT) at the University of California, Santa Cruz, and a group of stakeholders at MES, including the school principal (now deceased), a literacy specialist (who is no longer at the school), and a fifth-grade teacher (who was our school collaborator). MES stakeholders and Dr. Regina (Gina) D. Langhout, the faculty supervisor of CPRAT, met in 2006 to discuss the possibility of developing a program at MES that could serve students' needs. Based on their common values and their desire to support greater school-based student civic engagement, they agreed to create a program that would help young people develop their leadership skills as well as critical literacy. As a result of this meeting, the Change 4 Good YPAR afterschool program was established as a community-university collaboration between CPRAT and MES in 2008.[62]

Change 4 Good served youth from low-income and working-class families of predominantly Latinx descent. One young person was born in México; two other youth were born in Central America—one in Guatemala and the other in El Salvador. The rest were born in the United States. With the exception of three youth, all were a part of a mixed-status family where either one or both parents were undocumented, legal permanent residents, or citizens, naturalized or US-born (see table A.1 in the appendix). More than half of the youth are second-generation, except for three who are 1.5-generation.

Fourth- and fifth-grade students self-selected themselves into the program by completing and submitting their application to the coordinating Change 4 Good program facilitators, who subsequently randomly selected and invited students to participate. Modification of the selections occasionally took place to ensure diverse representation among race/ethnic and gender categories. Students often joined the program during the fall of their fourth-grade year, and remained involved for two years throughout the end of the fifth grade.

Change 4 Good met during the academic year every Thursday for an average of seventy minutes. Afterschool program sessions often began with young people leading an icebreaker or check-in question. Afterwards, youth helped distribute a small snack and juice to the group. A key aspect of the afterschool program was to cultivate youth leadership, critical literacies, and social science research skills. Young people in Change 4 Good were therefore engaged in the development of action projects to facilitate social change in their school. The action projects were developed and determined by young people through the curriculum and activities led by the Change 4 Good team. Youth-led action projects included the creation of two school-based community murals over the course of three years, with the first one created in 2009 and the second in 2013. For the second mural, the Change 4 Good youth were involved in conducting focus groups to document school, family, and community experiences of struggle and hope, discern themes from these stories, and produce a school-based mural that reflected their lived experiences, histories, dreams, and community.

During weekly meetings, youth learned how to conduct social science research via a participatory action research (PAR) paradigm. Through a PAR process, youth engaged as co-researchers with the Change 4 Good team, including the program facilitators, by identifying an issue or social problem in their school and/or community, collecting and analyzing data about the problem, and developing possible actions or projects to address it. Each session was structured on the lesson plan, activities, or tasks from the preceding session. For example, if youth learned about focus groups previously, in the next session they would practice how to co-facilitate a focus group. Sessions typically ended with a prompt that young people responded to as a group or in their journals. In addition to the once-a-week afterschool program sessions that took place during the academic year, Change 4 Good organized a three- to five-week summer program where youth developed or implemented an action project, such as a school-based community mural. The murals were informed by and rooted in their community's stories—data that they had gathered through focus groups. Change 4 Good youth then subsequently analyzed their data to discern themes and patterns to help inform their action project, and in this case the themes of their mural. The data collection and analysis often took place during the academic year, with further data analysis or the implementation of an action project happening in the summer. Youth spent a portion of the summer program designing and developing their mural draft, getting it approved by school stakeholders, and then creating the mural.

I began my participation in Change 4 Good in the summer of 2009, after Gina, the principal investigator for the program and supervisor of CPRAT, and Danielle Kohfeldt, the graduate student coordinator at the time, invited me to join the afterschool program. Before joining Change 4 Good I had been involved in a community-based photovoice project and a two-year community assessment of Maplewood. These previous experiences allowed me to familiarize myself with the community, have a presence in the area, and develop relationships with local community members and stakeholders. From July 2009 through August 2012, I served as one of the two coordinators of Change 4 Good. During this time, I developed relationships with MES teachers, administrators, and school staff. I formed friendships with Change 4 Good youth and had positive interactions with their family members. These connections gave me the opportunity to learn more about Maplewood and the challenges Latinx youth and their families experienced, as well as their aspirations. I viewed my role in Change 4 Good as an opportunity to connect with and support a community that resembled the one I had grown up in. I embraced the process of meaningfully supporting youth leadership, critical literacy development, and research skill training, especially for Latinx youth. My experiences with Latinx youth in Change 4 Good—specifically, thirteen youth who were foreign-born or born in the United States to Latinx immigrant families, some of mixed status—are the focus of *Growing Up Latinx*.

Youth Participatory Action Research (YPAR)

Unlike many afterschool programs that are designed to help students with homework and might provide some additional enrichment opportunities, Change 4 Good followed a youth participatory action research (YPAR) paradigm. By designing program activities and curricula in line with a YPAR process, we sought to engage with and support young people in developing their social science research skills. YPAR facilitates youth engagement via active participation in every step of the research process, including design, implementation, and dissemination of the project's findings.[63] Furthermore, YPAR supports youth critical literacy development and civic engagement through social science research action projects that center youth voices and position them as co-researchers and decision makers.[64]

YPAR is characterized by several phases that facilitate praxis (i.e., putting theory into practice).[65] The first phase involves researchers and young people engaging as co-researchers to identify a social problem or issue to be addressed. Once the problem definition has been identified and agreed upon, the second phase of data collection and analysis follows. Through this process of data gathering and discernment, potential structural solutions are identified to inform the third phase, which is to implement an action to address the problem. Changing social structures is followed by the fourth phase: evaluating or assessing the impact of the action on the initial problem. YPAR phases facilitate the democratization of knowledge, power, and decision making by young people who meaningfully contribute to the research process.[66]

Most YPAR projects engage youth of high school or middle school age. Recently, scholars in critical youth studies and education have advocated for the inclusion of youth of elementary school age. Studies have involved youth assessing and identifying key elements for the implementation of afterschool program curricula,[67] young girls conducting program evaluation to determine the effectiveness of a nonprofit organization serving young girls' needs,[68] youth developing data analysis tools to assist them in discerning and implementing action projects to foment community change,[69] and creating maps and visuals to support the participation of youth in research studies.[70] The growing interest in engaging young people in research attests to the importance of making space for their agency and participation. As Michelle Fine contends, YPAR embodies "a radical commitment to inquiry-inspired action" that allows for the reimagining and transgressing of structures and institutions that delimit and restrict the power of young people.[71]

Researcher Positionality and Reflexivity

The lives of Latinx youth in the Change 4 Good afterschool program reminded me of my own experiences as a Chicana, México-born immigrant to the United States, growing up in a Latinx community and an immigrant mixed-status working-class Mexican family. As a student, I had limited opportunities to center my own lived experiences in the classroom; I experienced a disconnect between my family, community, and school contexts, which constrained my capacity to meaningfully engage academically. Despite my limited access to education programs, however, my family afforded me with community cultural wealth and resources to thrive in school.[72] I learned through curiosity, frustration, and accompaniment with my parents, who instilled in me the value of storytelling to build community and sustain hope.

When I began my graduate studies, I had recently completed the US citizenship naturalization process. Although I had successfully "achieved citizenship," I witnessed others in my communities (fellow students, family members) being denied the status, or in some cases being detained, deported, or criminalized. Massive raids, arrests, and deportations in my communities were juxtaposed with a new citizen identity I had earned by virtue of conditions in my life that were compliant with the existing sociolegal system and the status quo.[73] I had a green card because my parents had one, and at that time immigration legislation was not as restrictive; hence they were able to petition to adjust my status while remaining in the United States. At present, this is not possible. In the eyes of some immigrants, including my parents, I embody the "American Dream" because I was an undocumented immigrant youth who became "documented," pursued a higher education (a PhD, no less), and live a modest middle-class life. Regardless of these labels, I felt (and still feel) inadequate in claiming my status as a (naturalized) citizen of the United States. I am unsettled by the fact that people are being deprived of their human rights and protections because of how legality is constructed. At the height of Secure Communities, and under the Trump administration, I witnessed communities being profiled and terrorized for no reason other than the color of their skin, their language, their religion, and the intersections of their positionalities. The tenor and terror of the political context, grounded in my lived experiences, continue to inform the development of my research, including the creation of this book.

It is because of my lived experiences and positionalities that I am compelled to write about citizenship and Latinx youth. Therefore, throughout this book I center my writing voice in relation to moments that reflected and in others refracted Latinx youth experiences. As a budding scholar, I find critical reflexivity an essential practice that enables me to learn about my dispositions, assumptions, desires, and refusals, especially when writing from within and outside the Latinx youth experience. In weaving the theoretical and empirical, the personal and political dimensions of my work, critical reflexivity serves an important purpose. For one, it highlights the inherent tensions that are unearthed in doing ethnography and YPAR. As a practice of being mindfully aware of my own positionalities, critical reflexivity allows me to pursue research with integrity and *conciencia con compromiso* (consciousness with commitment).[74] Developed by Linda Prieto, *conciencia con compromiso* refers to the social consciousness of being accountable to and in community with others, with the intention to leverage any acquired privileges and institutional resources to support community struggles that seek transformation and justice.

By engaging critical reflexivity, I strive to be intentional about decolonizing how research, theory, and practice reproduce power and hegemonic discourses. Therefore, throughout this book, I use the terms "young people" and "youth" interchangeably to denote the socially constructed categorization of children and childhood, including the positioning of youthhood vis-à-vis adulthood. "Youth" has particular associations and different meanings from "child," yet these words are often used synonymously to describe youth differential status from adults and adulthood. Young people experience different structural forms of adultism, discrimination based on their child or youth status, specifically their age, compared to that of adults.[75] Adultism reflects the inherent institutionalized sociocultural hegemony that relegates young people to a marginal positioning as youth, with less power and agency compared to adults in most Western societies.[76] In a US context, adulthood is typically achieved at the age of eighteen; youthhood—or childhood, to be specific—is constructed as a time period of suspended responsibilities, unburdened by the demands of adult life.[77] This is especially the case for preadolescents between the ages of eight and twelve, who are transitioning between developmental stages and social contexts from elementary to middle school.

In discussing the experiences of Latinx youth, I refer to their school, family, and community experiences in a US context specifically. There are instances where I may reference Western Eurocentric frameworks of childhood and citizenship to describe the differential positionality of young people. In the Majority World, however, some youth are viewed and treated differently—in more egalitarian ways, for example—than young people in Western societies, particularly the United States. This is because the colonialism rooted in Western Eurocentrism has produced strikingly different environments for youth in the Majority World. Most Western societies, while priding themselves on values of democracy, are often marked by limited and inequitable social, political, and economic opportunities for youth agency and participation. These systems of power are evidenced by United Statesians' views and treatment of Latinx youth, who are often denied full citizenship recognition and rights or are assimilated into a second-class citizen status.

Book Overview and Organization

In this introduction I offered an overview of *Growing Up Latinx*, its purpose and motivation, and the literatures of Latinx studies and critical youth studies that inform this work. I opened with a vignette, highlighting Lina's story, to show how discourses of citizenship, legality, and rights were unearthed and experienced by Latinx youth. Critical to the well-being and democratic engagement of Latinx youth in the United States is documenting how terms like "citizens" and "citizenship" are understood, troubled, and embodied by young people. US-based constructions of citizenship hold implications for Latinx youth sociopolitical development. Thus, documenting the meaning-making, complexities, and nuances of these terms as Latinx youth experience them is part of their coming of age in the United States.

Growing Up Latinx is organized into two parts that build from the introduction. Part 1 includes the first three chapters, which discuss Latinx youth meaning-making about citizenship, legality, and rights in relation to US-based constructions of citizenship as a status, practice, and rights-bearing construct. Chapter 1 describes Latinx youth conceptualizations of citizenship as a status. Specifically, this includes how citizenship is associated with the nation-state and sociolegal constructions of legality. I illustrate how Latinx youth citizen and citizenship definitions are informed by the possession of legal documentation (i.e., papers, *papeles*). I discuss how Latinx youth meanings reflected US-based constructions of citizenship, including an individual's immigration experience and immigrant status in the nation-state. Furthermore, Latinx youth meaning-making of citizenship as a status unearthed their associations with and experiences of immigration, family separation, and deportation.

Chapter 2 describes Latinx youth views on citizenship as a practice. I demonstrate how Latinx youth drew from their own lived experiences as students to define citizenship, as well as challenge what teachers and adults recognized as desirable or "good" citizen behaviors. In particular, I discuss how Latinx youth reflected on the limitations of defining citizenship solely as a practice, especially when specific behaviors like voting, which is considered a hallmark of citizenship, are denied young people. Additionally, I examine Latinx youth schooling experiences, particularly how the culture of the hidden curriculum, including Character Education, shapes their perspectives and meanings of "good" student citizens.

Chapter 3 describes Latinx youth experiences in school, family, and community contexts in relation to perspectives that undergird nurturance and self-determination rights. I offer a discussion and critique of the United Nations Convention on the Rights of the Child (UN-CRC) by highlighting themes in Latinx youth conceptualizations of rights. By centering Latinx youth views on rights, I examine how the UN-CRC positions youth as dependent on adults, and thus the nation-state. Furthermore, I contend that while nurturance and self-determination rights aim to protect, advocate for, and uphold the safety and well-being of young people, they pose limitations to youth agency and participation in decision making, especially in political matters that concern them. Consequently, I discuss how this holds implications for sociopolitical development among youth, as agents of change and as citizens in full.

Part 2 of *Growing Up Latinx* introduces sociopolitical citizenship as a standpoint for characterizing Latinx youth meaning-making about citizenship, as well as their agency and the embodiments and enactments of citizenship beyond US-based constructions. Comprising the last two chapters, this second part specifically focuses on expanding notions of citizenship toward characterizing Latinx youth sociopolitical citizenship and rights. Chapter 4 describes the processes and practices associated with sociopolitical citizenship, specifically, Latinx youth social and political subjectivities. How Latinx youth reflect upon and engage their positionalities to make sense of their experiences, as these relate to and seep through in their meanings of citizenship, is the focus of this chapter. I discuss Latinx youth sociopolitical citizenship through their developing understanding of their social identities, critical consciousness, socioemotional awareness, and political engagement in their school, family, and community contexts.

Expanding upon earlier claims, chapter 5 describes how Latinx youth both understood and troubled individualistic constructions of rights, especially in relation to community dynamics that resist or challenge individual roles and responsibilities to the nation-state. I describe Latinx youth definitions of rights, which they viewed as privileges, responsibilities, and actions. Latinx youth, for instance, critiqued voting because not all people, among them young people, are able to vote or participate in democratic structures to influence or effect change in matters that concern their lives. Thus, Latinx youth problematized—and at times refused—discourses that privilege individual roles and relationships to the nation-state over rights as responsibilities and opportunities to support their communities, especially their families.

The conclusion offers a review of the main themes in *Growing Up Latinx*. Of significance are the implications of this work on Latinx youth sociopolitical development. I conclude by restating how hegemonic discourses such as ageism and racist nativism render Latinx youth as second-class citizens with limited opportunities to engage and express their agency. Through the centering of their stories, via fieldnotes and interview excerpts, I offer examples of Latinx youth troubling US-based constructions of citizenship. Additionally, I demonstrate their agency in the creation of a school-based mural that was informed by their reflections on school, family, and community experiences. I posit that Latinx youth, through their stories and reflections, embody citizenship in the everyday. As young people, they make meaning of citizenship, legality, and rights as they reflect upon and experience these concepts in their lives. In the conclusion, I offer recommendations for how to support Latinx youth sociopolitical development and agency as citizens in the present.

As educators committed to the thriving and well-being of Latinx youth, we must cultivate and sustain opportunities for them. Creating and facilitating enriching opportunities for the participation of Latinx youth in the construction of citizenship is important because it helps them amplify their voice in the decision making about matters that concern them and the conditions that affect their lives. Cultivating and supporting the development of Latinx youth sociopolitical citizenship is necessary because part of what makes a well-functioning democratic society is its civically engaged youth. Therefore, researchers, educators, and youth advocates must strive to make space for Latinx youth stories and experiences to be acknowledged and understood. By centering Latinx youth lived experiences as citizens with agency, voice, and power, youth-centered programs can be developed.

The scholarly contributions of *Growing Up Latinx* to the theorizing of Latinx youth citizenship are significant, especially at a time when Latinx youth experiences of belonging are compromised by hegemonic discourses that position them on the margins. Youth-service providers, advocates, and scholars engaged in critical youth work must direct their efforts in support of youth sociopolitical development, which can further youth-led counter-hegemonic stories, as well as youth agency that cultivates their social and political subjectivities as citizens. Accounts of Latinx youth experiences must make visible their sociopolitical citizenship as a form of resistance to being othered and disenfranchised. Approaching citizenship from the perspectives of Latinx youth can aid in the transformation of US-based constructions of citizenship, legality, and rights. Latinx youth scholarship must strive to engage youth-centered intersectional frameworks to document and understand Latinx youth coming-of-age experiences in the United States, especially in a time of contested citizenship.

PART I

Making Meaning of Citizenship

Citizenship, like other terms entwined with social, cultural, economic, legal, and political meanings, is a complex concept to define. This has led scholars to theorize the philosophical as well as social implications of citizenship. T. H. Marshall, one of the leading political theorists on the study of citizenship, posited that citizenship is predicated upon an individual's sense of belonging within the nation-state, and the civil, political, and social rights that characterize individual-state relationships. In these early writings, citizenship is theorized as an individual's relationship to the nation-state. The right to citizenship was associated with privileges and responsibilities. Building on Marshall's theorizing, feminist political scholars Nira Yuval-Davis and Ruth Lister argue that citizenship constitutes a marker of identity and belonging.[1] Citizenship is constructed through historical, cultural, social, legal, and political discourses that operate to maintain the nation-state's social structures and institutions, which oversee its power to govern society, including people residing within its physical, geographic boundaries.[2] The social, cultural, political, and legal practices of a society create institutionalized structures that at times can serve to empower or limit people's rights, opportunities, and sense of belonging. The meanings associated with citizenship hold implications for the thriving of individuals and communities. It is these value-laden meanings attached to citizenship that make defining and characterizing the everyday embodiments of citizenship a convoluted and mundane task.

Citizenship and the Nation-State

Conceptualizing citizenship along nation-state–prescribed meanings delimits the agency, participation, sense of belonging, and rights of some individuals and communities. For young people, who are institutionally marginalized as noncitizens or future citizens because of their age, this is especially the case. Society's view of youth as future adults, specifically as citizens in the making, characterizes their citizenship. Because youth are not adults yet, but will be, they have limited institutional power.[3] Similarly, youth rights are constrained as these are transmitted through the structure of the state via the institution of the family.[4] Ageist discourses that reinforce adult-centered perspectives work to preserve the power and positioning of adults over young people. Ageism, when overlaid with the racism that upholds nativist constructions of citizenship, positions Latinx youth as noncitizens or, at best, citizens in the making. The ageism and racist nativism embedded in hegemonic discourses that surface in relation to youth rights positions and views young people as citizens to be. This further disempowers Latinx youth by limiting their agency, participation, and sense of belonging. The hegemonic discourses that imbue US-based constructions of citizenship have the potential to dehumanize and render unworthy the lives, humanity, and dignity of youth. In this case, how citizenship is constructed and how youthhood is understood intersect to marginalize Latinx youth on account of their age, race, ethnicity, and immigrant status, both their own and that of their families.

Latinx youth associations with citizenship, legality, and rights surfaced frequently as passing statements over the course of several Change 4 Good program sessions. At other times, these were brought up as playful, sometimes problematic remarks. Playfulness, manifested in subtle comments such as teasing, would often render visible Latinx youth positionalities and lived experiences. Yet Latinx youth were often encouraged by the adult Change 4 Good program facilitators to connect their lived experiences with the curriculum and share their own stories. We developed workshops, activities, and lesson plans centered on supporting youth critical literacies, via reflexive dialogues and project-oriented lesson plans.

During one of the Change 4 Good program sessions, focused on helping youth develop and determine what images they would include in their mural, several young people drew images of the US flag and people coming together holding hands around what appeared to be the world. While discerning and reflecting upon these drawings, youth conversed about what they were drawing and the meanings they wished to convey.

Lina and Iris were still intently working on their drawings. Lina wanted to draw something about freedom, immigrants, and papers [legal documentation]. Another youth asked what immigrants are. Lina tried to explain by saying, "They [immigrants] are illegal people in the country." The program facilitator said that immigrants are not "illegal people." We then tried to explain the differences in immigrant status and citizenship. Lina told us that they [the immigrants in her drawing] needed "papers"—and Feliz jokingly said, "Everyone has papers. Toilet papers!" Iris, Lina and Feliz, like the rest of us, laughed. But it was an awkward comic relief in relation to a word—"illegal"—that none of us felt comfortable hearing, yet the youth were familiar with.[5]

Because of the difficulties of defining citizenship and characterizing what constitutes it or who is a citizen, it was not surprising to observe Latinx youth like Lina, Feliz, and Iris ascribing different meanings and associations to these terms. Some of these meanings reflected popular or conventional discourses, whereas others resisted these as they reflected upon their lives and the significance of these terms for their families and communities. In defining citizenship, Latinx youth often responded with comments that reproduced hegemonic discourses, as Lina's remark demonstrates. Yet they also troubled these meanings when they could draw from their lived experiences in school, family, and community contexts.

Three of the most common tropes offered by Latinx youth were citizenship as the possession of papers (i.e., *papeles*), voting as the hallmark of citizenship, and good student behaviors as constituting citizenship. Latinx youth remarks reflected the complexities and contradictions of conceptualizing citizenship along social, legal, and cultural dimensions. Defining and characterizing citizenship have implications for how people view youth rights, as well as how youth are included, seen, and heard. Latinx youth meaning-making about citizenship, legality, and rights, while at times aligned with hegemonic discourses, was also laden with stories and even humor. These served to offer a critique of US-based constructions of citizenship determined by a nation-state that relegated them, along with their families, to a second-class citizenship that reinforced their marginalization as perpetual foreigners and "alien citizens."[6]

Interrogating Citizenship as a Status, Practice, and Right

Part 1 of *Growing Up Latinx* describes how Latinx youth troubled, engaged, and reproduced hegemonic discourses on citizenship as a status, practice, and right in accordance with US-based constructions of legality and belonging. The meanings, definitions, and associations Latinx youth offered in relation to the terms "citizen" and "citizenship" are the focus of chapters 1, 2, and 3. Latinx youth meanings, for instance, were often offered spontaneously as reflections that were grounded in their school, family, and community experiences, as well as their participation in the Change 4 Good program. Other meanings, however, were offered in the context of one-on-one interviews I conducted after their matriculation from the fifth grade and the program. In the context of these interviews, Latinx youth were asked to share their thoughts on citizenship, legality, and rights, as well as schooling experiences that made their age, race, ethnicity, and immigrant status, as well as gender identities, salient. Immigration experiences associated with nationality and place of birth, along with the possession of legal documentation and the practice of "good" studentship, were meanings that figured prominently in Latinx youth meaning-making. Latinx youth definitions are organized in the following chapters along three themes: (1) citizenship as a status of legality; (2) citizenship as a practice in relation to the nation-state's institutions, specifically the structure of schooling; and (3) citizenship as bearing rights to privileges and responsibilities.

Consistent with previous empirical studies demonstrating youth conceptualizations of citizenship, Latinx youth definitions were associated with having agency, accessing opportunities for meaningful active participation, and a sense of belonging. Developmental psychologist Martin D. Ruck, for example, has found that young people are more likely to describe citizenship as a status, a label that one either has or does not, or is given by the state. Similarly, Ruth Lister and colleagues have found that young people are likely to define citizenship as both a status and a practice, whether that person feels a sense of belonging or social responsibility to the state, and shown how that person in turn participates and contributes to society.[7] Citizenship as a status refers to the association between citizenship and legality, specifically legal status, which affords people social, civil, and political rights and privileges. As evidenced by Latinx youth remarks, examples of citizenship as a status included birthright and naturalized citizenship. The latter was associated with notions of legality, including a person's possession of papers, or legal documents, which grant the person lawful permission to reside in the nation-state. The former described citizenship as a practice associated with rights and responsibilities, bestowed upon an individual by the nation-state. Latinx youth definitions echoed these constructions of citizenship as a status, practice, and rights-bearing construct. In other instances, as further discussed in part 2, Latinx youth meanings of citizenship emphasized the social, relational, and political dimensions of citizenship untethered to the nation-state.

As a socially constructed concept that defines an individual's relationships to the nation-state, citizenship has meanings that extend beyond individual state affiliations as it also describes experiences of belonging. Dominant models of citizenship that rely on liberal and civic republican frameworks, such as those described by T. H. Marshall in *Citizenship and Social Class*, characterize citizenship as a status necessary for the possession of civil, political, and social rights.[8] Universalist models, on the other hand, emphasize communitarianism and pluralism, whereby citizenship is a practice of upholding individual rights and responsibilities in relation to the nation-state and its constituents.[9] These approaches have dominated public and scholarly theorizing, as well as the meanings, values, and practices associated with the construction of citizenship, including how an individual is seen and treated as a citizen.

Citizenship as a status, practice, and right is heavily informed by American ideologies of individualism and meritocracy aligned with the pursuit of the "American Dream."[10] Latinx youth meaning-making, rooted in their lived experiences, was inevitably shaped by these ideologies of *being* and *becoming* American, and thus a citizen of the United States. At the forefront of Latinx youth reflections were the complexities of defining a concept that they experienced in relation to legality and rights, yet were rarely asked to explain. Part 1 describes Latinx youth meanings of citizenship, and how these surfaced in relation to hegemonic discourses associated with *papeles* (legal documentation), specific practices like voting, and schooling experiences of discipline and belonging.

1

Legality as Having *Papeles*

Latinx youth are not empty receptacles of information and experience. On the contrary, they are in tune with their social contexts, actively constructing their understandings and relationship to those around them, including the institutions that shape their lives, and the discourses that inform citizenship, legality, and rights. A process of troubling citizenship and the ways it played out in their lives led them to question discourses associated with its meaning, and thus construct their own definitions. Feliz, a rising sixth-grader and daughter of a single parent and immigrant from El D.F. (Distrito Federal), the capital city of México, distinguished between birthright and naturalized citizens. As we sat in a warm and brightly lit living space, a convertible sofa bed inside Feliz's modest mobile home, located in one of the many trailer park neighborhoods that were characteristic of the community, we talked about her understanding of citizenship and legality in her life and that of her family.

> FELIZ: A citizen, I think it's—for example, a citizen to me means a person that was born here [in the United States] and they have citizen rights, so that means since that person was born here they have [more] rights than the rest of the people who were not born here, but live here, have. Citizens have rights—like the right to vote. They have the right to work, have a house, and the right to adopt kids.
> JESICA: So, who do you think are citizens?
> FELIZ: Yeah, well, just people who were born in that country or place. They are citizens of that specific country or area [nation]. If you were born in México you can't be a citizen of the US unless you get permission, like *papeles* [legal documentation]. Then you can have citizenship.

Woven into Feliz's definition of citizenship were notions of nationality, birthright citizenship, voting rights, and legal documentation. Yet Feliz's remarks seem to challenge sociocultural constructions of youthhood, which assume youth innocence, ignorance, and unworldliness in matters that concern "adult experiences."[1]

Feliz described the challenges of acquiring naturalized citizenship, or an authorized immigration status. She demonstrated her knowledge of *jus soli* citizens as distinct from naturalized citizens. The former are citizens who, by being born in a particular nation-state, are granted citizenship under the Fourteenth Amendment of the US Constitution. The Fourteenth Amendment declares that any person born in the United States, regardless of race, ethnicity, or parental heritage, is a US citizen. *Jus soli* citizens have rights, privileges, and protections that cannot be overturned or denied. Birthright citizenship constitutes part of the federal law under the Civil Rights Act of 1866, which repealed the Supreme Court decision in *Dred Scott v. John Sandford* (1857) that postulated that any person who was the descendant of a slave was not eligible for citizenship. To avoid overturning or altering the Civil Rights Act, the US Congress passed the Fourteenth Amendment in 1868, thereby upholding the right to citizenship for people born on US soil.[2]

Naturalized citizenship, unlike birthright citizenship, involves a person petitioning for US citizenship. The process for citizen naturalization is a lengthy and expensive bureaucratic procedure that requires a person to acquire legal permanent residence (LPR) before potentially applying for naturalized citizenship. To be considered for LPR, a person must submit required documentation to the US Citizenship and Immigration Services (USCIS). As part of the application process, the person must provide evidence that they entered the country lawfully, through some prescribed, authorized immigration status or document, such as a visa, which allowed the person to remain in the United States lawfully for a specific period of time. Additionally, the person must demonstrate exceptional moral character, law-abidingness, and the capacity to maintain financial stability and independence, through consistent employment and/or sponsorship through kinship. After a specific period has passed, in some cases at least five years, the person may then apply for naturalization through an adjustment of status process from LPR to naturalized citizenship.

US naturalized citizens are presumed to be statutorily protected from detention and deportation. Under the Trump administration, however, a task force was instituted to investigate and scrutinize certain naturalized citizens presumed to have committed fraud to obtain naturalization. In June 2018 the USCIS, in collaboration with the Department of Homeland Security and the Department of Justice, implemented two operations: Operation Second Look and Operation Janus. The former is a nationwide campaign to investigate and review cases of naturalized citizens who obtained citizenship by concealing in their application prior orders of deportation and removal from the United States. Unlike Operation Second Look, the latter began under the Obama administration and seeks to prevent documented immigrants (e.g., LPR) who received a removal or deportation order under a different name from obtaining or further applying for adjustment of status and immigration services.[3] Efforts to "denaturalize" US citizens appear to be justified under the pretense of protecting and securing the nation-state from presumed "criminals" or "illegal aliens" who nativist pundits claim have "cheated" the US immigration process. The inherent racist nativism that surfaces in the public sphere has the potential to shape the social, cultural, and political climate, as well as fuel hegemonic discourses, campaigns, and legislation like Operation Second Look. Under this hyper-scrutiny of people's presumed legality and their process toward naturalization, the guarantee of well-being, rights, and protection from deportation is severely compromised.

Legality, as Feliz claimed, is determined by nation-state–granted authorization or "permission" to lawfully reside in the country. Although Feliz did not name naturalization explicitly, she referred to the process of acquiring legality as gaining "permission"; this can be interpreted as "earning" a citizen status. Feliz's nuanced understanding of citizenship as being tied to nationality, rights, and legal documentation was associated with notions of belonging as determined by having *papeles* (papers, or legal documentation). The juxtaposition of a Latinx young person's immigrant status to that of their family members who are authorized or undocumented immigrants made their identity as US-born citizens salient. Latinx youth meanings of citizenship were complex, as well as implicitly and explicitly tied to notions of legality and rights.

Legality, like citizenship, is a concept that entails a sociolegal relationship to the nation-state. As a juridical status, the term "legality" describes the political subjectivities and identities of immigrants who are presumed to be undocumented.[4] The condition or status of legality materializes in the everyday lives of those who are labeled as or presumed to be unlawfully residing in the United States, or undocumented because of their race, ethnicity, language, and other markers of their identities and positionalities. Legality is associated with experiences of racialization and state-sanctioned exclusion or institutional marginalization, as well as vis-à-vis the false equivalency that to be a citizen is to be American, and to be American is to be racialized as white, as Nilda Flores-González documented among a diverse group of Latinx young adults in her book *Citizens but Not Americans*.[5]

Counter to the notion of legality is the construction of illegality. In recent years, the term "illegal" has become a pejorative, an offensive term that dehumanizes and curtails the rights of people presumed to be undocumented. The label or use of "illegal" is often deployed to dehumanize and disenfranchise undocumented people whose immigrant status is rendered unlawful or criminal. Latinx youth use of and at times rejection of the word "illegal" reflect the broader sociolegal, political, and hegemonic discourses they were exposed to, and how they often sought to make sense of contradictory messages that did not reflect their ways of understanding and experiencing citizenship in their school, family, and community contexts. Yet associations between citizenship and legality were often produced by Latinx youth in subtle ways. Feliz, for example, referenced the possession of papers, or legal documentation, as important for acquiring citizenship. *Papeles*, according to Feliz, afforded immigrants the security to live without fear of deportation. Latinx youth meanings at times reflected their knowledge, as well as critiques of the political climate, characterized by restrictive immigration policies, including the tightening and hyper-militarization of the México-United States border. When pressed further, however, Latinx youth unpacked their meanings to center and highlight the implications of citizenship and rights in relation to their lives.

Latinx youth described citizenship as a status determined by possessing legal documentation. Legality was equated with having legal documents or *papeles*, which Latinx youth understood as being conferred and legitimized by the nation-state. A legal document such as a visa, green card (i.e., LPR), or some other authorized immigration status maintains the nation-state's power over the person because it determines the extent of a person's free movement within and across borders.[6] These border-crossing experiences and constraints on movement across geopolitical landscapes have been of concern to naturalized citizens who under the Trump administration are presumed to be undocumented. In the absence of legal documentation, movement becomes constrained and restricted, and a cause for great concern and grief to individuals and families.[7] For undocumented and mixed-status families, this is especially the case.[8] Latinx youth associated legal status with citizenship because *papeles*, aside from their literal meaning, took on a significant value in determining the safety, stability, and well-being of their families.

Bearing Witness to Deportation

In the United States there are approximately 16 million people living in mixed-status families.[9] Reports estimate that 4.1 million young people born in the United States under the age of eighteen live with at least one undocumented parent, and 5.9 million have at least one undocumented family member.[10] The term "mixed-status" refers to families in which one or both parents or other immediate family members are undocumented or hold a non-US citizen authorized immigration status. Temporary protected status (TPS), legal permanent residence (LPR), or visas are examples of lawful or authorized immigration status. Citizen youth born in the United States as *jus soli* citizens living in Latinx mixed-status families do not experience the same liberties as youth whose families are not living under the constant fear or threat of deportation.[11] Latinx youth occasionally talked about their family's mixed status and how it impacted them or those they knew. Experiences with and fear of familial deportation occasionally surfaced in the context of Change 4 Good, especially in relation to discussions about family well-being, community safety, and belonging amidst a climate of heightened anti-immigrant sentiments ensconced in racist nativism.

During one Change 4 Good program session, as youth were cutting out newspaper and magazine articles, popular culture clippings, and images to include in the collages they were making to describe their community, I recall youth sharing among themselves the immigrant status of their parents and family members.

Celine said that her parents didn't have citizenship, but that they were allowed to stay here [in the United States] because they had a "green card" [legal permanent residence]. Diego, in a seemingly quiet tone of voice, uttered that his uncle was deported a few months ago. I asked him if his family was okay, and he said that it was very sad because his uncle had to leave the family and everyone missed him.[12]

The youth fell silent after Diego's comment. Although some of us, both youth and adults, had personal experiences with family deportation, I was unsettled by the realities of this among youth. Not knowing how to respond or engage with the youth in a deeper, more meaningful way, or perhaps to attempt to unpack that experience further and its impact on Diego's family, we turned to silence. To this day, glossing over it and shifting away our focus has caused me to reflect on how the lives of Latinx youth were significantly shaped by the nation-state and the racist nativism that informed their experiences of belonging and overall well-being. Assessing and understanding the conditions and risk of deportability seemed to be a part of their lives as Latinx youth.

Latinx youth were aware of and often witnessed instances of deportation and family separation in their families and communities. In September 2008, in the span of just a few days, more than a thousand people across cities in California were arrested by ICE in what has been described as one of the most massive immigration raids in the state.[13] Some of these raids took place in communities characterized by a growing immigrant population, as well as low-income and working-class families. Just a few months prior, in May 2008 in the Central Coast of California, a region known for its agricultural growth and migrant labor, approximately four hundred undocumented immigrants were detained and taken into custody by ICE.[14] These events left a catastrophic ripple effect on the already institutionally marginalized, unincorporated, low-income, and predominantly Latinx immigrant communities of the region.

The impact of these immigration raids reverberated across communities, including the families of Latinx youth in Change 4 Good. Shortly after the raids, testimonies from community members at grassroots community organizing meetings in Maplewood underscored the fear and anxiety many families experienced. The fear was so palpable that families stopped taking their children to school, going to work, and attending public events, including Mass and other religious and/or cultural gatherings important to their sense of belonging and community practices. The Maplewood community's response to the incidence of raids was indicative of the fear for their safety. Instead of seeking resources, support, and guidance, some Latinx immigrant communities residing in areas with a perceived high demographic population of undocumented and mixed-status families retreated to the shadows. Reports indicate that residents of communities that have experienced raids are hesitant to seek support and services from law enforcement, and less likely to report incidents of violence and delinquency in their neighborhood.[15] The distrust and ambivalence toward law enforcement position immigrant communities at a greater risk for experiencing crime and other incivilities that can further threaten the well-being and public safety of the entire community.

Unequivocally, anti-immigrant sentiments that often materialize in legislation, along with deportation campaigns and immigration raids, have a devastating impact on families and communities, including young people. Luis H. Zayas, in his book *Forgotten Citizens*, identifies parental deportability as having life-altering implications for healthy youth development and well-being; family separation has a detrimental effect on a young person's positive development.[16] For Latinx youth in undocumented and mixed-status families, this is especially the case. In fact, Latinx youth in Change 4 Good who talked about these incidents drew from personal experiences, including being directly affected by parental deportability.

One day after the Change 4 Good program ended, some of us were hanging around the school to wait for the youth to be picked up by a parent or older sibling. Usually, most youth would be picked up on time; however, on the rare occasions that they were not, we played tag, exchanged jokes, or talked about our day. Only a few times were we asked by a youth or a parent to walk with them home. Andrés was one of the youth who would regularly be picked up on time or even a bit early before the program ended to attend other extracurricular activities, particularly sports. It was springtime, and thus baseball season. On this occasion, however, his ride was late, so those of us who carpooled waited with him. As we stood around chatting about sports and how I knew little to nothing about baseball, I noticed Andrés's necklaces. My inquiry into the story of the necklaces unfolded into a salient memory that remains very present in my mind.

> I noticed Andrés had three necklaces that were hiding underneath his t-shirt but somewhat visible because of the contrasting colors of brown, blue, and white from his navy-blue shirt. I noticed the white necklace more so than the other ones because it was sticking out from his t-shirt collar. I asked Andrés about his necklaces. Andrés said "sure" as he began to take them out from under his t-shirt one by one. I identified the white one as a rosary, with a cross at the end and ten beads intersecting one larger bead. I also noticed the other two necklaces. The blue one was a cross, made from knitted material unlike the brown and white ones, which seemed to be made out of plastic. The latter one had somewhat of a white triangle-shaped pendant that was actually a shark tooth. I asked him where he had gotten these necklaces, and another youth interrupted to say that his dad had given him the one with the shark tooth. I asked, "Is that right?" and Andrés responded, "Yeah, our dads are friends." I then asked Andrés about the other necklaces, and he said that the rosary was given to him by his dad. I asked where his dad was from—recognizing it as a familiar rosary design commonly worn among my family in México—and he replied, "Jalisco." Before I could follow up with another question, and share that I was from a state near Jalisco, Andrés volunteered information that left me startled and disheartened. He shared that his dad was in Jalisco, and added: "He was deported back to México. So, I'm adopted." I then noticed that his eyes looked away from mine and he began to focus on the six Character Counts! posters that took up so much space on the crammed classroom walls. I asked, "Are you okay?" and he replied, "Yeah, I'm fine" as he nodded with at swift "yes." I asked, "Do you need a hug? Are you okay?" and Andrés nodded again emphasizing, "Yeah, I'm fine. I'm okay! Really!" I let him know that I just wanted to make sure he was okay, and that I didn't want him to feel saddened by our conversation. Before he joined the rest of the youth who were playing outside, I emphasized that if he needed someone to talk to he could reach out to me, if he wanted to, and I would listen. Andrés replied, "Okay, thanks" and he went off to join the other youth.[17]

The story of Andrés, a ten-year-old fifth-grader, is particularly striking. Andrés's experience is heart-wrenching for me because it demonstrates how parental separation, as a result of deportability, is not a new or recent phenomenon that surged under the Trump administration. Although there is some solace in bearing witness to Andrés's resilience, it is disconcerting to learn that such an experience is not unique. A 2019 report by the American Immigration Council on family separation involving parental detention and removal indicated that between 2010 and 2012, the US ICE issued more than 200,000 deportation orders for parents of citizen youth.[18] These orders have implications for determining whether a youth will be able to remain under the care of a parent or taken into the custody of the state. While a parent might choose to bring their youth with them to their country of origin, the state might again intervene if it deems that the youth will not be provided with a safe and stable environment, even under the care of the parent.

Deportation has significant implications for youth development. Yet regardless of these implications and robust evidence demonstrating its negative impacts on youth overall health and well-being, raids continue. In the span of one year, between October 2017 and May 2018, approximately 2,700 youth under the age of eighteen were separated from a parent.[19] More than half of these youth were separated from a parent who was detained or taken into immigration custody. In cases where a citizen youth is separated from a parent who may be waiting for a hearing or date of removal from the United States, the youth is taken into the custody and care of the welfare state, the Child Protective Services (CPS). Child welfare services oversee the care of the youth until a family relative is able to claim guardianship and responsibility for their care. In cases where both parents are deported or subject to removal, the high levels of anxiety and fear can inflict insurmountable socioemotional, psychological, and developmental stress upon a youth.[20]

The experiences of citizen youth whose parents have been subjected to deportation and removal underscore Andrés's story. The psychological and health consequences for a young person separated from their parent under such political and sociolegal conditions is likely to have a lifelong impact. Zayas notes that the intensification of anti-immigration policies, racialized criminalization, and zero-tolerance immigration law enforcement, particularly from ICE, has led to heightened psychological trauma among Latinx youth in immigrant and mixed-status families. Parental deportability, in addition to causing psychological trauma, can lead to economic hardships and precarity that exacerbate living conditions of poverty and a diminished sense of well-being.

Andrés's ability and willingness to reflect on his experience as an adopted youth from a Mexican deportee attested to the implications and life-changing consequences of parental deportation. Although Andrés appeared a bit soft-spoken, he was usually engaged and interested in Change 4 Good program activities. He showed positive socioemotional development as evidenced by his active engagement in the program, as well as clear expression of his thoughts and prosocial interactions with youth and adults. It is difficult to discern the extent to which his experiences with parental deportability left a scar in his overall well-being and development. Andrés's story, while unknown to most youth and adults in Change 4 Good, appeared to inform his understandings and meaning-making about citizenship; his lived experiences underscored the salience of legality in his young life.

Border-Crossing Immigrant Youth

While rehearsing for the focus groups youth would be conducting with students, school staff, parents, and community members as part of their action project—and which would help inform the making of their mural themes and design—youth often took seriously the task of facilitating discussions as well as sharing stories. Some Latinx youth, for example, often reflected upon and described instances when they felt they had the power, or did not have the power, to make a change in their community. This was also one of their focus group prompts, and the starting point for conversations on border-crossing experiences. Although stories of immigration and deportability were not specifically the purpose of their focus groups, these stories were occasionally shared when participants described experiences of limited or no power.

David, a ten-year-old recent immigrant to the United States, shared a story about his schooling experiences in El Salvador. Juxtaposing the porousness of his former school's physical infrastructure with that of the border made salient for some youth other people's experiences of migration and belonging.

David was very soft spoken, as he shared that he tried to "escape" [ditch] school once. When asked by other youth why he had done that, David gave no real answer, he just shrugged his shoulders. Hesitating to continue, Andrés then helped David tell his story by encouraging him to continue. Andrés shared with the group that David was bored [at school] so he walked out of the school. We wondered and asked why the teachers didn't notice him leaving, but David shared that no one had seen him, so he just walked home because his house was close to the school. However, his mother found him at home and brought him back to the school, where the teacher later disciplined him. As the youth continued to listen to David's story, it was revealed that this incident occurred while David was living in El Salvador. As David was telling his story, Diego, Iris, and Celine remarked that David had "illegally" crossed the border into the United States.[21]

After this story was shared, several youth and adults were taken aback by the remarks offered by Diego, Iris, and Celine. I certainly was surprised to learn that Latinx youth knew about each other's border-crossing experiences. Opting to maintain our attention on the focus group activity at hand, we adults encouraged the youth to follow the focus group script and prompt. Yet David's story and the remarks that followed made salient what Latinx youth knew or assumed about each other based on their presumed immigrant status. Furthermore, in reflecting on and discussing their schooling experiences of power, or lack thereof, some youth disclosed David's immigrant—and presumed undocumented—status, thereby demonstrating how they were attuned to the migrant experiences of their peers. Latinx youth knew that David was a recent immigrant from El Salvador who had arrived just a year prior. Although we could not (nor did we want to) confirm whether the comments by Latinx youth had any validity, it was evident that their border-crossing experiences circulated among themselves. Latinx youth were keenly aware of youth immigrant experiences, as well as the struggles of adapting to a new social context, culture, and language.

Recent immigration to the United States characterized the experiences of two other Change 4 Good youth, in addition to David. Joaquín and Yesenia had emigrated from México a few years before David, yet they all appeared to be well-adjusted to their new environment. David,

Joaquín, and Yesenia emigrated in the company of a parent or relative. When asked to share more, however, they claimed that they were too young to remember details of their border-crossing experiences. The intact families, academic engagement, and overall positive development of David, Joaquín, and Yesenia suggest a positive context of reception, with their immigrant experiences having little or limited impact on their lives. All of them spoke English well, with some subtleties in their accent, and were adept at speaking and reading Spanish with a modest degree of proficiency in their writing.

Data on the number of unaccompanied migrant youth who entered the United States are limited given the inadequate record-keeping and the fact that immigration law does not distinguish between youth and adult migrants.[22] Reports indicate that in the span of thirty months, between October 2013 and July 2016, approximately 156,000 unaccompanied migrant youth were apprehended at the México-United States border.[23] Most unaccompanied migrant youth are fleeing violent and poverty-stricken regions in Central America or countries with ongoing civil, political, and economic instability and unrest, such as El Salvador. Like most adult migrants, unaccompanied migrant youth make the journey to the United States in hopes of pursuing a more promising, financially stable, and safe future for themselves and their families, who might have been left behind. Family reunification is another reason why some unaccompanied migrant youth journey north of the México-United States border.[24] Anthropologist Lauren Heidbrink notes, in *Migrant Youth, Transnational Families, and the State*, that unaccompanied migrant youth experiences elucidate a set of predicaments and challenges within immigration law, as well as a problematic disjuncture between immigration legislation and family welfare services.[25] The circumstances of a young person's emigrating decision, their immigrant experience, and the conditions upon arrival unequivocally shape their lives and future.

The border-crossing immigrant experience for young people poses stark implications for their overall development and well-being. Research indicates that youth who immigrate in their late adolescent or early adulthood years struggle to adapt to new environments, and experience limited opportunities in education.[26] Additionally, immigrant youth are more likely to experience negative health, psychological, and developmental outcomes compared to youth who migrate in their early years of childhood or during preadolescence.[27] Some of these negative outcomes include depression and anxiety associated with uncertainty about their futures, as well as post-traumatic stress resulting from immigration experiences marked by violent or life-threatening incidents. Among Latinx youth who were recent immigrants to the United States, these outcomes were not evident in the context of our relationship and interactions in Change 4 Good.

The Value of *Papeles*

Joaquín arrived in the United States as a first-grader, and although he often described the difficulties of having to learn English, he was well-spoken and highly involved in school activities, such as playing soccer, excelling in math, which was his favorite subject, and looking out for his younger siblings. In describing his experiences upon arrival to the United States, however, Joaquín shared how he struggled to communicate with teachers who were unable to engage with or appropriately respond to his diverse cultural and linguistic strengths as a Spanish speaker and English-language learner.

As a proficient Spanish speaker, Joaquín often struggled to articulate his thoughts in English, yet he was confident in communicating complex ideas in Spanish. Seated at the small dinner table inside a tightly packed yet well-organized kitchen, in a two-bedroom apartment a few blocks from the local middle school, which Joaquín attended, we talked about his new friends. The linguistic nuances of his bilingualism surfaced as Joaquín attempted to articulate his associations with the word "citizen," which he referred to as *ciudadano* (citizen) or *ciudadanía* (citizenship) during our interview.

> JESICA: So you've heard of the word "citizenship" in school, but do you know what it means?
> JOAQUÍN: I can't, like, I can't describe it [citizenship]. It's hard for me. I think—wait, what's *citizen* in Spanish?
> JESICA: *Ciudadano.*
> JOAQUÍN: *Oh, ser ciudadano.* [Oh, to be a citizen.] Like having *ciudadanía* [citizenship]. Hmmm, yeah, I heard it on television. I heard

about what happens when you aren't a citizen. I heard that you—like, people could get citizenship. Like, you need to be in the United States for a certain amount of time and then you could be[come] a citizen. You could go get a visa and fill out paperwork. Then, like, you could go to México and do other things with it [citizenship].

Joaquín's statement made visible the privilege that comes with the possession of legal documentation. His response echoed Feliz's remarks, which alluded to the significance of legal authorization or permission to reside in the United States. Joaquín troubled the construction of legality when he stated that a person is a citizen of the nation-state when they are eligible and free to re-enter a country with the proper immigrant authorization documents. For Joaquín, the privilege of crossing the border without repercussions made visible the links between citizenship, legality, and rights.

The freedom that comes with possessing legal documents, or *papeles*, was a defining feature of Joaquín's meaning-making of citizenship. Despite initially struggling to define the term, Joaquín described it as the status of being a *ciudadano* (citizen), thereby conceiving citizenship as a label with material and social significance. Similar to Feliz, Joaquín associated citizenship with a discourse of "deservingness"—citizenship is earned and granted, not necessarily given or obtained through free will. Joaquín also constructed the term in relation to the amount of time a person has resided in the United States. He did not elaborate on what constitutes a "certain amount of time" to warrant citizenship or lawful status, however. Instead, Joaquín made causal assumptions between length of residence and legal status, consequently highlighting a common association that citizenship is a function of individual and nation-state relationships. Assumptions such as these further the construction of citizenship as a status and right that could be acquired over time. Yet this perspective implies that legality, like the status of citizenship, is not static, but instead shaped by the sociolegal structures, policies, and practices put forth by a system that ultimately determines a person's right to belong, and the conditions under which they can apply for citizen naturalization or some other authorized immigration status.

Critical immigration studies literature posits that citizenship, like other constructs such as legality, is presumed to be fixed and stable.[28]

The construction of citizenship—specifically the process of determining whether a person is or can *become* a citizen—is rooted in hegemonic discourses that reflect racist nativist assumptions about a person's lawfulness, and consequently whether they belong and are treated with dignity and respect. To underscore this point, Nicholas De Genova, in "Migrant 'Illegality' and Deportability in Everyday Life,"[29] as well as other critical immigration scholars,[30] explain that law-abidingness, criminality, and legality are refractions of the law, which over the years have become more constrictive and racialized to exclude certain ethnic communities. The impact of these practices manifests as the terrorizing of Latinx communities, as they attempt to work the boundaries of their belonging.[31] Laws and policies shift and change to constrain as well as disenfranchise those who transgress the interests of the nation-state.

Dominant social group members have the power to determine the conditions and circumstances under which citizenship, legality, and rights are afforded to immigrants as well as other institutionally marginalized groups. The status of being a legal citizen implies recognition of a person's rights and enfranchisement, along with the freedom to move across borders. A visa, like other sociolegal authorizations, for example, represents the nation-state's legitimate recognition of a person's entry or rightful movement across borders, under the conditions prescribed by the nation-state. In simple terms, as Joaquín remarked, a person can "go to México" if they have a visa or some other sanctioned document—but the visa, like other conditional legal authorizations, has a limit.

The possession of legal documentation as a criterion for citizenship was a common topic among Latinx youth. Given the contemporary sociolegal and political rhetoric on immigration, these connections among Latinx youth were not surprising. Furthermore, the permanence of detention and deportability campaigns that threaten families and youth rights was reproduced in Latinx youth citizenship associations with legality and rights.

One example of a policy that affords some presumed relief from deportation, but does not allow for the privilege of mobility across borders, is the Deferred Action for Childhood Arrivals (DACA). DACA is an executive order instituted under the Obama administration in 2012 that grants some undocumented immigrants a very modest degree of legal protections and opportunities. Under DACA, youth and young adults under the age of sixteen who arrived before June 2007, have demonstrated exceptional moral character, and are enrolled in a higher education institution or military service are eligible to apply to the program. A major benefit of DACA is being exempt from deportation, as well as obtaining a two-year work permit, social security number, and driver's license. Although the Trump administration has continued to challenge the terms and conditions of DACA, as of this writing, the program is still in effect. Yet it must be clear that DACA does not provide a pathway to citizenship. DACA grants permission to temporarily reside and work in the United States legally.[32] To nativist pundits, DACA signifies the state's refusal to protect its borders and "American" citizens.

The Trump presidential election heightened anti-immigrant sentiments and racist nativism among a very powerful subsector of United Statesian society, primarily white supremacists. In this context of rising fascism and white nationalism, the Trump administration fiercely advocated for rescinding DACA along with other immigrant and social service programs. Additionally, it has enforced restrictive immigration legislation and heightened the militarization of the border, which has further criminalized undocumented immigrants, all while continuing to detain, deport, and separate families. The cumulative impact of these practices and policies has been the introduction of draconian anti-immigration legislation, such as the Muslim ban (Executive Order 13769, Protecting the Nation from Foreign Terrorist Entry into the United States). These actions have been rightfully met with resistance from activist and grassroots organizations, and a coalition of states has sought to halt anti-immigration policies, including the repeal of DACA, which made its way to the Supreme Court.

DACA is viewed as a hopeful initiative in line with efforts toward comprehensive immigration reform, as well as protection from deportation, access to lawful work, financial stability, and educational opportunities; attacks on DACA have led many undocumented people to experience fear and insecurity, however. The precarity of undocumented youth is well underscored by the work of Roberto G. Gonzales in his book *Lives in Limbo*, which demonstrates how undocumented youth are coming of age in the United States to face uncertain futures and lives in legal limbo. The current state of the executive order is still being debated; the future of more than 800,000 DACAmented youth and young adults hangs in the balance.[33]

The aspirations and desires for legality among people who have resided in the United States for most of their lives are significant—and this was also reflected in the stories of Latinx youth in Change 4 Good. On an unusually hot summer day, Yesenia and I met at her former elementary school for an interview. At the time, the elementary school was not gated; there were no fences around its parking lot or main school grounds. The school would usually remain open and accessible to the public, especially considering the community's unincorporated status, which was characterized by limited access to recreational areas like parks and other open spaces. The school was centrally located in the community, and because it was also near Yesenia's home, we agreed to meet there.

Seated on a metal picnic bench beside the newly added solar panels, Yesenia and I talked about her time in Change 4 Good and how she missed everyone and wanted to know what we were all up to. It had been a little over a year since she had matriculated from the fifth grade and moved on to attend the local middle school. Well into our conversation, we began to talk about what she was looking forward to this summer, and she explained that she was going to begin her process for acquiring "citizenship."

JESICA: So, you were explaining the process for getting citizenship. Can you tell me a little bit more of what that process is like?

YESENIA: Well, they ask for a lot of papers. They need your passport. They need your birth certificate. They need to know—like, they need to have proof that you've been here for a certain time and they need *a lot* of papers. Like, not even my mom could get all those papers that they're asking her for. It's a long process.

JESICA: For getting citizenship?

YESENIA: Hmm, yeah, and I think the [visa] status—I think it's that one I'm eligible for. I'm not sure, though. It's a temporary one, and then after three years—after you have that, you can fill out papers again and this time you can get your green card [legal permanent residence]. And later you can apply to get the [naturalized] citizenship. Yeah, um, you also have to fill out—you have to write an essay explaining why you should get it [name of specific visa], and you have to explain what happened to you back then [country of origin] for them to give you the status or some permission to stay [in the United States].

JESICA: So, you have to write an essay about you?

YESENIA: A letter, like, a statement about, like, what happened to me. I had to write and explain why I should get the [name of specific visa].

JESICA: That must be difficult to write?

YESENIA: Um, well, pretty much I just wrote that I should get it [name of specific visa] because that way I could help my mom more with the rent payments and bills. I could actually—like, when I'm legal [documented], I can have a job, and I could help my mom with money and stuff like that. I could go to college and get a good education.

Yesenia, an eleven-year-old immigrant from Guatemala, stated that education and work opportunities are her primary motivations for becoming a citizen, for being "legal." She described these as opportunities accessible via the attainment of a lawful or authorized immigration status. In drawing from her lived experiences, Yesenia expressed knowledge of the process for acquiring lawful residency in the United States. For Yesenia, legality and citizenship, although associated, were not one and the same, however.

Legality, either through a visa, green card, or naturalized citizenship, appeared to be more significant. That is, Yesenia equated legality with the capacity to access certain opportunities, such as lawful employment and an education. She aspired to obtain citizenship, yet her priority was acquiring lawfulness or a legal status to help her mother. If granted legality, Yesenia would be able to pursue education and employment opportunities that would benefit her and help support her mother. Yesenia's knowledge of the legalization process, along with her motivation to obtain legality to work and go to college, underscored her aspirations, as well as those of other undocumented youth who are impacted by anti-immigration legislation.[34]

Yesenia troubled US-based constructions of citizenship by making a significant distinction between legality and citizenship. Nonetheless, her response subscribed to a rhetoric of deservingness reflecting the neoliberalization of citizenship.[35] The presumption that legality should be granted on the basis of capital and labor—namely, a young person's future potential to contribute to the neoliberal structure of the nation-state—reifies sociocultural constructions of youthhood that position youth as citizens of the future who will become workers and consumers.[36] As Ruth Lister notes, a future-oriented perspective on youth citizenship is limiting and problematic because it overlooks the present-day agency of young people to engage politically, civically, and socially in creating social change.[37] These perspectives presume a prospective expandable worker, whose lawfulness will continue to rely on and be determined by the nation-state. Furthermore, it demonstrates that because youth are underage, youth citizenship is conceived as futuristic or *in the making*.

In contrast, Yesenia's motivations to work and financially assist her family troubled such assumptions and highlighted her social and political subjectivities. Additionally, they resisted or pushed against the presumption that youth are acritical, apolitical, and invested in play rather than work.[38] The desire to assist the family is a common explanation provided by unaccompanied migrant youth.[39] Responses similar to Yesenia's are also noted, in general, among youth in low-income and working-class Latinx immigrant families.[40] Yesenia was not alone in her desire to obtain an immigrant status that would afford her opportunities for a stable, more prosperous future for herself and her family.

Conceptualizing citizenship as a status determined by the nation-state via the possession of legal documents was a common theme among Latinx youth. The statements by Joaquín and Yesenia made visible their familiarity with the legal system, the bureaucracy of legalization, and the implications of residing in the nation-state unlawfully. Consequently, these conditions have implications for accessing opportunities, services, and resources, as well as cross-border mobility. Latinx youth troubled and at times problematized US-based constructions of citizenship that were associated with notions of legality in accordance with individual-state relationships. These remarks were often a part of the conversations that unfolded among them in Change 4 Good, especially during the summer sessions when we met for longer periods at a time, approximately four hours, instead of one hour a week as we did during the academic year.

On one occasion, youth were engaged in developing and discerning themes and symbols to represent their community in their mural. As they were immersed in their community stories, through their focus groups and lived experiences, we transitioned into talking about their summer plans and travels. Some Latinx youth, however, hesitated to share about their plans.

> Lina raised her hand and appeared somewhat coy, hedging about what she was about to say. She said that "Some people might not have papers, you know—and I'm not saying this because I'm referring to anyone or anything, but some people—some parents, cannot go or leave the US." Although no one responded or questioned her comment, the conversation shifted to talking about people who don't have citizenship. One of the program facilitators commented: "So, people that don't have citizenship also don't have certain rights?" and most of the youth agreed, with one remarking, "Because people that can't travel might not be able to because they are immigrants"—and another adding, "Some immigrants also can't vote because they might not be citizens." Finally, one stated: "They also cannot leave the country because they are illegal." In my attempt to respond, however, Lina intervened to say, "Some immigrant workers are not treated equally too"—adding, "They also don't have the rights that other people can have." Lina talked about the inequality in pay and workload that her father receives, while Feliz followed up sharing: "Sometimes people ask you for a bunch of stuff that you don't have, like papers [legal documents]."[41]

Latinx youth conceptualized citizenship as a status, largely determined by either having or not having papers, and were aware that a person's lived experiences and opportunities are informed by such status. Citizenship was understood in relation to legality, with social, economic, and political implications; this was illustrated by the remarks offered by Latinx youth, specifically by Feliz and Lina.

Some Latinx youth believed that citizenship as a label could be earned over time, through either legal mechanisms or nation-state–determined procedures. Latinx youth referenced the possession of legal documents in relation to the nation-state because *papeles* were identified as an important signifier of people's rights to belong, to be seen and heard, as well as to have access to opportunities, including travel, fair wages, and an education. Latinx youth meaning-making demonstrates the complexities of defining citizenship, and how associated concepts like legality are constructed as having or not having *papeles*. The sociolegal binaries of belonging, being labeled a citizen or "not from here," according to Latinx youth, were determined by the possession of *papeles*, which—like toilet paper—they believe everyone has a right to have.

2

Socializing Future Citizens

The education of children has a direct bearing on citizenship, and when the state guarantees that all children shall be educated, it has the requirements and the nature of citizenship definitely in mind. It is trying to stimulate the growth of citizens in the making. . . . The aim of education during childhood is to shape the future adult. Fundamentally, it should be regarded, not as a right of the child citizen to go to school, but as a right of the adult citizen to have been educated.
—T. H. Marshall, "Citizenship and Social Class"

Education in the United States serves a fundamental purpose. T. H. Marshall's quote makes this quite clear: "The aim of education during childhood is to shape the future adult." A central function of education is to prepare and socialize the future adult citizen to participate in and contribute to the democratic structure of the nation-state. Individual practices and behaviors within that structure prescribe citizenship as fundamental to a democracy. Accordingly, a citizen is assumed to be an adult individual who follows the laws and takes on rights and responsibilities, like voting, that are determined by the nation-state.

Constructions of "good" citizenship focus heavily on upholding laws, rules, and expectations as informed and shaped by US democracy. The nation-state maintains its power to decide who is a sanctioned member of society according to who upholds the values and norms of its democracy. The law-abiding citizen is constructed as the ideal "good" citizen; the preferred citizen is one who conforms to the status quo.[1] When citizenship is associated with law-abidingness, practices attached to certain meanings of civility develop to constitute an individual as a citizen, or not. US-based constructions of citizenship informed by the law therefore reify a person's relationship to the nation-state.

Stories of law-abidingness were part of the reflections Latinx youth in Change 4 Good often expressed in discussions of citizenship. Seated at a small corner table in the Starbucks closest to the local elementary school, Celine and I talked about her adjustment to a new school. Of the youth in Change 4 Good, Celine, a ten-year-old Latinx youth of Salvadorean descent, was the only one to attend the farthest middle school from the community. Because her cousins attended that school, it was more convenient for her family to coordinate pickups, drop-offs, and day care. Since everyone at her new school seemed to know each other, and she knew only her cousins, Celine shared that she missed her friends from the Change 4 Good program. As we moved through our conversation and eventually incorporated some interview questions, I observed Celine's hesitance to respond to questions about citizenship. When she did offer a response, she often prefaced her remarks or spoke softly. In terms of citizenship, Celine stated,

> I've heard it [the word "citizen"], like—I've heard, like, "citizen," like, "citizen of the state." And there's laws that a citizen—that we should follow, but I don't know much about it [citizenship], other than, like, citizens must follow the laws.

Celine connected the terms "citizen" and "citizenship" to the nation-state; her response reflected her understanding of citizenship as a set of individual responsibilities, including following the laws. Characterized as citizen practices, responsibilities were viewed as important to determine an individual's role in and accountability to the nation-state, as well as a commitment to upholding laws, values, and social norms accordingly. As noted in Celine's remark, the conditions for recognizing a person as a legitimate "citizen of the state" lie in their capacity to follow the rules, or laws. Celine defined citizenship as a practice of law-abidingness by claiming that "citizens must follow the laws."

Individual practices that demonstrate being a well-functioning member of society often include contributing to the capitalistic structure as a worker and consumer, as well as abiding by the laws and social norms of the nation-state. Together, these practices exemplify what society considers "good" citizenship.[2] Latinx youth like Celine presumed that following the law was a necessary requirement of all citizens of the nation-state.

Thus, to be acknowledged as a citizen or deserving inclusion within the nation-state and its polity, a person must demonstrate the capacity and will to follow the law. The performance of law-abidingness among individuals seeking to obtain permanent or authorized immigration status is often imperative for perceiving individuals as "good" or "bad" citizens, deserving or undeserving of citizenship.

If the value of citizenship is to be legitimated, roles and responsibilities must conform to the social norms of a society. Similarly, in the context of schooling, certain expectations and rules are instituted. Education therefore becomes an important institution and setting where structures of power are enforced, along with the socialization of the "good" citizen. Broadly speaking, a nation-state maintains its status quo by reproducing a social order for its constituents through systems of power embedded within institutions that begin and extend beyond schooling. The organizing of these systems transcends institutions and contexts, in turn shaping cultural, social, legal, economic, and political structures informing the types of actions that are recognized as legitimate citizenship practices. In the context of schooling, the hidden curriculum operates as a totalizing system, a mechanism of hegemony that produces a culture of power over students. Deconstructing notions of citizenship as a practice in relation to the nation-state, including the institutionalized contexts wherein certain behaviors are sanctioned or punished, as is the case with schooling, is a central theme of Latinx youth citizenship meaning-making.

The Hidden Curriculum of Schooling

The culture of the hidden curriculum shapes student behaviors. Within the structure of schooling, specific curricula communicate to youth what is good and bad. As described in the literature on critical education, as well as the work of educator and author John Taylor Gatto, the hidden curriculum is a system of beliefs, values, and practices that are institutionalized within the structure of schooling to maintain the social order.[3] In the US education system, the hidden curriculum operates as an organizing yet invisible structure in the context of the classroom that reifies and subsequently determines who is and is not a "good" student. Adults sustain the status quo of schooling by perpetuating the hidden curriculum through interactions of authority and control over students and what they learn or the curricula they engage with, including Character Education.

Implicitly integrated in education curricula are schooling practices that encourage or often expect students to adopt particular behaviors, such as being on-task and acquiescing to authority in the classroom setting.[4] Although some schooling practices might encourage students to express themselves via opportunities for critical literacy and civic engagement, other practices—and certainly the overwhelming majority—emphasize and reinforce student behaviors that align with the status quo. The unsaid and unseen messages in the classroom environment, including their entrenchment in seemingly quotidian student-teacher dynamics, characterize the hidden curriculum of schooling.[5]

As a form of power in the classroom, the hidden curriculum reinforces and instills among the students specific behaviors, such as compliance, to reproduce a culture of hegemony that views students as being able to be molded and educated to fit or conform to desired social norms.[6] The practices that structure schooling, which include classroom student management strategies and discipline, have compelling lifelong implications for students' critical literacy. For boys of color, particularly Latinx and African American students, this is especially the case. More than any other demographic, youth of color are disproportionately disciplined and pushed out of schools at higher rates than white students.[7]

The institutionalized racism that characterizes the hidden curriculum seeps through the classroom to create an environment where teachers and administrators praise conformity, reward obedience, and offer little to no consideration for the diverse experiences and needs of students. These were particularly the outcomes of a study by Regina D. Langhout and Cecily A. Mitchell, who documented the hidden curriculum and student-teacher interactions in a public elementary school classroom.[8] They found that teachers reprimanded Latinx and African American boys more frequently for behaviors that teachers perceived as "deviant." Deviance was characterized by student behaviors outside the bounds of desirable classroom etiquette, such as talking out of turn. Yet similar behaviors were not problematic when performed by white boys and girls. These findings are supported by critical race scholars who argue that the intentions behind *Brown v. Board of Education* (1954) are yet to be realized. In other words, the outcomes of this decision were meant to be more "symbolic than real." Instead of equity and equality in education, students of color have experienced disproportionate levels of punitive disciplinary consequences leading to school pushout and disenfranchisement.[9] Students' academic performance, including their critical literacy development, as well as their sense of belonging in school, were often informed by how they had been racialized and gendered by adults and classroom peers in the context and culture of schooling.

Seated under a tree on a windy day in the park, just across the local middle school parking lot, Santiago and I caught up with each other by sharing jokes and recent travels. We talked about his trip to Guadalajara to meet his mother's family. I asked whether he had been there before and he mentioned that they tried to go every summer; he preferred going to México than anywhere else because he could visit his cousins, play soccer, and learn new "bad" words in Spanish. I then asked him how he was feeling about being in a new school as a sixth-grader, and he began to describe his frustrations with a teacher, Mrs. L, who seemed to constantly "be in a bad mood" and "picking on some of us." Santiago, a Latinx and African American ten-year-old youth, shared his classroom experience with emotion, clearly expressing annoyance over some of his interactions with Mrs. L.

> SANTIAGO: My language arts teacher, Mrs. L, if you had—if you had your hood all weird, she'll, like, put it into place, like, she randomly just puts your hood into place and stuff. And takes your stuff [notebook, pencil, book] out of your backpack, like—I could do it myself.
> JESICA: Why does she do that?
> SANTIAGO: Because she wants—she wants to control everybody, to get ready in *like a minute*.
> JESICA: How does it make you feel when she does that?
> SANTIAGO: Like, kinda sad or shy because, like, when she does that, everybody starts laughing, so yeah.

Santiago's descriptions of his classroom experiences and interactions with his teacher, Mrs. L, highlight the subtle yet palpable practices that characterize the hidden curriculum. Practices that socialize students into performing citizenship in conventional, often acritical and apolitical ways require students to look, act, and behave according to the norms of the classroom culture. In the context of schooling, teachers rewarded actions perceived to align with classroom norms and expectations. On the other hand, the disciplining of student behaviors took place when these acts deviated from the norm, such as posing questions or attempting to nuance a dialogue. Conditional responses of praise or punishment such as these are unwittingly part of the hidden curriculum culture of schooling. Teachers rebuked youth like Santiago for engaging in seemingly nonconforming, disapproved classroom behaviors.

Latinx youth also appeared critically attuned to the way adults, especially teachers, shaped their perceptions and views of students as deficient or "in development." Santiago evidenced this in the unspoken rules and expectations that students, particularly boys of color, experienced and were expected to subscribe to. Santiago highlighted how his body, clothing, backpack, and personal school-related belongings became props to impart a lesson on classroom etiquette and student expectations. The teacher disapproved of Santiago's inability to have his things "in place" and "be ready" for class. This turned into a spectacle for other students to learn from and/or mock.

As if the spectacle were not enough, in some cases student disciplinary consequences of varied degrees followed. These experiences were noted by Yesenia, an eleven-year-old Latinx youth of Guatemalan descent, who shared the following in an interview: "In school, if students don't listen to the rules we're supposed to follow—if we break them, then you're in trouble." Instead of fostering youth critical literacy in a supportive learning environment, disciplinary and punitive classroom strategies can legitimize the exclusion of students of color, especially Latinx who may feel that certain classroom dynamics and student-teacher interactions in the context of the hidden curriculum of schooling challenge their learning experiences.

Latinx students, who might be best positioned to identify social problems impacting their lives and discern solutions to address these, are rarely afforded opportunities to develop their critical literacy, including their capacities to exercise agency to create social change. Such opportunities could help foster students' civic engagement. Yet because Latinx students' academic experiences are continuously challenged by a culture of schooling rooted in the hidden curriculum, more time is spent policing, disciplining, and punishing students than actually cultivating their critical literacy, agency, and voice to speak to issues of concern to them. The behaviors Latinx youth display inside and outside the classroom and school reflect the disparate, often problematic schooling conditions Latinx youth experience. It is worth noting that these schooling practices both demonstrate and reproduce a sociocultural mismatch for students' learning that exacerbates the problem.

Embedded in the culture of the hidden curriculum are ageist, racist, and sexist assumptions about young people, especially Latinx youth. The hidden curriculum rests upon authority figures—namely, adults—foreclosing opportunities for students to challenge social conditions of disempowerment and institutional marginalization. Indeed, teachers play an important role in upholding the hidden curriculum; however, they are not the sole perpetrators. School administrators and supporting staff, such as courtyard supervisors and lunch assistants, similarly reinforce the disempowering and disciplining culture of the hidden curriculum.

During one of the Change 4 Good program sessions, we were reflecting on experiences of belonging at school and what makes students feel included. Initially, no one seemed interested in responding to our prompt or engaging in a discussion about this topic, which was building upon our previous conversations about themes to include in the mural and their expectations about its potential impact beyond the school. As was often the case with Iris, who would occasionally remark, "awkward silence" when things got too quiet even for her rather timid self, a young person spoke up after a few minutes.

> Yesenia raised her hand and said that sometimes there were teachers at the school like Mrs. M and other yard duties [courtyard supervisors] that were very mean to the students, and would call the students "mental." Some of the students shared their experiences with Rosa [the lunch lady]. Lina raised her hand and shared that the other day she had asked Rosa if there was anything else for lunch, and Rosa said, "No! That's all we have and all you are going to get until the end of the year!" Lina said that when Rosa made that comment, she was really sad and angry because she couldn't do anything about it. Yesenia reiterated that Rosa was always in a bad mood, and Diego said that she was in a bad mood because she

was the only one working and "there are too many students." Lucia then added, "There are mean people at the school." Lucia was asking Iris to tell the story, but Iris didn't want to. After several requests by Lucia, Iris said that the other day it was raining and "Ana" [the yard duty]—"The nice one!" Yesenia interrupted—asked her to go get one of the little kids away from the grass. Iris went out to get him, but he didn't want to come, so Iris had to go into the grass, and "the mean [yard duty] Ruth began to shout out 'What are you doing?'" and that's when Yesenia heard Ruth say, "Kids are mental!" Iris said that she felt hurt by that.[10]

In reflecting upon their schooling experiences and relationships with school staff, Yesenia, Lina, Lucia, and Iris described their interactions with adults at their school. By reflecting upon and retelling stories of their schooling experiences, specifically their interactions with Rosa and Ruth, Latinx youth described contentious interactions with school staff outside the classroom.

Latinx youth like Yesenia, Lina, Lucia, and Iris recognized that school staff felt overworked. However, they also noticed their unwillingness to engage with students in positive ways. Latinx youth characterized these exchanges as unpleasant because they made salient their positionality as subordinate to adults. Additionally, these interactions silenced students' voices and concerns. As noted in Diego's response to Lina, some Latinx youth understood the circumstances that led adults to behave in such ways. Yet they did not justify or excuse the school staff's reactions. Instead, they took notice and occasionally discussed these among themselves to validate one another's experiences, and come to a consensus as to which teacher and/or staff they should avoid, or whom they saw as an ally or a source of support. The culture of the hidden curriculum in schooling is symptomatic of the hegemony that reproduces oppressive and disparate power relations among students and school administrators. To be specific, it underscores the hierarchies of differential status and power between youth and adults.

By delimiting what are questionable or unquestionable, desirable or repugnant, and appropriate or transgressive youth behaviors, the hidden curriculum works to disenfranchise students. Furthermore, it regulates and polices youth agency into a culture of silence and marginality that limits their critical literacy. As a result of these disciplinarily strategies, Latinx youth voice, agency, and determination are suppressed, while adults' power over them is maintained. Feliz offered an example of the silencing of Latinx youth when she described their response to school administrators' disapproval of their initial mural draft design. Latinx youth questioning, however, began as we proceeded to debrief with them the feedback we had received from school administrators and their requests for changes to the mural draft. As we crowded around the mural draft, each youth and adult glancing over the design and ideas, Feliz challenged the school administration's response and their narrow assumption that "kids are stupid."

> Feliz then said, "Ohhhh," and asked why they (e.g., the Principal and Superintendent) don't think that the students came up with the symbols and images in the mural. Lina responded with, "'Cause they think kids are stupid." We then explained that some of the stories and issues are controversial, and so adults might not think that the students have a place to discuss those issues. Lina, still flustered, ranted about how these were also their stories, and that they too had marched out there with the teachers when the rally against pink slips (i.e., teacher layoffs) was going on. Both Lina and Feliz explained that when teachers get pink slips, it's not only the teachers that are being hurt, it's the students too because some students might like or feel connected to the teachers, and so it makes them sad to see some of the teachers leave.[11]

Change 4 Good youth discerned that a mural would help cultivate a sense of belonging to the school and improve the relationship between the school and community. However, the mural draft design served to make salient the tensions and power dynamics between students and school administrators. This became evident in the mural draft design that illustrated a protest sign with the message "No More Pink Slips"; the school administrators felt that such an image and message would be too complex to represent in a mural created by youth.

The story and its illustration represented quite the contrary. For the youth in Change 4 Good it was a story of students and teachers coming together in solidarity to protest teacher layoffs. Latinx youth sought to meaningfully represent an illustrative mural that highlighted their caring relationships with and support toward some of their teachers.

Despite their efforts to illustrate solidarity in action, youth felt that they were misrecognized by school administrators who strongly disapproved of their initial mural draft design. Drawing from their previous schooling experiences of being disregarded when they expressed their concerns, youth felt indignant.

The mural sought to represent stories from school and community members that highlighted experiences of struggle, solidarity, hopes, and dreams for their community's future. These motivations underscored youth efforts to create a mural at their school that, while viewed by school administrators as problematic or "too controversial" for youth to engage, would reflect youth voices and experiences. Young people like Lina interpreted adults' disavowal of youth voices and agency as oppressive. Although Latinx youth tried to push back on such remarks, the culture of the hidden curriculum, which also shaped the Change 4 Good program's standing relation to the school, limited their agency to challenge the school administrators' decision.

In implicit ways, the hidden curriculum entwines with ageist and racist discourses about youth. As noted by Feliz and Lina, adults presumed to know what was best for young people. Adults, from school administrators to teachers to even the Change 4 Good program facilitators, at times assumed a patronizing role that involved them deciding on behalf of youth or unintentionally limiting their active role and contributions to the decision-making process. Some Latinx youth met these adult reactions with frustration, anger, and indignation because they felt silenced. On one occasion, the experiences of silence and invisibility compelled some Latinx youth to want to organize a protest at their school to oppose the school administrators' mural draft design feedback. Although a protest did not take place, Latinx youth reactions demonstrated their agency, specifically their desire to be seen and heard, as well as included in the decision-making process. Furthermore, it illustrated the constraining culture of the hidden curriculum in the schooling environment where the Change 4 Good program was located.

The final mural design was a compromise between Latinx youth in Change 4 Good, program facilitators, and school administrators. Two silhouettes replace the image with the "No More Pink Slips" slogan and related symbolism. The first silhouette shows an adult holding a

Figure 2.1. Maplewood Stories Mural. Photo by Regina D. Langhout.

picket sign with the words "La unión hace la fuerza" (In unity there is strength). The second features a young person holding a picket sign with a heart drawn at the center. Together, they symbolize the power of unity, organizing, protest, and communities coming together.

The culture of the hidden curriculum characterizes disempowering schooling practices, including certain curricula and disciplinary norms that reinforce hegemonic discourses on the definition of a "good" student, and thus a citizen. Embedded in the classroom are student socialization and behavior management norms and expectations that include, but are not limited to, classroom attendance, punctuality, completion of homework assignments, and compliance with adult and teacher authority.[12] Schooling practices associated with the hidden curriculum discipline students to abide by the formalities and expectations of "good" studentship, which reflect curricula on character development that align with the status quo. Compliance with expectations and prosocial behaviors lead to praise and reward, whereas resistance, often labeled as deviance, is repelled and punished.[13] Taken together, these practices of the hidden curriculum presume that "good" students will be or become upstanding future citizens in adulthood.

Socializing Citizens via Character Education

Character Education, also known as Citizenship Education and Character Counts!, among other names, are curricula instituted in US public schools nationwide. The purpose is to promote the prosocial behavior and positive moral development of students from kindergarten through high school.[14] The Character Education Partnership, a prominent new advocacy group, defines Character Education as "the deliberate effort by schools, families, and communities to help young people understand, care about, and act upon core ethical values."[15] Highly praising the program, and education scholar Nel Noddings's book *Educating Moral People: A Caring Alternative to Character Education*, Margaret Price writes,

> As a means of stemming the growth of violence, disinterest, and disrespect commonly reported in today's schools, educators seek programs that will help instill moral and ethical behaviors in students and promote a sense of community within the culture of schools. Character Education programs have been adopted in many educational entities to promote ethical, moral, and virtuous behaviors in the students who attend them.[16]

As an institutionalized and structured curriculum in predominantly public schools, Character Education is an example of a hidden curriculum within schooling.

Citizenship Education purports that good students are upstanding classroom citizens. With this assumption, Character Education strives to foster among students six core values: trustworthiness, respect, responsibility, fairness, caring, and citizenship. The values purported as core practices for positive youth development are associated with good studentship. Proponents of Character Education vow that students will gain skills that will lead them to become "moral, civic, good, mannered, well-behaved, non-bullying, healthy, critical, successful, traditional, compliant, and socially acceptable beings."[17] Although these six values are important skills to foster among young people, they leave intact the inherently oppressive social structure of the hidden curriculum in schooling. Additionally, the curriculum fails to account for the ways young people are constrained by the culture of schooling. When students are socialized into developing these specific skills, potential opportunities for critical literacy, oriented toward fostering youth agency, are limited. Character Education's alignment with the socialization and construction of the "good" student and subsequently the future citizen is premised on assumptions of conformity to the status quo. Character Education endorses disciplinary practices to maintain classroom norms and individual skills development among students to keep the hegemony of the hidden curriculum intact.

Character Education attempts to socialize students into seeing themselves as individuals who must perform specific behaviors that conform to the culture of the classroom and align with the hidden curriculum. The promotion of said values views young people as individual "blank slates" who are to be shaped into adults and eventual citizens.[18] The implicit message for students is that to be awarded and rewarded for certain behaviors advocated by Character Education will lead to recognition, inclusion, and positive schooling experiences.

Research on Character Education demonstrates that students are likely to relate kindness and care with citizenship.[19] Associating care with citizenship is consistent with the construction of "good" citizenship that is predicated on law-abidingness. Complex views among preadolescent and middle school-age youth demonstrate young people's understanding that citizenship is more than a label. Youth view citizenship as extending beyond their experiences in schools. For example, they describe the significance of citizenship in terms of a person's sense of belonging and participation in contributing to the betterment of their communities.[20] The work by Ruth Lister examining European youth meaning-making about citizenship is consistent with the research of Irene Bloemraad and colleagues, which demonstrates that among Mexican-origin US-born youth in the San Francisco Bay Area, young people characterized citizenship as a status with a prescribed label granted either at birth or through naturalization; the latter being granted on the basis of a person's character, civility, and social responsibility to the nation-state. Young people view citizenship as a practice of social responsibility often expressed through civic engagement to participate in society or in a particular community or setting, such as school.[21]

Aligned with the hidden curriculum, Character Education socializes students into a culture of classroom behavior management. The Maplewood Unified School District, which oversees Maplewood Elementary

School (MES), endorses Character Education. The classroom where the Change 4 Good program met displayed four-foot-tall posters associated with Character Education. The values, displayed as six pillars, were promoted and visibly present in the classroom. Latinx youth meaning-making about citizens and citizenship was therefore heavily informed by what they saw and experienced in the classroom, as well as the messages conveyed there. Learning about these terms like "citizenship" in relation to the six pillars associated with Character Education helped inform Latinx youth meaning-making about citizens and citizenship. On one occasion, as we were engaging Latinx youth in an activity to help them discern themes from their focus group data, which they had collected and wanted to represent in their mural, the youth turned to the posters hanging around their classroom to describe how some of the Character Education values related to their themes. Drawing insights from their classroom surroundings, looking around and reading each of the posters, they returned to the activity.

> The process for discerning meta-themes and sub-themes from their focus group data proved to be a bit more complex, yet they seemed deep in thought, carefully reading through each slip of paper. Each slip of paper had written on it the theme and its definition, which was then taped onto a candy bar to facilitate youth engagement. Lina added that sorting through themes and creating categories based on their definitions was like the posters, "Like 'Citizenship'" (pointing to the poster in the classroom that described citizenship, and read: "Be Cooperative, Be a Good Neighbor, Obey Laws & Rules, Protect the Environment"). Celine pointed to another poster that was on the back wall that had bolded words like "Caring" and "Citizenship," and smaller non-bolded words around them like "sharing" and "voting." Lina added that it was easier to send a message by using one word instead of many. She listed off the qualities of having good citizenship that were on the poster—reading them out loud, "Be Cooperative . . ." She, like the other youth, did not question these; they read them and suggested that we do the same with our themes and corresponding definitions. "Keep them short. Like rules," Celine remarked.[22]

Latinx youth readings of citizenship in relation to displays on the Character Education posters were summarized in their descriptions and read out loud. While unquestioned by the youth, however, these posters reflected the meanings and associations Latinx youth made with citizenship: following the rules and not breaking the law. The posters reinforced and even socialized Latinx youth views on citizenship, which consequently shaped their schooling experiences and perceptions of desirable citizen behaviors.

Practices and behaviors—being kind, cooperative, and obedient, for instance—conveyed a type of citizenship that, in students' view, conformed and complied with the culture of the hidden curriculum as well as Character Education. Lina and Celine associated citizenship with the context of schooling and the behaviors students should perform to be seen and treated as good or bad students, and thus citizens. The process of associating citizenship with socially acceptable behaviors informed Latinx youth binary thinking about the term, specifically what constituted a citizen as either good or bad, deserving or undeserving of citizenship. Latinx youth, for example, drew parallels between citizenship and "good" student behaviors by identifying certain practices consistent with maintaining the culture of schooling. Conceptualizations of citizenship in relation to Character Education were rather constraining and limiting because these notions did not allow youth to enact their agency. In the context of the classroom, any potential for critical literacy development as well as agency and participation in decision making was constrained by the hegemony of the hidden curriculum, including Character Education.

Latinx youth at times described citizenship in relation to Character Education because that is where many of them came to experience and engage with the word "citizen." Diego, for example, described citizenship in association with actions that were keenly constructed to sustain hierarchical student-teacher relations. For Diego a citizen is a "good," cooperative, and law-abiding person, and this presumes that there is only one type of citizenship that is most desired. An interview response from Diego, an eleven-year-old Latinx youth, demonstrates this point.

JESICA: Where did you hear the words "citizen" and "citizenship"?
DIEGO: I got three awards for it [citizenship], and that's where I heard it.
JESICA: Three awards, where?

DIEGO: At school, for being a good citizen, and having citizenship.
JESICA: Congratulations! What did they tell you about that?
DIEGO: Nothing. They [stakeholders at school] just gave it to me.
JESICA: What did you do for it?
DIEGO: I don't know; I had to be a good person.
JESICA: What do you mean by a good person? Did you do certain things?
DIEGO: Yeah, I had to be kind. Um, share. Be polite.
JESICA: Be polite to who?
DIEGO: Everybody.

As we spoke outside one of the few local coffee shops in the community, across from a building that formerly housed the family resource center, Diego's remarks made evident how school undeniably preferred a very specific type of citizenship. The kind of citizen who is promoted within the culture of schooling is one who is conventionally and institutionally defined to abide by the culture and norms of the school environment. Diego perceived the "good" student to be or eventually become a "good" citizen.

A person who follows the rules of the nation-state—or in students' case the classroom—and does not disturb or disrupt the norms is conceived of as a "good" and deserving citizen—and in the classroom, a "good" student. Given these associations, Diego referenced the "citizenship award" to describe the context where he first encountered the word "citizen." Diego described why he believed he had received the award; he referenced classroom behaviors, such as being kind and polite to everyone. As evidenced by Diego's statement, "good" citizenship practices in relation to individual behaviors were often characterized by acts of sharing. The citizenship award that was granted to students like Diego reflected what teachers deemed appropriate in the classroom. However, these practices focused on maintaining the social order of the classroom, while encouraging student behaviors to align with the values of Character Education.

Diego was not the only youth who conceptualized citizenship in relation to the award. Daniela, an eleven-year-old, equated socially acceptable behaviors with citizenship because "good" students were often recognized and praised by teachers and administrators. As we sat around the kitchen table in Daniela's home, a newly renovated two-bedroom apartment right on the border street of a city known for its quaint downtown, she shared with me her reflections on the citizenship award.

> In my second-grade class, I got a certificate of [for] citizenship, and I never—I never got what that meant, though. I think I got the certificate because I read, I helped—I helped, like, in the classroom. My class was a combo class, so it was second grade and third grade, and sometimes the third-graders wouldn't get the instructions and I would always listen. So, when the third-graders wouldn't listen, they'd ask me if I could help them with the addition, multiplication, the math. And I think that's why I got the citizenship [award]. I don't remember—I think 'cause I was helpful and I always listen, I always—I always read aloud. I think that's why I got it.

Daniela believed that to be a citizen was to be recognized and valued. The citizenship award informed her—and many other students'—sense of these terms. In the process of naming these characteristics, the youth referenced practices associated with Character Education values and concepts. When I initially asked Diego about the citizenship award, he claimed that he did not know what it meant in detail, only that he "had to be a good person." Daniela, however, remarked that she "never got what it meant."

Upon further reflection, Diego and Daniela suggested that the citizenship award was determined on the basis of prosocial classroom behaviors, such as being caring, kind, and helpful toward others. Diego's and Daniela's responses highlighted features of Character Education values. Among these were caring practices that valued sharing, helping, politeness, and kindness. Daniela offered more explicit examples of what she believed helped her earn the award. These included practices that were more community-oriented, as they involved Daniela providing guidance and support to students who were struggling with math. Daniela's offering of guidance and help to her peers illustrated some features of Character Education. For Diego and Daniela, Character Education sought to facilitate positive classroom behaviors and prosocial values among students. To a degree, Diego and Daniela internalized the praise, which was rooted in set rules and expectations regulated by teachers, who determined what counts as "good" behaviors in the classroom and consequently who are labeled "good" students.

Latinx youth meaning-making about citizenship as related to student behaviors had implications beyond the context of the classroom. Some Latinx youth remarked that in the classroom a "good" student is someone who follows the rules and complies with the teacher's expectations. A "good" citizen is one who abides by the rules and laws of the nation-state. The "good" student is a future citizen, constructed in relation to behaviors that conform to the hidden curriculum and value the principles of Character Education. The assumptions that "good" students will become "good" citizens when they conform to the sociocultural norms and conventions of the classroom environment—and, in turn, society at large—are evident in the culture of schooling.[23]

The associations Latinx youth made between their behaviors and citizenship, or the practices that were rewarded when perceived to be "good," are not surprising given the socialization and conformity that are expected in schools.[24] Such behaviors are especially reinforced for Latinx students. In fact, no matter how many awards Latinx youth are granted or the number of accolades and recognitions they receive, the broader sociocultural context of schooling along with the ageism and racist nativism inherent in society create an environment where Latinx youth feel excluded and disenfranchised.[25] Messages of conditional inclusion and liminal belongingness produce what postcolonial Chicana feminist scholar Chela Sandoval describes as an oppositional consciousness, an identity and embodiment of resistance to the status quo structures that impinge upon the authentic being, voice, and agency of a person, in this case Latinx youth.[26] Subscribing to these hegemonic discourses about citizenship and good studentship has detrimental consequences for Latinx youth agency, belonging, and sociopolitical development.

Latinx youth occasionally referenced the six pillars to remind their peers to behave, even in the context of Change 4 Good. In doing so, they reproduced similar practices of policing their peers. In accordance with the curriculum of schooling, youth often took on the role of disciplining and reprimanding their classmates. Although we strived to cultivate a different learning environment in Change 4 Good, the practices and behaviors they engaged in the conventional classroom sometimes made their way into the program. On one occasion, I observed youth explicitly calling each other out by saying "shut up," which some frequently heard used in the classroom by their teachers.

> Joaquín told another youth to "shut up!" We reminded the youth to be careful of what they say, and how they should try to be nicer to each other. We asked if they knew a nicer way to express what they were feeling. Santiago spoke up and said, "Yeah. Be quiet, please." I thanked Santiago. But then others started telling everyone to "shut up." Once again, I told them to watch what they say and how, Santiago again remarked, "Everybody, shut up!" I asked again if he could say it in a nicer way, but Santiago joked, "What if I said it like this: Shut up peeps!" I explained to him that what he said was not a nice way of telling someone to be quiet. Santiago smiled and said, "Just kidding."[27]

While we understood him to be joking, we also knew that such behavior was not conducive to the environment we were trying to cultivate in the Change 4 Good program, and was akin to regulating student actions in problematic ways. The Change 4 Good program facilitators strived to ensure that the norms of schooling and discipline would not permeate the program; in practice, however, this was more challenging than we imagined.

In the culture of schooling, youth were expected to subscribe to and practice disciplinary values and enforce them on other students. Change 4 Good youth would often reproduce what they observed, enacted, or stated in the classroom because the context of schooling and the hidden curriculum were so entrenched in how they saw themselves in that environment. Latinx youth often held up their "peace" fingers in the air, expressed a loud "shhh," told each other to "shut up," or reminded their peers that they would be "in trouble" for engaging in some behaviors, like "not raising their hand" or "not paying attention." Explicit subtle actions like these worked to perpetuate the socialization of Latinx youth as second-class citizens.

Schools are a training ground for shaping adulthood and citizenship. Students acquire competence in certain skills and behaviors, as well as knowledge of the rules and expectations of a given context. Yet the culture of schooling that is decided by teachers, or adults in positions of power, rarely attends to or considers the perspectives, needs, and experiences of students. The rules that students, particularly Latinx youth, are expected to follow are predetermined and offer few or limited opportunities for youth to practice more critical and participatory forms of engagement that could very well help cultivate their agency and sociopolitical development.

Good Students Getting in Trouble

The construction of the "good" student, deployed in the classroom and in early years of schooling via the hidden curriculum, socializes students into certain norms associated with adult citizens. The practices that characterize "good" citizen behaviors are learned, rehearsed, and reproduced among students in a culture of schooling that reifies the hidden curriculum, as well as individualistic student values and behaviors. Students are viewed as citizens of the future who will take on certain roles and responsibilities in society. As Peter Levine, author of *The Future of Democracy*, purports, young people are viewed as future citizens because of their potential economic, social, and political contributions to society.[28] The socialization of the future citizen begins in the classroom, through the hidden curriculum, where young people learn who "good" and "bad" students are, who will be rewarded or disciplined, and what behaviors are treated accordingly. Schools are organized according to specific values, rules, interactions, and relationships that are determined and reinforced by the hidden curriculum. Some students will take on full citizen rights as adults, while others will be relegated to second-class citizenship, or will be denied citizenship and rights because of their age, race, ethnicity, and gender, along with other markers of identity, including their own or their family's immigrant experiences.

Latinx youth schooling experiences helped inform the meanings they attached to and associated with citizenship. Schooling experiences that positioned students with limited agency in the context of the classroom were stories Latinx youth occasionally shared. During one program session, while debriefing some of the focus group data in the form of stories associated with experiences of having or not having power to make a change, the youth reflected on those moments at school where they felt powerless. Joaquín, for instance, shared that he has felt powerless in school when other students call him names and he is not able to do anything about it because he does not want other students to get into trouble with teachers in the ways that he has. Diego and Yesenia similarly agreed that they too often got in trouble—in most cases for no reason or for petty behaviors. For Latinx youth, the seemingly minor yet recurring instances of getting in trouble in school communicated a specific desirable behavior, one characterized by obedience to rules and social expectations in the classroom.

The hidden curriculum, along with Character Education, conveyed meaning on what a "good" student should do and be like. These associations are similarly ascribed to who a "good" citizen is. The assumption of "good" students as future "good" citizens underscored roles in and responsibilities to the nation-state, which included but were not limited to voting and following the law. In the context of the classroom, the teacher set forth guidelines and expectations that structured Latinx youth experiences with rules and labels as either "good" students or troublemakers. Joaquín and Yesenia, who were first-generation immigrant youth and English-language learners, often openly shared their experiences with "getting in trouble" in school for reasons they were at times unsure of or they felt were unjust. One day, Yesenia came to the Change 4 Good program with a rather deflated and sad expression.

> Yesenia asked Joaquín if they had really hung out as friends in the second grade, and Joaquín said they did because they were both in Mrs. G's [English-language learners, ELL] class. I asked if they had gone out for recess today, but Yesenia said they had not because of the rain. She then proceeded to tell a story about her day, recounting why she had gotten in trouble with her teacher, who then went on to call Yesenia "a crazy woman" because she had defended herself from a boy that was picking on her all day by calling her names—names that Joaquín had also been called in the past, like "dumb" and "stupid." Names that also reminded them of being picked at in their ELL class because they could not say certain words in English. Yesenia shared that the teacher had also called her "nasty" because she hugged a boy she considered a friend. Her expression of sadness and disappointment in having had a bad day could not be overlooked for the rest of the program session.[29]

Shortly after she had checked with Joaquín about their earlier schooling experiences with the teacher who coordinated the English-language learners program at the school, Yesenia described a vivid memory that made her feel sad. Through Yesenia's story the culture of schooling informed by the hidden curriculum is noted, especially its implications for the varied meanings youth attach to what kinds of behaviors are rewarded or disciplined, and in turn what makes for a "good" or "bad" student. This, in turn, has implications for how students come to perceive themselves in relation to adults, especially teachers who will often label them according to the judgments ascribed to or associated with a student. The associations are also shaped along categories of race, ethnicity, gender, and language proficiency, as noted in Yesenia's experience.

Yesenia's story of getting in trouble was not the last reflection that she shared in the Change 4 Good program. Just one week prior to sharing this story, she recalled when a teacher had wrongly disciplined her in the context of a school field trip to see the symphony. Yesenia added that while at the symphony, students were not allowed to chat. In telling her story, Yesenia described the following:

> A few girls behind me started talking and chattering, and "blah blah blah," so I turned around just to say "hello" and then "shhh" them, hoping that they would be quiet. But then when I turned back around I saw Mrs. K in front of me and I got in trouble because she thought I was the one that was doing all the talking. When we returned to school Mrs. K embarrassed me in front of the class, telling everyone how disrespectful and impolite I had been, when I wasn't even talking. They, those girls were talking, and I just got in trouble for saying "hi" and reminding them to be quiet.[30]

What happens when a student is constantly being reprimanded, disciplined, and scolded even for behaviors and actions they have not engaged in? A particular experience is constructed for these students that conveys to them how teachers perceive them, as "bad" students despite their attempts to do and be "good," and as "troublemakers." The constant experience of being disciplined functions to further marginalize certain students, in this case Latinx youth like Joaquín and Yesenia, and make them feel powerless, unintelligent, and unworthy of being treated with dignity and respect by their peers and teachers.

Education curricula like Character Education create conditions where students are expected to be upstanding citizens in their school environment, especially the classroom. To uphold and abide by the norms, values, and behaviors of the culture of schooling, as Yesenia's stories demonstrate, are what make for a "good" student. Yet despite her attempts, she was not seen that way by teachers. On the contrary, she was viewed as deviant and even promiscuous. Social justice scholar Monique W. Morris in *Pushout: The Criminalization of Black Girls in Schools* articulates how these views toward young girls of color, especially Black girls, are significantly racialized and gendered in problematic ways, a pattern that then accounts for the disproportionate rates of school push-out and discipline.[31]

Latinx youth conceptualized citizenship as a practice that aligned with the status quo, which associated it with discipline, and thus socially acceptable "good" student behaviors. In other words, Latinx youth equated citizenship with following the rules and conformity; yet at times they pushed back against these meanings, especially when they described their lived experiences of feeling wronged by teachers or unheeded and ignored by adults. The limited forms of support further underscored the opportunities Latinx youth were afforded to cultivate their agency. Latinx youth were attuned to the structures of power that curtailed their opportunities for agency, participation, and decision making. When reflexivity and dialogue about these experiences were facilitated in the Change 4 Good program, Latinx youth were open to sharing, as evidenced in this conversation on how adults could better help students learn.

> I asked the students if they could think of ways in which adults could help them do well and better at school, and the students couldn't come up with very many good ideas at first. They did however say that adults could help students learn better "by showing them instead of telling them." Iris remarked, "Like they could tell a student about something important, and they can show them and teach them about what it is that they want to have them learn and know." Diego added that "if a teacher or an adult wants to teach students about hexagons they can go out and look for that shape in things that are out there, like a stop sign!" Jackie emphasized "learning by doing things" and "having fun is more engaging." Feliz said

"and showing them [students] instead of telling them." After this brief exchange of learning by doing and what this means, Diego emphasized that "adults could also tell students what they are doing right and what is good for them instead of getting them in trouble." Yesenia agreed and added that "sometimes kids at school don't even know why they're in trouble. We might say a word that is bad but we might not know what that word means. Instead of telling our parents and getting us in *more* trouble, they could teach us what those words mean."[32]

US-based constructions of citizenship that begin and are formed in the context of the classroom, often through the culture of schooling that subscribes to the hidden curriculum, limit possibilities for Latinx youth to express themselves in authentic, agentic ways. Latinx youth might strive to uphold the status quo and norms of schooling; however, because of how they are racialized as "troublemakers," their attempts at being "good" student citizens might be futile. Latinx youth citizenship embodiments as well as their meanings are often misunderstood by teachers, and further limited because teachers focus on Latinx youth behaviors that they view as nonconforming. The experiences of Latinx youth being disciplined and socialized in schools in particular ways surely has implications for how they come to perceive themselves in institutionalized settings within and beyond school.

A discussion of the hidden curriculum in the US education system opened this chapter, and was followed by a critique of Character Education and the construction of the "good" student. Despite echoing constructions of citizenship as a practice, Latinx youth problematized these meanings by arguing that citizenship should be determined by the social and relational experiences that allow them agency. Together, these experiences, if provided in the classroom setting, can help cultivate schooling environments where students can actively participate and develop their critical literacy, alongside their agency. Schools represent an institutional microcosm of society, and an essential structure for sustaining democracy and shaping citizen behaviors.[33] In this critique of US-based schooling, the troubling of citizenship is discussed in relation to the "good" student discourse that seems to ignore Latinx youth attempts to embody a student citizenship that extends beyond but also challenges the tenets of Character Education.

3

Rights as a Privilege

The United Nations Convention on the Rights of the Child (UN-CRC) frames much of the social, cultural, and legal constructions of youth rights. Although the United States has not ratified the articles with the UN-CRC, nurturance and self-determination rights are purported as necessary for the positive development and democratic formation of young people. The curricula, contexts, and experiences through which Latinx youth learn and are engaged in exercising rights must constitute part of the theorizing of citizenship. That is, how Latinx youth learn about rights is as important as the definitions youth provide, especially when these inform their associations with the terms "citizenship" and "citizens." Highlighting the significance of rights as a privilege are Latinx youth stories. Their reflections illustrate associations between nurturance and self-determination rights and notions of citizenship, legality, freedom, and access to opportunities. The meanings Latinx youth ascribed to rights reflected their lived experiences, as well as resistance to being excluded, especially when they associated rights with claims to belong and participate in society.

Latinx youth described rights as being related to yet also extending their capacity for self-determination, including access to opportunities and decision making. In relation to or against the backdrop of social structures, Latinx youth problematized these meanings by drawing from their experiences. Latinx youth meaning-making about rights often reflected a critique of social structures, or how power was maintained to determine what people can or cannot do and what they can or cannot access. While conceptualizing rights, Latinx youth provided powerful critiques of how rights were often unequally distributed, particularly among those who are positioned as subordinate to the dominant social group. Additionally, they drew on their experiences and those of their communities to reflect upon and construct meaning about rights. That is, they connected their experiences to contexts where power was deployed to limit or constrain their rights; these moments often served as the basis for their understanding of rights. Because of this, Latinx youth endorsed human rights values whereby all people, by being members of a community, are citizens and afforded full rights. Latinx youth claimed rights for themselves as well as on behalf of their families and communities, often at the same time as they troubled the individualistic, sociolegal liberal constructions of citizenship and rights that do not reflect their pluriversal understandings and embodiments as citizens.

Sociolegal constructions and meanings of citizenship and legality surfaced in Latinx youth discussions and reflections about rights within and beyond an individual's relationship to the nation-state. At times their understanding of rights prioritized the full enfranchisement of all people regardless of their age, race, ethnicity, and immigrant status—from being undocumented to holding an authorized immigration status. In their conceptualizing of rights, self-determination was described as individual privileges, specifically as freedoms or opportunities people can pursue. This was supported by their experiences in the context of the Change 4 Good program, where they were encouraged to exercise their agency and center their experiences. In other settings, however, such as the classroom, these experiences were constrained by the structure and culture of schooling, along with the hidden curriculum. Latinx youth therefore discussed self-determination rights more than nurturance rights, especially when challenging the limited opportunity structures in which they were embedded. This was often in relation to situations where they were not able to exercise agency or where their agency was limited or curtailed. Given these experiences, Latinx youth interrogated the value of individualized constructions of rights, particularly when they felt that they were being denied rights and their communities were disenfranchised.

The United Nations Convention on the Rights of the Child

Efforts to center Latinx youth agency were central to the Change 4 Good program. To act upon these intentions, we aligned the program's curriculum with Freirean critical pedagogies and literacies, such as youth empowerment perspectives, and children's rights. With regard to the latter, the Change 4 Good team saw value in the UN-CRC, and we drew from it to guide and support our approach to developing positive youth-adult interactions. As an organization, the United Nations (UN) strives to hold countries accountable to preserving the humanity, dignity, integrity, and human rights of all people regardless of their identities, beliefs, and legal status in a nation-state.[1] The right to safety, self-determination, freedom, and dignity to live a healthy and thriving life as a human being is a cornerstone of the UN.

In line with these values, the UN has committed its institutional resources to raising awareness of youth needs, as well as to their development, strengths, and agency. Established in 1989, the UN's charter for children and youth is tasked with overseeing the implementation of fifty-four articles outlined in the UN-CRC treaty. In accordance with the Universal Declaration of Human Rights and the International Covenants on Human Rights, the UN-CRC specifically advocates for the rights to safety and freedom of all young people.

> The family, as the fundamental group of society and the natural environment for the growth and well-being of all its members and particularly children, should be afforded the necessary protection and assistance so that it can fully assume its responsibilities within the community. Recognizing that the child, for the full and harmonious development of his or her personality, should grow up in a family environment, in an atmosphere of happiness, love and understanding. Considering that the child should be fully prepared to live an individual life in society, and brought up in the spirit of the ideals proclaimed in the Charter of the United Nations, and in particular in the spirit of peace, dignity, tolerance, freedom, equality and solidarity.... The child, by reason of his physical and mental immaturity, needs special safeguards and care, including appropriate legal protection, before as well as after birth.

The UN-CRC came into effect in 1990 and was ratified by 196 countries, all of which are members of the UN. Although the United States is affiliated with the UN, it has not signed the treaty, nor has it implemented it in full. The robust number of young people in the United States who are in the juvenile justice system, for example, as well as unable to access quality education, health care, and safe housing and living conditions, indicates that the United States is far from adequately caring for and upholding the rights and dignity of young people.

In the United States one key reason for not endorsing the UN-CRC in full is the assumption that granting youth self-determination and autonomy will limit the role of the family. Opposition to the UN-CRC is in part due to political and religious conservatives' concerns about the nation-state's potential influence in the socialization and development of young people. Critics of the UN-CRC believe that this should be a task reserved exclusively for families, without state intervention. The divided support for the UN-CRC underscores liberal and conservative political agendas in a secular nation-state that strives to maintain plurality while suppressing the rights and autonomy of young people. Because the United States has not ratified the UN-CRC, efforts to implement policies and practices to protect the rights of youth are yet to be developed.[2]

Most of the UN-CRC articles fall under two broad categories: nurturance rights and self-determination rights. As purported in the treaty, these are meant to uphold the thriving and well-being of youth in the jurisdiction of the nations that have endorsed it. Nurturance rights are concerned with providing youth with the material resources and care to help sustain their safety and well-being. Self-determination rights, on the other hand, are meant to cultivate youth positive development via opportunities that foster youth agency and participation in the decision making that affects their lives.[3]

The UN-CRC was created with good intentions to address youth needs. Yet it must be acknowledged that Western Eurocentric frameworks of youth and families, which limit youth participation as well, largely informed the development of the UN-CRC. Thus, it is likely to presume that the articles were developed with limited explicit engagement by youth. The centering of youth experiences—how the articles might reflect a young person's needs, agency, and rights—must be understood through a critical lens. Accordingly, there is a need for further empirical research on Latinx youth understandings of their rights. To be clear, how Latinx youth experience their rights holds implications for their understanding of citizenship as well as their expressions aligned with sociopolitical development.[4]

Nurturance

A central mission of the UN-CRC is the right to grow up in a caring and safe community. According to the UN-CRC, rights to safety fall under nurturance rights. Rights to well-being that include access to resources and forms of support—and fundamental nurturance rights of all youth—are stipulated in the UN-CRC. The protection of and care for young people that are emphasized purport to uphold the social welfare of youth under guidance by the nation-state. Nurturance rights posit that young people must be guaranteed and provided with shelter, food, health care, and an education, along with other forms of sustenance and wellness. Under nurturance rights, young people are cared for and looked after in most cases by an adult who is either a parent, relative, or legal guardian. Unlike self-determination rights, which grant young people opportunities for decision making over aspects of their lives that are of concern to them, nurturance rights are not necessarily concerned with the promotion of youth agency and self-determination.

It was not surprising to initially encounter silence among Change 4 Good youth when we started to talk with them about the meaning or implications of rights in their lives. There was some hesitation in talking about rights, but then the youth proceeded to discern its significance.

> We asked the youth if anyone had heard of the United Nations, but none of the youth responded. The program facilitator leading the activity shared that the United Nations (UN) was a name given to a group of people who each represented different countries. The UN's purpose was to "unite" these different countries and have them work together to address social issues affecting communities and people around the world. In our discussion, we emphasized that one of the things the UN did was to make sure people were treated as full human beings with rights, and their basic needs were met. It was further explained, "In 1989 the UN decided to develop a set of human rights to help meet the needs of children around the world." We asked the youth: "What kinds of rights do you think were on this list?" Celine exclaimed, "Underwear!" Some of the youth and adults laughed out loud; however, the program facilitator rephrased Celine's comments to mean: "Having the right to have and wear clothing. To not be poor." Iris, another youth, added, "Education," and Jackie shared, "A

right is also having a place to live and food to eat." The rights stated by Celine, Iris and Jackie were identified as examples of nurturance rights.[5]

Latinx youth discussed rights often in relation to aspects of their lives, like housing, food, and education, that they identified as being important. More specifically, rights to care that include social and material resources, which are key elements of nurturance rights, were discussed by Latinx youth as rights every youth should have. Their remarks, to a degree, reflected the significance of nurturance rights in their lives as young people growing up bearing witness to poverty and social inequities in their community. Almost all Latinx youth, however, appeared to experience family conditions where they were provided with sufficient resources to ensure their care, safety, and well-being.

Education was an important right as well. According to the 1982 Supreme Court decision in *Plyler v. Doe*, public education for youth in K-12 grades in the United States is a common good, a right of all youth regardless of their immigration status. In most states young people are required by law to attend school if they are under the age of eighteen. Because education holds a meaningful role in the lives of young people, it was unsurprising to document education as a topic of discussion among Latinx youth, especially when they interrogated how notions of agency were constrained or supported in school. The social value placed upon education can help explain why Iris identified education as a right.

Not all youth reflected upon rights or the UN-CRC in the same way, however. Celine's earlier remark about "underwear," later rephrased as clothing, although not explicitly stated, signifies the importance of young people having access to material goods. Having the "right to have and wear clothing," as well as the right to choose what to wear, demonstrates the mutuality of nurturance and self-determination rights. Thus, to a degree Latinx youth rights were associated with notions of freedom. In making such associations, they saw freedom connected to choice, particularly in regard to how or whether they could decide freely without adult influence or interference.

Although conversations about rights among Latinx youth did not explicitly reference the UN-CRC, their dialogues reflected what rights meant to them, and whether (or how) these rights were being fulfilled in their lives. In describing the importance of the UN-CRC, as well as the Human Rights Declaration, Lina stated that "food" and "home" were essential rights. Because of the limited power young people have in accessing rights as youth and as individuals, these may at times remain unachieved or unfulfilled.

A year later, in the context of an interview, Lina described rights in much more nuanced ways, as the pursuit of well-being, democracy, and social mobility. Such ideologies underscored the importance of a caring, safe, and well-resourced environment that can sustain youth well-being and thriving. As Lina carefully ate her food, making sure not to spill any in my car, I eased her concerns with humor; she and I joked about the right to not have to clean all the time. I asked Lina when and where she had learned about rights, and she explained that a week prior to our interview she had learned about them in her classroom.

> LINA: Last week we were learning about human rights—that's when Eleanor Roosevelt was still alive—but, hmm, so there it [Human Rights Declaration] states everyone has the right to food, home, and things like that, but the thing is that having the right is different from *actually having the things* [material goods and access to resources]. In the Human Rights Declaration it said that you have the right to having food, but not everyone has it, not everyone is able to access food or things like that.
>
> JESICA: Why do you think that is?
>
> LINA: Well, I don't really know anymore, because things are so different now than what they used to be. What I've noticed is that everything's about money now. If you don't have money, you don't have food. If you don't have money, you don't have shelter. It's just everything! And then the government, I don't get it sometimes and I feel kinda *mad*.
>
> JESICA: What makes you feel kinda mad?
>
> LINA: Well, here's the thing, if children were to grow up thinking that everyone had a right to everything—and we're gonna be the future, you know. So, if everyone thinks this way, things would change for better. Well, if everyone thought that. Like, I know some people think it's right to keep Mexicans or other cultures away from [outside] the United States, but if we were all to combine as one, and if there weren't fights with North Korea, or the past wars we've had, then we,

we'd be all just *one* country, and not ruled—yeah, not ruled over by one person, but, like, by several countries and their people. And not just whites [white people] or Americans' ways of thinking—then maybe, just maybe, we'd all be able to have the *rights we want to have.*

Lina powerfully stated that even when rights are presumably granted, this does not necessarily mean that all people will have rights. Rights are differentially and disproportionately allocated based on people's positionalities and status in the nation-state. According to Lina, access to opportunities and material resources is limited for some people because of how they are perceived or positioned by social structures in specific contexts. Lina's initial response referenced and challenged discourses on human rights. Lina, like other Latinx youth, interrogated the meaning of rights in her life by troubling how the Human Rights Declaration purported and bestowed certain rights. The granting of rights along with protections and privileges to some people but not all does not necessarily mean that all youth will have access to rights. Lina's associations with rights challenged assumptions of nurturance rights that rely heavily on the individual and are rooted in a micro-level analysis. The response offered by Lina underscores a critique of rights, pointing out that rights are constrained by economic, legal, cultural, and social structures. To further this point, Lina stated, "If you don't have money, you don't have food." Lina recognized the impact of neoliberalism in people's lives and how this shaped and affected their rights.[6] For youth with limited access to resources and opportunities, and for whom nurturance rights are limited or nonexistent, the pursuit of well-being is a struggle.

Lina contested human rights in a social, political, and economic context where she noticed rising inequities. Situating her experiences and identities as a young person, Lina discussed youth agency in shaping the future of US society. By advocating for meaningful and intentional representation in the United States, especially the public sphere, for example, Lina purported that democratization and justice can be fulfilled. Yet fundamental human rights to equality and freedom are commodified under neoliberalism and hegemonic discourses where those who are in positions of power—and whom Lina identified as "whites" or proponents of American ideologies—maintain the status quo by determining the structural arrangement of institutions and resources. The power that reproduces systems of oppression has its roots in the colonial racial formations of the United States, which Lina's response illustrates when she referenced efforts to "keep Mexicans or other cultures away." The restrictive immigration policies that she identifies are entrenched in a US history of colonial power that continues to shape social, cultural, political, and economic conditions, specifically for Latinx and México–United States relations.

In line with these remarks, Lina emphasized cultural diversity as an asset to US democracy. Poignantly, she described how the differences that set communities apart should also bind them as a nation to create what she described as "*one* country"—in other words, a pluralistic society where people are not ruled by hegemonic discourses and structures that uphold whiteness or sustain the status quo rooted in US imperialism. As Lina's response demonstrates, troubling and reimagining the nation-state requires engaging a process of reflecting and challenging what it means to belong, and to claim rights regardless of one's immigrant experience and status. This reconceptualizing of rights facilitates sociopolitical development and supports critical literacy skills about what it means to build a more just society, one where rights as freedom and opportunities are not merely an illusion but a lived reality for all people. Lina's understanding of rights highlights the continuous struggle to build thriving communities for young people, Latinx, and immigrant communities. By troubling meanings of rights that do not characterize or reflect the conditions experienced in their lives, Lina challenged the American narrative of freedom and justice for all.

Self-Determination

Self-determination rights are characterized by the ability to act with agency. Self-determination rights, unlike nurturance rights, align with values of freedom and choice, as well as actions that support agency, autonomy, and free will. Self-expression and independence characterize self-determination rights, which emphasize active participation by youth in making decisions about their lives. In practice, however, self-determination rights are not always exercised or fulfilled, especially by youth from institutionally marginalized communities with limited resources and opportunities.

Latinx youth conceptualized self-determination rights as different from but related to nurturance rights. Santiago conceptualized rights as the capacity to act or take action. When asked to describe what he understood by the term "rights," Santiago responded with a story about a time when he felt that his right to act was minimized because of his age.

> JESICA: Have you heard of [the term] "rights"? What do you understand by that term?
>
> SANTIAGO: Like, I have, hmm, rights—is, like, you could do something and nobody can tell you, you can't.
>
> JESICA: Do you think that kids have rights?
>
> SANTIAGO: Yes—*no*. Hmm, they're different from adults. Like, they [adults] can have a driving license, they can have cars, hmm—a job, ehh, and retirement, yeah [*laughs*]. Mmm . . . they get allowed into school campus grounds.
>
> JESICA: Are kids treated the same as adults?
>
> SANTIAGO: No. Adults treat them like, like, dogs.
>
> JESICA: *Really?*
>
> SANTIAGO: Yeah, some of them. Well, if somebody's babysitting you, like, they're doing everything when you could do all the things by yourself. Like, like get stuff off the shelf—they'll be like, "Uh, I'll get it for you, little baby!" and then I'd be like, "*Really. I'm only like two years younger*," so, yeah. It makes me feel kinda mad since—*I could do it myself.*

Santiago defined rights as actions, as "things you can do." Yet when asked to further elaborate, he juxtaposed youth and adults' access to certain rights, or opportunities, such as having a license or being allowed on school grounds, as differential forms of power expressed as agency. Specifically, Santiago discussed youth rights in relation to how they are treated and positioned by adults, including older youth. Through a comparative process, Santiago engaged in a critique of instances where he felt he was disparaged and viewed as incompetent by older youth.

Santiago's lived experience as a youth compelled him to reflect on and interrogate ageism—even by other youth themselves—in an adult-centric society. As evidenced by his remarks and definition, Santiago reflected on the ways that age worked to limit youth agency to decide and act for themselves and how adult-centric structures worked to disempower youth. Santiago referenced age, a specific positionality in relation to adults, to make salient the source of his limited capacity to engage agency. In situations where he felt that his agency was being minimized or subverted by an older youth, for instance, age was the defining determinant of his rights. Because of the power that is ascribed to age, specifically the construction of adulthood, Latinx youth meaning-making about rights included a critique of adults' power over youth. Latinx youth understood their rights in relation to broader structures, even as they conceptualized rights as privileges that all people can access. Santiago viewed rights as entitlements to be claimed because people in positions of power often deny them to those whom they view and position as subordinate.

Rights were also regarded as equivalent to having freedom, that is, the capacity to exercise free will without external force or influence. The curtailing of Latinx youth rights, in some instances, led them to perceive and experience a sense of limited freedom. Reflections about perceptions of limited rights and freedom were brought up by the youth in Change 4 Good, especially when discussing history or topics related to social justice, rights, and bettering their community and school. Celine and Yesenia, for example, explained this by arguing that an important but missing aspect of the UN-CRC is the right to choose what to do with one's time.

> Youth described self-determination rights as "the right to participate in having a say on the things that affect your life." Choice, specifically freedom of choice, seemed to be an important right for them that was referenced in the UN-CRC. The rights of children to have their opinions heard and respected fell under self-determination rights. To further their critical thinking about rights, we asked and encouraged the youth to think of something they would change if they had the opportunity to do so. We asked: "If you could have the power to make a change in your community, what would that be?" Celine raised their hand enthusiastically and stated, "No homework!" Yesenia joined her, and exclaimed, "Yes, I agree. We get too much homework." Yesenia and Celine explained that students do work in class all day, and when they go home they have to do more homework, which is unfair. Yesenia shared that she would rather spend time with family and friends, and doing other things in the community.[7]

For Yesenia and Celine, the right to have their opinions and thoughts respected, validated, and acknowledged was key to their conceptualizing of rights. Having the right to socialize and engage with one's family or community was identified by Latinx youth as important to them. Although not explicitly stated as a characteristic of self-determination, the right to grow up spending time with family and in community with others has implications for the well-being and positive development of young people. This aligns with self-determination rights, as well as important tenets that strive for the cultivation of youth nurturance.

Central to self-determination rights were opportunities for engaging agency, participation in decision making, and political engagement. In fact, some Latinx youth defined rights in relation to what youth could and could not do. According to Celine,

> Uh, everyone has the rights to, like, to do something, to do what they want to do. It's something everyone has, it's, like, something everyone is able to do, I guess, sort of.

Consistent with Celine's response, Joaquín extended his definition to include privileges in relation to agency.

> Rights are like privileges. To have some privileges and, like, to do it, like—you have the privilege to do, like, what you want. Yeah, I think that's what it means. . . . I think all people have rights. Rights like, for people 'cause they're grown up and they could, like, have their own life, and for kids, I think they have rights too.

Celine defined rights as "something everyone has" and "something everyone is able to do." Joaquín, on the other hand, drew on his positionalities to emphasize that youth have rights regardless of their age. Of most significance, however, is that both Celine and Joaquín argued that rights are for everyone. Yet rights are often understood as privileges that can facilitate people's opportunities to act, or express agency to claim their power and make demands to better their lives. Celine's and Joaquín's responses demonstrated that youth conceptualized rights as inalienable. All people have rights that grant them certain privileges, including the capacity to have a choice or engage in decision making.

Despite their understanding of adults' power over youth and a young person's capacity for self-determination, Latinx youth referenced these dynamics as opportunities they could access. For instance, and as noted by Celine, Latinx youth demonstrated an awareness of their social circumstances of limited power in relation to adults. Some youth understood what they could and could not do in the presence of adults. At the same time, however, they also recognized how adults constrained their agency as well as their capacity to act with self-determination. These views reflected sociocultural constructions of youthhood that position youth knowledge and experiences as subordinate to those of adults. Additionally, these constructions assume that youth experiences, opinions, and knowledge are insignificant in comparison to those of adults. Ideologies like these posit that youth experiences do not warrant attention or importance because they are immature or irrelevant to the concerns of adults. Yet there are critical implications for failing to engage youth views on rights, especially with regard to their agency and sociopolitical development.

Lina's response challenged this when she described her schooling experiences and interactions with teachers and staff during one of our Change 4 Good program sessions.

> Lina was reminded of all the discussions we had with the youth about the school lunch food. Lina shared that one time she was out by the blacktop chewing gum. She explained: "And we're not allowed to chew gum, but Gloria, one of the nicest yard-duty ladies, let me chew it and she told me, 'Don't let Mrs. K [teacher] see you with the gum in your mouth!' and I told her that I wouldn't let her see me with it. But I forgot to throw the gum away before I walked to the classroom with Mrs. K—so I put it in the top of my mouth! *But Mrs. K noticed it* and she asked me what was in my mouth and I told her 'Doritos!'" Lina continued her story, adding, "I asked Mrs. K if I could go to the restroom and she wouldn't let me go because she said, 'You just came back from lunch!' and she reminded me that I had to go to Mrs. M's [teacher] room because I had math class." Lina shared that students aren't allowed to chew gum at school, or go to the restroom without a teacher's permission: "We always have to ask for permission if we need to go to the restroom."[8]

Lina continued her story by sharing how she got in trouble for chewing gum; she had forgotten to throw it out, and then Mrs. K noticed that there was something in her mouth, because she was chewing it.

> You know I forgot I had it, and then she looked at me chewing and said, "Throw it out!" and then she asked me to get my materials box and go to Mrs. M's room for math. I could tell she was mad.

A key theme of this story is Lina's expressed desire for wanting freedom as she strategically tried to avoid the consequences of her presumed transgression. As young people, they were not able to have the freedom to do even minuscule things like chewing gum. Of course, there might be valid reasons for not chewing gum, yet precluding youth from understanding these reasons challenges their self-determination rights. Additionally, it limits their capacities for engaging agency, decision making, and critical literacy development. Lina assessed the situation further, however.

> Students should have the freedom to go to the restroom when we want, and also to chew gum. We're not going to throw it on the ground, but some students are afraid at getting caught so we do throw it on the floor.[9]

As Lina explained, chewing gum was an unacceptable behavior in school. The wrongful disposing of chewed gum, in Lina's view, stemmed out of youth fears and anxieties about being caught chewing gum in the first place. The fear, along with the schooling culture of discipline and punishment, reflected the power embedded in the classroom that emphasized zero-tolerance for particular student behaviors.

The zero-tolerance practices in some classrooms are intended to maintain power over students and to discipline some youth into certain socially desirable behaviors. Young people of color, especially Black and Latinx boys, are often disproportionately chastised for behaviors that do not warrant harsh punishment. This has been documented by sociologist Victor Rios in *Punished: Policing the Lives of Black and Latino Boys*, which features the disproportionate disciplinary consequences that boys of color predominantly experience in US public institutions, especially schools.[10] The zero-tolerance experienced in school significantly curtails youth agency, freedom, and self-determination, and is another example of the culture of the hidden curriculum in schooling.

In providing a critical perspective of the issue, Lina argued that if young people were afforded the choice and trust to chew gum and dispose of it appropriately, they would not get rid of it haphazardly. Lina described how chewing gum was constructed as a problem because it was policed, surveilled, and sanctioned by teachers. Chewing gum became emblematic of other problems, limitations, and constraints as experienced by Latinx youth in a culture of schooling. The disciplinary sanctions that resulted from chewing gum were an example of the ways youth self-determination rights become limited and constrained by the structures, or in this case rules, that were determined by adults, specifically by teachers. Perhaps to some youth, chewing gum was a subtle form of resistance, their attempt to exercise agency and to push the boundaries of what was permissible in school.

Undergirding their demands for choice as well as discernment for themselves was Lina's critique of the superficial meaning of self-determination rights for young people. Lina articulated that although youth were often told to participate and exercise their agency, in practice this was significantly difficult for young people to do. Because of the limited opportunities to engage self-determination fully, Latinx youth offered their reflections on the significance of rights often in the context of learning about them.

Latinx Youth Learning about Rights

Latinx youth definitions of rights differed from those reflected in the citizenship literature.[11] They often conceptualized rights beyond nurturance and self-determination to include rights for their families and communities. School and family settings served as meaningful contexts to expose Latinx youth to rights-related meanings and their implications. Latinx youth viewed rights as necessary for the fulfillment of citizenship, which they associated with legality, access to opportunities, and a sense of belonging. Because schooling and family experiences helped inform Latinx youth meaning-making about rights, understanding where and how youth learn about rights deserves some analysis. School, family, and community contexts, given the associations and experiences Latinx youth offered in their reflections and dialogues, are discussed as important for learning about and engaging rights.

Historicizing Struggles for Enfranchisement

In Change 4 Good, young people were encouraged to develop their critical literacy about rights in relation to their lived experiences and the program's activities, including their mural and its depicted themes. In this context, what ensued were often nuanced conversations and reflections about rights, histories of struggle, and activists.

> For several weeks now, we had been engaging with the topic of rights—what these are and mean to the youth, and how they experience these, or witness them or not in their contexts of school, family, and community. We began our discussion by asking the youth to describe what they associated with the word "rights." Initially there was silence, but after a few minutes, the youth facetiously stated some associations, such as "The opposite of left" and "To be correct." These responses were technically correct; yet, they were not what we were hoping the youth would say. Their responses made for good laughs however. This encouraged us as program facilitators to be more specific with our questions. In our following discussion we acknowledged that the word "rights" could mean very different things, including what some of the youth had stated. The question about "rights" was then rephrased in relation to social justice to encourage the youth to give more nuanced responses that reflected our earlier conversations on human rights and the civil rights movement. After a few minutes, a few hands were raised, and youth shared that they had learned about rights in relation to people like Dr. Martin Luther King Jr. and César E. Chávez. We asked the youth to elaborate on what Dr. MLK had done for people. Yesenia shared that "He tried to stop people from being racist." And, in a quieter tone, she added, "But it didn't come true." Celine nodded in agreement, and some other youth followed nodding their heads as well. Iris, nodding in agreement with others, stated out loud that some changes were made, adding: "Rosa Parks made busses equal for all people because there used to be separate busses for African Americans." Celine agreed and added that Rosa Parks refused to give up her seat on the bus to white people.[12]

Schools are an important context where young people learn about rights. Curricula centered on historical perspectives that expose young people to civil rights and social justice–related topics can facilitate youth critical literacy and sociopolitical development.[13] Such enriching learning experiences can introduce youth to discourses on rights that frame these as statutes or laws. In these courses, students often learn about histories of struggle, like civil rights, for example, as well as an individual's relationship and responsibility to the nation-state. Most importantly, there is the potential for learning about social justice and collective action in relation to rights and freedoms.

Among Latinx youth, language arts class was identified as a setting for learning about rights. In defining the term "rights," Latinx youth referenced course material such as the civil rights movement to give context and meaning to the word "rights." For Iris and Daniela, as previously stated by Lina, language arts class was an important setting to engage with topics about rights. In the context of our interview, each conducted at a separate time, Iris and Daniela offered the following:

IRIS: We learned about that [rights] in language arts.
DANIELA: Yup, I heard it today in language arts.

At the time of our interview, both were sixth-grade students, and at a different public middle school, which Daniela described as "more open" to learning about "different things." Daniela elaborated on what she had learned by explaining the significance of the civil rights movement.

We were talking about it, the civil rights movement. . . . My teacher said that Dr. Martin Luther King Jr. was fighting for his rights but at the same time he wasn't violent, and the ones that—the powerful people, like the government and whites [white people], they were the ones looking bad on the news because they were the ones that were hurting other people. They were hitting people, the African Americans, just because of the color of their skin.

Daniela contextualized her learning about rights in relation to the civil rights movement, specifically the legacy of Martin Luther King Jr.'s nonviolent protest and activism. By naming the "powerful people" and how they were "hurting other people," she implied that these were acts of racism and violence perpetrated by white people with power over African Americans. Daniela's response demonstrates her critical understanding of how racism operates to oppress people of color. Through a critical analysis, Daniela questioned and challenged institutions, including the role of the government, in perpetuating segregation, discrimination, and violence. Daniela's critical analysis reflected her understanding of the intersections of power, racism, and violence. The racism she described was rooted in her understanding of the significance and implications of the civil rights movement for actualizing racial justice.

Another key feature of Daniela's response was that she viewed rights as freedoms and opportunities that must be demanded through collective action, grassroots organizing, and protest, similar to King's activism. In other words, the work of activists and leaders like King is synonymous with rights, especially rights to inclusion, enfranchisement, and full citizenship. Consistent with Daniela's remarks, Iris described rights in relation to being recognized as a full human being. Iris, for instance, attempted to explain how race and racism played a significant role in contributing to discrimination toward people of color because this was embedded in the fabric of the United States.

At a quaint coffee shop across the street from Iris's mother's place of work, a small catering business, Iris and I talked about her new school and how her older brother was helping her adjust to the demands of schoolwork and making new friends. As we continued the interview, I asked Iris about rights.

> IRIS: When people say human rights, like, some people don't have them, and human rights is when you have freedom of speech and stuff like that. But some people don't have rights because they're from other places and sometimes they'd be treated differently.
> JESICA: Do you think that's right?
> IRIS: No, because we're all the same. We watched a human rights video, and we'd see some people mistreated, treated differently because, you know, some people are, like, racist and all that, and that's what we learn about, how some people treated people from different places differently.

Iris was one of the most soft-spoken youth in Change 4 Good; however, every now and then she would express her sassiness by calling out students and adults when we were not following our community agreements, which we had developed collectively as a group. As evidenced by her response, Iris noted that rights can be limited or in some cases denied to those who are immigrants or perceived to be foreign to the United States. Iris argued that their perceived differences, including country of origin or nationality, do not justify the mistreatment and dehumanization of people. According to Iris, rights emphasize an equal and shared humanity; the right to express oneself as guaranteed under the First Amendment is a right of all people. Using one's voice can become a powerful tool to make claims to freedom, opportunities, and enfranchisement, yet, as Iris described, racism can significantly curtail people's rights and power.

Iris has a strong personality, and although she was shy in discrete moments, she was quick to contribute and help other youth follow along, perhaps modeling her behavior on her brother's. Thus, when Iris identified the mistreatment of people of color, as well as other social groups whose physical features or cultural practices are perceived to be different, as "racist" and unjust, I was not surprised, because Iris was unapologetically blunt at times. In an explicit remark, Iris insisted, "We're all the same"—claiming that people deserve to be treated with dignity and respect. Iris's remark echoed Daniela's claims about inclusive perspectives of citizenship and pluralistic rights. Both responses reflect their experiences in learning about rights, and how this knowledge was informed to a degree by language arts curricula, but most importantly by their lived experiences.

Daniela's and Iris's responses demonstrated the context and discourses through which Latinx youth were exposed to rights. Iris's response, like Daniela's, demonstrated that when youth talked about rights in relation to social justice, their firsthand experiences with racism and forms of exclusion became more salient. The articulated connections made by Latinx youth reflected their nuanced understanding about rights, often in relation to a language arts topic like history, as well as the oppression of immigrants and people of color. The significance and value of language arts curricula, especially ones that are ethnic studies–oriented, cannot be understated, as they provide youth with critical and meaningful learning opportunities to discuss systems of power and oppression from a historic and contemporary perspective.

Community Experiences of Political Engagement

The social context that surrounds young people plays an important role in shaping their understandings about rights, political engagement, and solidarity. Latinx youth often learned about their communities' experiences with injustice by witnessing their communities' resistance to conditions of oppression. In these contexts and through their experiences, they developed an understanding of the significance of collective action. The research by Amalia Pallares in *Family Activism: Immigrant Struggles and the Politics of Noncitizenship* demonstrates how Latinx families, including youth, often participate in community organizing events or political mobilizing efforts that help shape their political subjectivities.[14]

A story that illustrates this is that of Sophie Cruz, a five-year-old who took center stage in US media in the fall of 2015 when she approached Pope Francis to deliver a letter advocating for comprehensive immigration reform. The Obama administration's deterrence of undocumented immigration through the use of detention and deportation campaigns made immigration a critical issue of concern for politicians, activists, and communities. During Pope Francis's visit to the US Congress, immigration was a central issue of discussion because of the several Immigration and Customs Enforcement (ICE) raids that were taking place across the nation. Against the backdrop of such hostility and fear, Sophie's activism was viewed as a powerful act of resistance because it interrupted the racist nativism while challenging presumed assumptions of youth apolitical engagement, specifically views of youth as naïve or ignorant about social justice issues that affect them.

Family, as a unique context that helps shape the building of communities, is an important influence on Latinx youth understandings of rights. Because Latinx youth are embedded in the everyday lives and sociocultural practices of their families, community settings are instrumental in forming the social and political subjectivities of youth. It is in the context of community that Latinx youth often experience, engage with, and voice their rights alongside family members who are also claiming rights. Families and communities making claims to rights through their activism can in turn shape Latinx youth meaning-making about rights. Among the Change 4 Good Latinx youth, some families provided meaningful opportunities for political participation through grassroots community organizing.

Community organizing groups often strive to hold the nation-state accountable for trampling on people's rights, dignity, and humanity. Therefore, in addition to family experiences and language arts classes, there were two other contexts in which Latinx youth learned about rights. First, youth learned about rights outside structured schooling environments, such as programs like Change 4 Good. Unlike what youth were exposed to in the traditional classroom environment, the curriculum of Change 4 Good was centered on youth engaging in projects that they determined and developed, such as the mural. The program allowed for significant flexibility in curriculum development, and we veered into other topics of relevance to support the critical literacy and leadership of the youth. Second, Latinx youth learned about rights through social justice–oriented community events, and some political demonstrations and gatherings. Examples of these events often aligned with and reflected histories of social movements, like the United Farm Workers (UFW), while others centered on local efforts associated with grassroots community organizing. In these contexts or environments, Latinx youth were often accompanying their parents and learning about rights by demonstrating and campaigning for specific rights.

As we were discerning themes to represent in their mural, Latinx youth were exposed to murals over the course of several Change 4 Good program sessions. The murals youth engaged with were mostly presented visually in the form of slideshows of images. We also facilitated a field trip to the local university, where youth were able to visit several murals on campus. During the field trip, we visited mural sites that depicted political and social justice–oriented images, stories, and themes. Our campus visit provided youth with an experience to engage with public, often political artwork and recognize murals as part of the ethos of the college culture and campus.

During one Change 4 Good program session we analyzed one mural's symbols. The intent of this analysis was to gather ideas for the mural that youth would create at their school. We began by having Latinx youth observe and interpret the symbolism represented in a mural image featuring the face of UFW organizer César E. Chávez. Historicizing Chávez's organizing on immigrant workers' rights, Latinx youth discussed one of the images on the slideshow.

> One of the photographs on the slide deck was taken at the Mural Moat. The photograph shown was about César E. Chávez, and I was pleased to see that some of the youth knew who he was. Andrés was the first to respond by saying that César E. Chávez had "fought for the rights of the farm workers." I smiled and I said to Andrés that he was right, that was the person that had fought for the rights of the Mexican farm workers. I asked the youth if they knew what quote he was famous for and they didn't respond for a couple minutes, and then Jackie and Diego simultaneously replied: "¡Sí, se puede!" I replied with an enthused yes, and then I asked them if they could translate it to English and they said, "Yes, we can!"[15]

Learning about rights through stories of community organizing was a central feature of Change 4 Good Latinx youth conversations on what to include in their mural. Rights discourses were engaged by Latinx youth via their focus group stories about community organizing and collective action to make a positive change in the community. Together with the associations they drew to histories of struggles for social justice, the connections they made to their community experiences took on a significant meaning for Latinx youth who were familiar with the content of these stories and their slogans. As we facilitated opportunities for Latinx youth to process their campus visit and viewing of murals through reflections and dialogues, they began to think about how to tell a powerful story about their community. Drawing inspiration from the histories of social movements, community organizing, and their own community's strength, Latinx youth sought to illustrate some of these themes in their mural.

Stories of community organizing and action were not exclusive to social movements; yet these were meaningful in helping Latinx youth understand contemporary struggles for rights and the opportunities that were being systematically denied to Latinx, immigrants, and communities of color. Learning about rights in the context of and through reflections about community experiences required Latinx youth to name those rights and resources that they felt both they and their communities were being deprived of. The opportunities they experienced as being foreclosed or denied to their communities were often at the root of social problems affecting their quality of life. In discussing and reflecting upon the rights that people have or do not have, Latinx youth identified several interconnected themes related to their limited agency as youth. This was evidenced in Lina's story and the bold but lucid and thoughtful claims that were shared in the context of Change 4 Good.

> According to Lina, "Youth don't have access to certain things like the teachers' lounge, which has the vending machines." She then added, "Students [unlike teachers] don't have access to certain rights and privileges." This remark, and the other stories and experiences shared by the youth, related to students not having certain rights, or not having equal rights as adults. Yesenia brought up a story from a youth in the community who was involved in gangs. She related it to other stories that were shared by students, such as not having rights equal to those of adults or teachers, limited access to things in the school, like the lounge with the vending machine, and having a limited capacity to decide for themselves and speak for themselves. Yesenia added, "I don't know, I just remembered that [youth and gangs] story because it was sad." Lina said, "That story should be depicted in the mural because some people don't have certain things, and so they get on the wrong path and they make bad decisions." Lina raised her hand again and said she had another story to share. She told us about the Futsal story that was shared by an adult who participated in the focus group. Lina reminded us that the Futsal story was about "youth not having access to certain things, and not having power." She elaborated by adding, "The power to change something or prevent something from happening, or getting people together to make something happen, like Futsal!" Together, the youth concluded, "The Futsal story was about parents organizing to help make something positive for kids in the community." Youth understood that in the absence of resources in their community, some youth would pursue activities that would pose challenges to experiencing positive and healthy lives.[16]

While Lina and Yesenia briefly described seemingly separate stories, their reflections demonstrated a similar awareness of the conditions that impact youth well-being and frequently lead to student disengagement and school pushout. Latinx youth reflections interrogated the culture of schooling, including the hidden curriculum, and why their limited access to resources and material goods led them to reject certain practices and discourses. Youth felt that these experiences, compounded with the patronizing role of adults—often disguised as protecting youth—prevented them from exercising agency and discerning what could be most beneficial to their well-being. The disenfranchisement and invisibility that were described by young people stem from what Lina identified as schooling experiences of marginalization, conditions that are exacerbated as these intersect with their student identities as both youth and Latinx.

In describing the limited sense of agency and thus self-determination among Latinx youth, Lina's and Yesenia's stories show how the absence of meaningful opportunities for participation in decision making affected young people. Because of these limited opportunities, as Yesenia described, youth turned to affiliations with groups that provide a sense of belonging and community. Gang-affiliated groups and their environments are not always conducive to the positive development of youth. As Lina explained, involvement in gangs offered some youth in her community "certain things," such as material and social support. Forms of support like these can track youth on "the wrong path and they make bad decisions," as Yesenia reflected. The decisions youth make to affiliate with gangs should be understood in the context of a structure of power that limits youth opportunities for engagement, a sense of belonging and care. Thus, when Lina elaborated on this story by explaining the significance of the Futsal program, she underscored the value of providing young people with activities that supported youth and community well-being. The creation of the youth Futsal program was possible through the collective efforts and mobilizing by parents and community members. Moreover, the joint efforts to create a Futsal program illustrated the outcomes of community organizing to demand resources, particularly sports and other positive youth development opportunities for young people in the community. Stories of community organizing to bring about social change, like the Futsal program, shaped how and what Latinx youth learned about rights in the context of community experiences, often with their parents.

In Change 4 Good we strived to facilitate these opportunities for story sharing among Latinx youth because these also reflected their focus group stories. The stories pertained to their school and community, as well as the history of agricultural farmwork in the area. Community organizing stories were also complemented by the experiences of program facilitators. We occasionally offered our stories to help support Latinx youth critical literacy and engagement, especially when developing the mural design. For example, during one program session, some of the Change 4 Good program facilitators were late because of their participation in a student protest at the university. The purpose of this demonstration was to challenge tuition increases and budget cuts that affected student support services and programming. The late arrival of some of our team members prompted us to discuss with the youth the meaning of protesting, as well as the value of a free education. In discussing these topics—especially a free education—youth connected their reflections to social change and justice, as well as the right to voice such demands.

> Youth conversation about the cost of attending a university and how expensive it was, and how some college students were protesting the university's decision to raise tuition seemed to resonate with some of them as they remarked how students often cannot pay to go to college. Some youth said that students couldn't pay to go to school, especially college. A few others exclaimed, "Education should be free!" They began to chant "Education should be free!" and asking: "Why do we need to pay to get something that should be a right for all students?" I asked the youth if they paid to go to school now, and they said no. I asked them what they would do if they had to pay to go to school, and they said, "I wouldn't pay, I don't have money." Daniela then raised her hand and said that she went to a protest once with her grandmother, she said that they were walking with posters and signs, and they were chanting "¡Sí, se puede!" When she shared this, several of the youth laughed and said that they too had done that. That is, they had been a part of protests. Feliz told the youth that protesting was a way to "have [our] voices be heard so that change can happen." I added that sometimes protesting could lead people to notice something needing to be changed. Joaquín said, "pro, as in good, right?" Mrs. K overheard this comment and said, "Yeah, pro is right, and con is

bad." Joaquín then said "*Protesting*," putting emphasis in the "PRO" part of his sentence to help him make the association more explicit.[17]

Learning about rights in the context of community organizing provided Latinx youth with opportunities to reflect on, discuss, and interrogate not only the meaning of rights in their own lives but also the broader significance of rights for their communities. Some Latinx youth expressed powerful reflections on the importance of a free education. Similarly, others called for collective action and protest to amplify their voices and demands. Latinx youth discussed rights as privileges and opportunities they must claim for themselves and for their communities. Rights to opportunities, including a free education, must not be taken for granted, they concluded. Instead, according to Latinx youth, rights must be *demanded* because they are not equally granted or allocated to people. Protesting, as Joaquín and Feliz described, is necessary because it allows for silenced voices to be heard. As neoliberalism begins to take hold across various institutions, including education, the prospect of pursuing a free education, especially at the college or university level, is significantly compromised.

Latinx youth echoed the words of Chávez, "¡Sí, se puede!," in chanting demands for a "free education." Through reflection and dialogue, youth made connections between education rights and social justice. These connections were informed by historic experiences of injustice and disenfranchisement, and how these conditions to a modest degree were rectified and challenged by change agents, activists like Martin Luther King Jr., Rosa Parks, and César E. Chávez. Latinx youth interest in protest, social change, and justice exemplified their sociopolitical development as citizens expressing their hope for a more just society, one where they are heard, included, and able to exercise their rights. It also expressed their hope for school settings and community contexts that welcomed their participation and encouraged their agency, including their political determination.

Theorizing the meaning and significance of rights for a non-adult group like Latinx youth is warranted, especially given the limitations of characterizing rights and citizenship broadly along adult-centric-informed notions. Situating the literature on youth rights in a sociopolitical citizenship standpoint demonstrates Latinx youth capacities to define and make claims to rights. Latinx youth conceptualizations of their rights often included being recognized as holders of rights, who can and must be meaningfully involved as active participants in an adult-centered society. When provided with such opportunities to exercise agency and participation in decision making, Latinx youth made explicit how they conceptualized and made claims to rights. Theorizing Latinx youth rights beyond the UN-CRC's conceptualizations toward a youth-centered approach that illuminates Latinx youth lived experiences aligns with perspectives of youth as agents of change who are coming of age in the United States in a time of contested citizenship.

Summary

As Latinx youth reflections and stories demonstrate in part 1, citizenship is more than a status or label, a practice of learned skills, or a prescribed set of rights. A healthy democracy, characterized by social justice–oriented values, must center the voices and agency of Latinx youth as active citizens in the present. The socialization of citizenship, as Latinx youth experiences attest, often begins with the shaping of "good" students in the classroom. The valuing of certain citizenship practices over others intersects with US-based constructions of citizenship as a status, practice, and rights-bearing construct. Latinx youth troubled citizenship as a status and practice determined and established by an individual's relationship to the nation-state, and thus the rights it affords or denies certain people. Furthermore, individualistic rights understood as privileges ascribed to citizenship challenged Latinx youth opportunities to exercise agency as sociopolitical citizens.

A central theme among Latinx youth constructions of citizenship as a status, practice, and right was that they viewed the term as a set of behaviors aligned with the status quo, as well as the culture and norms of the classroom. The hidden curriculum and Character Education, which support "good" student socialization practices, can constrain the critical literacy development necessary to support a thriving democracy of socially, politically, and civically engaged citizens.[18] The challenge of instituting obedience in the classroom is the focus of much critique, as it should be. Thus, I underscore the urgency for creating conditions that are counter to the hidden curriculum of schooling, and instead cultivate spaces that support youth agency and participation in decision making on matters that concern them.[19] An interrogation of education curricula that socialize students into specific norms or conventions of citizenship is necessary.

Equally important is understanding Latinx youth conceptualization of rights. First, this understanding can provide educators, youth advocates, and service providers—who are involved in supporting and cultivating the sociopolitical development of young people—with valuable information on what youth view as important, of concern to their lives, and affecting their rights. Second, acknowledging how Latinx youth conceptualize their rights involves the situating of their voices and experiences in the construction of citizen rights and citizenship. Asking youth about their rights validates their experiences and needs, and acknowledges them as having agency to name and describe their citizenship embodiments. Third, in knowing what Latinx youth view as rights, educators and researchers, alongside youth, can create conditions to better meet youth needs, as well as support their agency and development as sociopolitical citizens beyond a mere status and practice.

PART II

Embodying Citizenship

Growing Up Latinx documents Latinx youth sociopolitical citizenship development in relation to how youth understand, engage with, and trouble meanings of citizenship, legality, and rights in their school, family, and community contexts. Although nation-state–defined meanings of citizenship as a status, practice, and right were a part of Latinx youth meaning-making, citizenship for Latinx youth meant much more than these labels. Definitions provided by Latinx youth often went beyond associating these labels with US-based constructions of legality and belonging. For instance, citizenship was often understood as a verb, as an action or expression, which under certain circumstances and social conditions was either constrained or supported in a given context. The thriving and well-being of Latinx immigrant families and youth agency, participation, and belonging hinge on the contexts or conditions that support pluriversal embodiments of citizenship. The meanings Latinx youth associated with citizenship were often shaped by their identities, which intersected with their social and political subjectivities within and outside their specific contexts, such as schooling.

Sociopolitical Citizenship

Latinx youth citizenship meanings were more capacious, as their reflections nuanced constructions of terms that often fail to fully value and honor the dignity and humanity of immigrants regardless of their status. The disempowering schooling experiences Latinx youth encountered, like the anti-immigrant sentiments they were exposed to, were enmeshed within their family and community settings. Additionally, this created for Latinx youth a liminal in-between space where they felt simultaneously included and excluded. Latinx youth posited in their definitions that all people are important members of a democratic society. Through these claims, they troubled US-based constructions of citizenship, legality, and rights, which Latinx youth understood as having implications in shaping their lives. Making the case for Latinx youth sociopolitical citizenship as a response to the limited rights and disenfranchisement of youth is the focus of part 2.

The second part of *Growing Up Latinx* consists of chapters 4 and 5. In chapter 4, the domains of sociopolitical citizenship are described through examples and reflections that center Latinx youth voices, agency, and experiences within and, to a degree, outside the context of the Change 4 Good program. Sociopolitical citizenship is illustrated through Latinx youth accounts of agency, participation, and belonging, and the meanings they attach to these experiences as they informed their understanding of citizenship. Experiences that surfaced the salience of citizenship, legality, and rights tended to intersect with positionalities along age, race, ethnicity, and immigrant status. Features of Latinx youth social identities, critical consciousness, socioemotional awareness, and political engagement are characterized as interconnected domains that supported their sociopolitical citizenship development.

Expanding upon sociopolitical citizenship, chapter 5 presents Latinx youth views on their rights. Reflections and discussions about rights surfaced in the context of Change 4 Good program activities, as well as in one-on-one conversations—notably, how particular meanings are formed, and the implications of these meanings in shaping their rights—and together, these illustrate Latinx youth claims to rights. Furthermore, Latinx youth meaning-making sought to trouble the relationship between citizenship, legality, and rights, especially when constructions of these terms excluded them and their families. Rights, often presented as privileges and responsibilities, are not equitably granted, protected, and upheld, nor are the freedoms and opportunity structures set up to be accessible for all people, in this case Latinx youth. Immigrants, communities of color, and low-income or working-class individuals and families, whose rights are conditionally afforded and essentially expendable, experience forms of liminal enfranchisement, as Latinx youth appeared to understand. The following brief discussion on youth perspectives on rights provides evidence in support of these points.

Perspectives on Youth Citizenship and Rights

The research on youth citizenship and rights—specifically, the meanings they attach to these, and their enactment of and claims to rights—centered on white populations of middle- or upper-middle-class status, including some outside a US context. Most of these studies examined youth knowledge of rights as civil liberties, as well as youth conceptual understandings about rights. More than four decades ago, clinical-community psychologist Gary B. Melton examined youth meaning-making about rights and described how these are shaped by specific factors, such as age and socioeconomic status.[1] About eighty young people in the first, third, fifth, and seventh grades, with half of them in the fifth and seventh grades, were interviewed about their rights. Seventh-graders from families with a higher socioeconomic status were found to have more positive attitudes toward youth rights, compared to youth from lower-income families. Most participants (85 percent) were white and from higher socioeconomic status families; thirteen youth identified as African American and one as Asian American. Demographics for Latinx were not provided. However, 40 percent of the participants in the lower socioeconomic group were labeled bilingual in Spanish or Portuguese. It is unclear as to whether the participants were of Latin American or European descent. The grouping of these participants based on language yields unclear information about Latinx youth.

To examine these results more meaningfully, Melton and colleagues conducted two-part semi-structured interviews with youth about their understanding of and meaning-making about rights. The first part consisted of questions from the Children's Rights Interview (e.g., What is a right? Who has rights? Do children have rights? Should children have rights?). The second part included twelve vignettes illustrating a youth-on-youth or youth-adult dynamic, such as a teacher or parent conflict. Participants discussed their judgments about the conflict-laden scenarios and how youth might exercise their rights. Results indicated that most youth, especially older youth regardless of their social class status, held abstract notions about the meaning of rights.

Melton's study set the foundation for subsequent research on children's rights. For example, expanding Melton's work, Isabelle Cherney and Nancy Walker Perry conducted an international study of eighty-seven young people between the ages of eleven and thirteen from the United States, Canada, and Switzerland, and found that rights to self-determination were identified as being most important to youth.[2] Self-determination rights were characterized as having the right to participate and engage in decision making on matters that concern them and affect the quality of their lives. A goal of the international study was to consider the broader globalized context that informed youth rights, and how as youth age into adulthood they develop more abstract conceptualizations of rights to freedom, agency, and power. Results indicate that rights to self-determination appeared to be more important to youth than nurturance rights. One explanation for this is that self-determination rights support youth agency and participation in ways that nurturance rights do not. Nurturance rights often emphasize paternalistic and/or maternalistic values that reinforce hegemonic discourses and sociocultural constructions of childhood that youth found to be especially constraining of their agency. The implications of this work are consistent with other studies on youth attitudes and knowledge about rights.[3] Most of this work, it should be noted, has not explicitly examined the intersecting identities or positionalities of youth according to age, race, ethnicity, and immigrant status—and especially of Latinx youth coming of age in the United States.

What it means to have or not have rights—how youth conceptualize rights in their own lives—must be theoretically and empirically discussed further. Research examining Latinx youth understandings of and engagement with rights is warranted given the broader political climate that surrounds their lives. Documenting Latinx youth social and political subjectivities in relation to rights and citizenship is imperative in the US context, where the question of *who a citizen is* (or is not) continues to be contested. Yet few empirical studies have examined Latinx youth citizenship and their relationship to and understanding of rights as these relate to and differ from notions of legality.[4] The voices of Latinx youth, who will inevitably come to constitute a significant US demographic, must be centered in the conceptualizing and theorizing of their rights. Theorizing about young people's lives must make Latinx youth agency visible; this can also help demonstrate their resistance to hegemonic discourses that curtail their rights as citizens.

Hegemonic discourses, together with a lack of resources, services, and forms of support for Latinx communities, immigrants, and low-income and working-class families, are exacerbated by practices that support the criminalization and/or assimilation of Latinx youth along with divestment in public education. The intensified structural inequities that surround Latinx youth in their upbringing reproduce conditions of oppression with long-lasting impacts. How Latinx youth experience and wield rights in their own lives, along with the values they attach to rights—what rights mean to them and which rights are most salient—must be addressed in the critical youth and citizenship literatures. The dearth of research examining the connections between citizenship, legality, and rights as experienced by Latinx youth in the United States seems to reflect the invisibility of or lack of concern for more fully understanding Latinx youth development. The erasure of Latinx youth perspectives is problematic because it assumes that youth are unaware of concepts like citizenship and rights, and how these shape their school, family, and community contexts.

Latinx youth are aware of the ways that citizenship and rights are manifested or denied.[5] Certainly the racist nativism that surrounds their lives has a direct impact on their experiences of belonging and their capacity to exercise their agency. In this regard, Latinx youth are not immune to or ignorant about hegemonic discourses, policies, and practices that affect their families and communities. Understanding Latinx youth views on their rights can help make visible the social conditions, discourses, policies, and practices that affect them. Relatedly, it can foreground how sociopolitical citizenship develops in response to—or perhaps in resistance to—being othered and excluded. Examining these dynamics through Latinx youth sociopolitical citizenship necessitates unpacking Latinx youth meaning-making and embodiments as citizens, particularly as they are exposed and socialized into a particular form of second-class citizenship with differential rights—points that I elaborate on in the following chapters.

4

Citizenship as a Sociopolitical Process

Sociopolitical development theory, a prominent framework in the community psychology literature to describe the critical consciousness that develops among institutionally marginalized youth, is the foundation for what I conceptualize as *sociopolitical citizenship*.[1] Informed by sociopolitical development theory, sociopolitical citizenship is a standpoint that can help make visible how young people cultivate their agency through an understanding of their social identities and the development of a critical consciousness and a socioemotional awareness, which together support their opportunities for political participation in decision making on matters that concern them. As sociopolitical citizens, young people seek to challenge injustices rooted in systems of power.

Consistent with positive youth development perspectives, sociopolitical development theory is fostered through opportunities for critical literacy development and collective action beyond civic engagement.[2] Sociopolitical citizenship extends sociopolitical development theory and positive youth development perspectives by emphasizing the importance of youth social and political subjectivities in shaping their agency. Although sociopolitical development theory strives to cultivate among youth a systemic structural analysis, in practice it prioritizes an individual-level analysis characterized by a young person's understanding of themselves in relation to others and the social context. As such, it does not explicitly engage with the colonial, sociohistorical, and intersectional dimensions of youth development, specifically among Latinx youth, in relation to citizenship, legality, and rights.

As a framework for characterizing aspects of critical literacy, sociopolitical development theory challenges deficit views of young people as being "at-risk," acritical, and apolitical.[3] The theory posits that when young people are provided with the adequate resources, forms of support, and opportunities for critical literacy, as well as civic engagement to transform their experiences with oppression, a critical consciousness develops. Unique to Latinx youth critical literacy is their consciousness of citizenship, legality, and rights as youth growing up in Latinx immigrant and mixed-status families. The social and political subjectivities they develop—in relation to their social identities, critical consciousness, socioemotional awareness, and political participation—are what I characterize and name as sociopolitical citizenship.[4] Sociopolitical citizenship, in practice, is something Latinx youth do. It is embodied and enacted as a response, and often in resistance, to conditions that disenfranchise them as young people coming of age in the United States.

Because Latinx youth grow up experiencing their lives as embedded within systems of power—which intersect with broader sociocultural constructions of age, race, ethnicity, and immigrant status, for example—opportunities for agency and participation are limited, yet necessary to cultivate their sociopolitical citizenship. Entwined with these systems are also hegemonic discourses that reify deficit views about Latinx youth, including their families and communities. By reflecting upon their experiences and encounters with US constructions of citizenship, legality, and rights, I argue, Latinx youth embody sociopolitical citizenship. As Latinx youth engage their social and political subjectivities, thinking through what citizenship means and how it manifests, they are expressing their agency as citizens. As they experience the hegemonic discourses in their lives, they simultaneously trouble notions of citizenship, legality, and rights that limit their agency and participation in decision making on matters that concern them and can contribute to their sense of belonging. Latinx youth positionalities and unique location in a context of contested citizenship and rights compel them to trouble and reimagine US-based notions of citizenship that position them, along with their families, as second-class citizens.

Sociopolitical citizenship as a practice offers an important standpoint to help transform and challenge deficit views and hegemonic discourses on Latinx youth development. By supporting and advocating for youth agency, sociopolitical citizenship underscores youth capacities to create change and improve the quality of their lives and communities. The critical consciousness that characterizes sociopolitical citizenship is rooted in an understanding of how systems of power operate to disenfranchise groups, and what *is* done or *can be* done to create change.

To illustrate, in the context of our interview, Diego demonstrated knowledge of collective action as he reflected upon a few of his experiences in political demonstrations.

> DIEGO: People can write a letter. Like a petition and people can sign it. They can try to get a group of people together. To, uhh—what's it called? Protest.
> JESICA: Protest? Have you gone to any protests?
> DIEGO: Yeah, I went with my mom. I went downtown because she wasn't getting paid the amount of money she was supposed to get paid, so they got a group of people and started protesting in downtown.
> JESICA: How old were you?
> DIEGO: Seven.
> JESICA: Have you gone to other protests after that?
> DIEGO: I don't know, I think it was for the rights—for the rights of people to stay in the US so they wouldn't get deported. I went with my mom.

In between sips of his smoothie and bites of his bagel, Diego named some strategies he saw people engage as they brought attention to issues of concern and social change during a demonstration he attended. Diego explained that the first protest he participated in was with his mother, who rallied for equal pay. The second protest, a presumably larger gathering of people, concerned organizing demands in favor of advocating for humane and just legislation toward immigration reform. Diego also described actions people can take to be heard. Examples of these included writing a letter and circulating a petition. Additionally, he emphasized the importance of protesting, which is a form of collective action via community organizing. Diego described how mobilizing people to come together to address an issue or injustice can be a way to create social change. Unlike US-based constructions of citizenship that define it as a status, a practice, and a rights-bearing construct in relation to the nation-state, sociopolitical citizenship is characterized by the interlinked social and political subjectivities of Latinx youth—specifically, how these subjectivities, rooted in their lived experiences, have shaped their practice of exercising agency, including demanding opportunities to participate in decision making as an example of collective action. Diego's reflections on collective action, such as rallies, marches, and protests, demonstrate the development of his sociopolitical citizenship, largely informed by his family's experiences.

Collective action, civic engagement, and political participation are all important practices associated with and characteristic of sociopolitical citizenship. Experiences to cultivate sociopolitical citizenship via collective action often unfolded among Latinx youth in ways consistent with literature that highlights the significance of intergenerational political socialization. The value of family and community settings involving youth in community organizing efforts, and how this is critical to supporting their political development, is well documented.[5] Adults, often parents, model political participation, civic engagement, and activism for Latinx youth. The modeling of such behaviors provides them with opportunities for critical literacy development. Opportunities like these can further cultivate Latinx youth agency, along with youth development perspectives that view young people as capable of embodying sociopolitical citizenship as they contribute to create social change.

Domains of Sociopolitical Citizenship

Sociopolitical citizenship is an embodiment and enactment of citizenship characterized by four domains: social identity development, critical consciousness, socioemotional awareness, and political engagement. Latinx youth engaged these domains in various ways, through their lived experiences and across multiple settings. Though some domains can be more salient or visible compared to others, or appear independent from each other, these must be understood as interconnected and mutually constitutive. Critical consciousness, one of the domains, involves engaging reflexivity toward the development of a social analysis of power or injustice, which is necessary for political engagement. Both critical consciousness and political engagement are complemented by the development of a socioemotional awareness of social issues that might compel, in this case, Latinx youth to reflect upon their social identities with more intent. Regardless of the salience of some domains, these must be understood as key elements of sociopolitical citizenship. Certainly, some of the examples of sociopolitical citizenship among Latinx youth draw from their marginalized experiences in the classroom. However, other examples are of their reflections and agency within the Change 4 Good program. Below I illustrate each domain as enacted and experienced by Latinx youth, and discuss them in relation to the relevant literatures that inform them.

Social Identity Development

> JOAQUÍN: I'm thirteen years old, and I like to play soccer. My favorite soccer team is Barcelona. Oh, and I like tamales.
>
> CELINE: I'm a bit crazy. I talk too much. Sometimes I'm too energetic at school. I, like, I just run around like crazy and I just talk way too much in class.
>
> DANIELA: Okay. Well, I'm fast. I'm athletic. I like soccer. Hmm, I have long hair, and I'm short [*laughs*]. I like math. I like music—I like to play the piano. And I think that's it. Oh yeah, and I like to laugh a lot.
>
> DIEGO: I'm a guy. I'm eleven. I'm a student. And I'm Mexican.
>
> FELIZ: I would describe myself as a girl who likes to think a lot, and when something isn't right she likes to fix it, and she cares a lot about her grades, and she appreciates everything that her parents do. I'm a kind person, and not rude. And also, I'm . . . I'm also a pretty smart person.
>
> IRIS: I like to read and that's, like, the only thing I actually like to do at school, but I'm good at other subjects. But, like, language arts is the best.
>
> JACKIE: Well, I guess, I was born in America [United States], I grew up here. And I like cake.
>
> DAVID: I'm eleven. I'm in sixth grade and I go to a new middle school.
>
> LINA: Well, I'm part Mexican, and part American [United States]. I have a stepdad that's taken care of me and my family my whole entire life, so technically he's like my real dad. My mom and I have the same name. I have one older sister that has autism, so that kinda makes me like the oldest one, and I have a younger baby brother.
>
> LUCIA: I'm twelve, and I'm in seventh grade. Well, I really like kid-superheroes. I like doing activities, like sports. I'm Mexican American. Half American [United States] and half Mexican. And I'm a girl.

SANTIAGO: I'm eleven, and I'm in sixth grade. *Shabang shabang!* I would describe myself as a little funny and, like, yeah, that's it. If I had to describe myself to someone I would say—I would tell somebody, "He's awesome, he's cool, he's the best guy in the world." And "He's the best of the best." Yeah!

YESENIA: I could be a quiet girl at times, like, if I don't know you, but I can, hmm, I can also be loud at the same time. I'm kind of unique compared to other people. I like different takes [perspectives, viewpoints] on what I think and why.

In the context of the Change 4 Good program, Latinx youth embodied and enacted their identities in a multitude of ways. These expressions reflected their positionalities and understandings of themselves in relation to activities they were involved in and the experiences that were most salient to them. In interviewing twelve of the thirteen Latinx youth about their experiences in school, family, and community contexts, including the Change 4 Good program, I encouraged them to describe themselves in terms of what they held most important. Latinx youth were asked, *How would you describe yourself? If someone were to describe you, what would they say about you and what makes you unique?* In responding to this question, they used different words to name their social identities, as well as personality characteristics and individual preferences to describe themselves. The process of having them name their identities, both the social and more personal elements of these, is consistent with the social identity development literature.[6]

As evidenced in their responses, social identities were constructed along categories of age, gender, and ethnicity, as well as descriptions of their interests or self-concepts. Latinx youth social identities as reflected in these brief statements were rooted in their positionalities and most salient experiences. In other words, Latinx youth viewed themselves in relation to others, the groups or communities they are a part of, and the personal and social experiences that to them were most meaningful. Age, gender, and ethnicity were the most significant identities Latinx youth named to describe aspects of themselves they considered important. Personalities, activities, and preferences, such as sports, food, and academic subjects they enjoyed, were also part of how they described some salient characteristics of themselves.

Most of the Latinx youth mentioned belonging in a social group that was characterized by age, gender, and ethnicity, as well as grade level and/or nationality. Identification with these groups was shaped by how Latinx youth believed they were perceived by others, especially at school. As illustrated in Latinx youth excerpts and descriptions of themselves, social identities were informed by their everyday lived experiences and the interactions that cultivated a positive or affirming sense of themselves. Although such identities and their descriptions could be considered problematic in the context of schooling, as noted in Celine's response about being "too loud," she understood her expressed identity to be at odds with the culture of the classroom, yet she nonetheless embraced it. Celine stated that she is "too energetic" in school and talks way too much, but ultimately, those characteristics are part of who she is. Unlike Celine's description, Yesenia recognized that her shyness was a response to her social context and whether she felt comfortable in a setting. Comfort was determined and shaped by the conditions that would support or allow her to express herself. Similarly focused on individual experiences, Iris, Lina, Diana, Feliz, and Santiago embraced and affirmed themselves as smart, responsible, caring, fun, and academically engaged youth. These qualities, although often interpreted as individual personality traits, are social identities that reflect a person's positive self-concept.[7]

Latinx youth understandings of themselves in their cultural, social, and political contexts, such as schooling, informed the development of their social identities. For instance, Latinx youth often referenced aspects of their identities that they believed were most visible to others. The visibility of some of these often led them to form connections and friendships with each other. Joaquín and Diana expressed their love of soccer, similar to how Lucia conveyed her fascination with kid-superheroes. The activity- and hobby-centered descriptions reflected Latinx youth interactions with their peers. The social groups they participated in and contributed to were those with whom they identified the most, and these, in turn, informed their social identities.

Some Latinx youth described the intersections of their identities, while others focused on only one aspect of their identities and/or interests. For example, Diego characterized his identities along age, gender, and ethnicity, stating that he is eleven years old, a guy, and, like

Joaquín, he, too, identifies as Mexican. Unlike Lina, Lucia, and Feliz, Joaquín and Diego described their identities as hybrids. Rather than merely describing themselves as Mexican or American, they choose both: Mexican American. As Mexican Americans, they saw their identities as a blend of Mexican *and* American cultures. Iris, who described herself as American, offered quite a different view of her identities. Iris emphasized age and gender, as well as academics, including the course subjects and learning activities she enjoyed the most, as formative to her self-concept. The social identities, including ethnic identities and nationality, Latinx youth named and claimed as theirs were informed by their positionalities, lived experiences, and everyday encounters with others who resembled, validated, and affirmed (or denied) their identities. Communities characterized by specific social markers that aligned with those markers that Latinx youth identified with were more significant to their sense of belonging.

Alongside ethnicity, two other salient identities Latinx youth expressed were age and gender. In a society that constructs and determines how age and gender are expressed and practiced, these identities were significantly legible and visible. Identities such as these were at times superimposed upon Latinx youth through sociocultural practices or other forms of socialization. For example, Yesenia stated, "I could be a quiet girl," and then immediately followed her comment by adding that she can also be "loud." By making such a remark, Yesenia was engaging with sociocultural norms of gender expression that characterize girls and women as docile, meek, and quiet. For Yesenia, being loud meant being a different kind of girl, who does not conform to sociocultural gender expectations. The slight qualifier in Yesenia's response—"I'm kind of unique compared to other people"—could be understood as an attempt to trouble or interrogate meanings or associations of what it means to be a "girl" in a gendered and adult-centered Western society.

The identities Latinx youth embraced, as well as how they described these in their own words, were informed by their associations with certain social groups and experiences. In Yesenia's case, the assumption was that girls can be quiet and boys can be loud; however, these constructions of quiet girl and loud boy are gendered and problematic because they constrain what youth can do as an expression of their gender. Despite not being able to fully articulate the limitations and problems with such constructions, Latinx youth to a degree were able to describe how their identities did not easily or "neatly" fit within certain sociocultural expectations of, as in the case of Yesenia, gender and more broadly what it means to be a Latinx youth coming of age in the United States. Still, Latinx youth described aspects of themselves by referring to the social identities that were most important and significant to their lives.

Social identities, according to the literature, are fluid. Because identities are informed and significantly shaped by context, social identities evolve and change over time in response to lived experiences and exposure to knowledge or perspectives about the self in relation to others and society. Some social identities might be more durable and stable over time compared to other identities. However, change is possible and largely influenced by a person's experiences, together with the social circumstances or contexts that shape their participation and sense of belonging in a community or social group.[8] The non-static nature of social identities is due in part to the social, cultural, and political conditions people experience as individuals and members of social groups. Experiences like these can compel people to engage as a collective in cultural, social, and political contexts.

The perception a person holds about themselves in relation to others or to a specific social group, according to social psychologist Henry Tajfel, characterizes a person's social identity.[9] Similarly, Chicana feminist social psychologist Aída Hurtado, in writing about Chicanx identities and political engagement, defined social identity as a person's social identification with and sense of belonging to a group based on shared experiences, values, and perspectives.[10] Social comparison, self-categorization, and identification are three interconnected elements or phases that characterize social identity development.[11] All three phases are interconnected and mutually inclusive such that these shape the formation of social identities among people, including youth.[12] Unlike other identities, such as a personal identity or self-concept, social identity is shaped by social, cultural, and contextual factors and the relationships and experiences with communities or social groups who ascribe to or identify with those identities, and thus how the individual constitutes themselves as part of a collective.

The social identity development model presented by Hurtado and colleagues is characterized by three phases that offer a clear description of a person's process of constructing, expressing, and embracing their social identities. The first phase, or process, that characterizes social identity is social comparison.[13] A person acknowledges their positionalities, where and how they are located or positioned in society, and to what extent they are similarly or differently positioned from others, often in terms of privileges and access to decision-making power and resources. Although it is a highly individualistic process, social comparison is a common practice that involves finding commonalities or differences and developing a sense of belonging to a collective based on perceived similarities. The sense of belonging that develops in relation to the social group characterizes the second phase of social identity: self-categorization.

In the social psychological literature, self-categorization, unlike social comparison, involves a person affiliating with those with whom they share experiences, values, affinities, and social conditions. Self-categorization allows for bonding and the strengthening of a group identity predicated on what is found or perceived to be common or shared among individuals.[14] The strengthening of social identity facilitates the development of the third phase: identification. The psychological work of identification can be both affirming and difficult because it might facilitate a sense of belonging while surfacing an awareness of conditions of oppression associated with a subordinated or stigmatized identity or status. Considered the third and final phase, identification is where the identity is embraced, yet malleable to change. Identification serves to further validate a person's positionalities, along with their sense of belonging in a community or social group with whom they might share similar lived experiences, interests, and values.

The stigma associated with some marginalized social identities can be challenging, however. In cases where social identities surface in response to experiences of oppression, this is especially significant.[15] Ethnic and racialized identities, as well as age and gender identities, are examples of social identities that are often salient, visible, and socially constructed. Understood in these interconnected ways, processes of social comparison, self-categorization, and identification with a specific identity, or category, lead to the formation of social identities. The ascribing to or embracing of a social identity, however, does not necessarily mean that the person will experience fewer forms of othering, exclusion, and institutional marginalization. On the contrary, among some Latinx youth, social identities can be significantly laden with stigma because of how contexts that reflect the status quo are set up to subordinate and disenfranchise young people, especially youth from Latinx immigrant and mixed-status families in low-income communities. Social identities among Latinx youth developed in relation to the contexts they occupied and their everyday experiences growing up Latinx in the United States.

Sociopolitical citizenship purports that social identities are tied to Latinx youth social and political subjectivities that inform their understandings of how certain social groups are disenfranchised or positioned on the margins. Seeing one's self as rooted in cultural, social, and political contexts—which consequently influence the ways people are positioned—facilitates a critical consciousness of the conditions and experiences that produced such social identities. Social identities, described as perceptions of oneself as a sociopolitical citizen with the capacity to exercise agency to engage in self-determination and collective actions beyond their individual needs, can cultivate conditions of social change. Such opportunities are necessary for the restoration and actualizing of self and community well-being. Sociopolitical citizenship brings together the social and political subjectivities of Latinx youth, in relation to their agency, participation, and belonging in school, family, and community contexts. Understanding the connections between social identities and young people's lived experiences, in this case Latinx youth, can help us better understand how they come to constitute themselves as agents of change, and thus sociopolitical citizens.

Critical Consciousness

Critical consciousness is characterized by the capacity for critical literacy that includes an analysis of how systems, structures, and institutions operate to perpetuate hierarchies of power at the intersections of multiple forms of oppression. The capacity to engage in a critical social analysis of systems of power is a characteristic of having developed a critical consciousness. Paulo Freire's notion of *concientización* is often associated with a critical consciousness.[16] Although related concepts, *concientización* and critical consciousness are not necessarily synonymous. Critical consciousness is rooted in *concientización*, which involves a critical social analysis of social issues, learning how to mobilize resources and efforts to redress injustices, and understanding the roots of systemic oppression that constrain the power and well-being of communities.

Critical consciousness is a process and a practice; it requires developing a social analysis of inequities via opportunities for reflection, dialogue, and collective action. Therefore, critical consciousness, like the development of a social identity, is an ongoing and purposeful experience. A person who engages in critical consciousness must deeply reflect, discern, and deconstruct how systems of power within institutions and settings operate to disenfranchise certain communities. The process of deconstructing or interrogating injustices, which often may manifest as experiences of oppression, is best illustrated in a story shared by Feliz. In this example, Feliz reflects on how she supported other youth rehearsing and practicing to facilitate their focus groups, specifically with regard to reflecting on stories of experiences with limited power.

> Lina began talking about the inequality in pay and labor that her father experiences at work. Feliz then shared: "Sometimes people ask you for a bunch of stuff that you don't have, like papers and information." Then, she added: "Sometimes kids feel ignored by adults" and went on to tell the story of a time when her brother, uncle and her went to the flea market. Feliz shared that she had asked the man that was attending to the items being sold a question; she had asked him for the price of a doll, and he just looked at them and did not respond. Feliz continued sharing, "We were standing there, and the man was just looking at us, and then a few minutes later an older man and woman came up to him, and they asked him for the price of this other item, and he responded and gave it to them." Feliz's story was telling of the invisibility and lack of attention she experienced. Some of the students asked Feliz what the man looked like, and Feliz said, "He was pale." I asked, "Was he white?" and Lina jokingly stated, "White like the whiteboard!," causing some youth to laugh. Feliz said, "He looked American [white]." Then Lina asked if the other people the man talked to also looked "American," meaning white, and Feliz said that they looked the same. A program facilitator asked, "Did the white man only respond and interact with the white people, but ignored you?" Some of the students felt uncomfortable hearing the phrase

"white people." One youth remarked, "That's racist." It seemed the youth did not want to refer to people based on the color of their skin because they thought that was being racist. Feliz added, "The man was only listening to people that looked [white] like him, and *we* didn't look [white] like him."[17]

Feliz's story motivated other Latinx youth to share and reflect on their experiences of invisibility as these surfaced in relation to their conversation. Like Feliz, they too described experiences of othering and exclusion, demonstrating perhaps that this is commonplace among young people. Some Latinx youth described these experiences as forms of race- and ethnicity-based discriminations, given how Feliz and her family were perceived in relation to these categories. Collectively, Latinx youth reflected and unpacked Feliz's story, including her feelings of being misrecognized and unheeded by a white adult man at the flea market.

Unsurprisingly, some of the youth wanted to know more about the "look" of the man, making remarks that alluded to his race and whether the other people he interacted with looked "similar" to him, which the youth interpreted or understood as being white. Feliz responded to these inquiries, carefully explaining that they looked like each other and remarking that they looked "American," which was read as pale and therefore "white." How an aspect of her identity led Feliz to such an experience made visible for her the significance of what she looked like, and why she was treated in such a way. Although the youth did not name this as an explicit example of racism and ageism, they understood it as an act of discrimination because it was explicit and directed by the white adult man toward Feliz and her family. Instead, when an adult facilitator mentioned "white people," the youth remarked, "That's racist," perhaps feeling uncomfortable with the racialization of a person being articulated explicitly. Yet Feliz experienced a subtle form of racism that imbued her with unsettled feelings, even though she was unable to articulate it as such.

As sociopolitical citizens, Latinx youth were critical of the ways their identities and positionalities, such as age along with their ethnicity, relegated them to a subordinate status where they often felt ignored or not taken seriously. In their question-posing reflexive dialogues, Latinx youth demonstrated a critical consciousness that aligned with a sociopolitical citizenship process of interrogating hegemonic discourses and deficit views. Rather than immediately assuming or making a judgment call that the white adult man was racist, youth engaged in a process of discerning why the interaction unfolded as it did. Sociopolitical citizenship is predicated on the ability to engage and develop a capacity for critical consciousness, and the dialogues that the youth engaged in helped cultivate their critical literacy.

Aligned with sociopolitical citizenship, critical consciousness is characterized by a process of de-ideologization.[18] A unique feature of this process of de-ideologization toward the development of a critical consciousness is that of questioning social conditions, asking why these are as they are and what can be done to change conditions of oppression. In the process of gathering ideas for the creation of their school-based mural, Latinx youth viewed slideshows of community murals with social, cultural, and political messages. Additionally, they visited mural sites at the local university. The visit to campus included a tour of murals that represented themes of justice, community, diversity, education, and hope for social change. One of the first murals Change 4 Good youth saw was the Oakes Mural, officially named *La promesa de Loma Prieta: Que no se repita la historia* (The promise of Loma Prieta: That history not repeat itself). The mural, painted by renowned San Francisco artist Juana Alicia, was created in collaboration with Oakes College students between 1991 and 1992.[19] A staff member at Oakes College introduced Latinx youth to the history and process of creating the mural. In sharing the story of the Oakes Mural, as it is known among the campus community, the youth learned the value, impact, and power of muraling, especially the significance of centering communities' stories.

A week after our visit to the Oakes Mural, we processed our tour of the campus with the Change 4 Good youth. Reflecting upon their tour, several of them expressed excitement over their visit, sharing anecdotes of what they learned, while others described what they saw and what stood out the most from their experience.

> Celine said that they had gone to see a big mural on a wall, and that they had sat around it as they talked about the drawings and images in the mural. Lina added that one of the program facilitators had given them

an explanation about what each of the symbols represented. Lina added that it showed people coming together, holding hands and being united. Yesenia raised her hand and said, "We also saw this other mural that was done with gold or something, and that was about immigrants, and about people coming to the United States." Feliz said, "The Oakes Mural had invisible people." Jackie raised her hand and shared, "The invisible people wanted to come to a new place, and there were other people holding the hands of the invisible people." I agreed and I told the youth that those were good interpretations of the Oakes Mural, and the art piece outside the classroom. Feliz shared, "They are telling a similar story but in a different way." Yesenia agreed, stating that they were telling the story of "immigration and people coming to another place, but the Oakes Mural shows people fighting together for their rights." Lina then shifted the focus of our conversation to share that they had also gone to see the murals in another part of the campus. There, she said, they saw a mural about two kids that were standing on top of a mountain of guns and weapons with a heart-shaped balloon that was flying over them. Lina said that she liked that mural a lot because it made her think about love.[20]

Latinx youth reflections began with Celine recalling and describing some of the images depicted in the Oakes Mural. In describing these representations and illustrations, she also highlighted some of the themes that stood out to her. Building on Celine's reflections, Lina remarked that the mural represented themes of unity, community, diversity, and justice. Similarly, Yesenia stated that it symbolized "people coming together" and "fighting for their rights." Some Latinx youth reflections following their engagement with the mural demonstrated their critical consciousness, particularly their social awareness of injustice, histories of oppression, and the significance of collective action.

The mural juxtaposed the story Yesenia saw illustrated in another art piece. Located in a stairway outside the Oakes Mural room, the bronze art piece told a different story of US immigration. The three-dimensional bronze art piece was a representation of colonialism, specifically manifest destiny and Western expansion, depicted by a silhouette of Columbus reaching above what appeared to be ocean waters with people in boats. As Latinx youth continued to reflect, Jackie and Feliz described how the Oakes Mural resonated with them the most, and how the bronze art piece seemed bland compared to the mural's symbolisms, which reflected stories of community struggle rooted in people's lived experiences. Latinx youth interactions with and reactions to the Oakes Mural served as a tool to facilitate their critical consciousness, specifically their social analysis and reflections about justice and freedom, and how these were represented meaningfully through mural art. Latinx youth drew inspiration from the Oakes Mural as they too attempted to tell a story of justice, diversity, and hope for their community.

Discerning themes in both art pieces via reflexive dialogues served to cultivate Latinx youth critical consciousness, which aided them in discerning themes from their focus groups to consequently inform their mural design. Among the themes they discerned through these art pieces were immigration, diversity, education, and justice, yet each theme was represented differently. In the three-dimensional bronze art piece, a Eurocentric narrative of settlement and conquest was depicted. In the Oakes Mural, however, it was a story about diverse histories, cultures, and communities that formed the fabric of US society. The Oakes Mural also featured the contentious struggle by communities of color for justice, freedom, and liberation from oppression. These were the depicted images and illustrations that young people were most interested in talking about. The "invisible people" illustrated in the Oakes Mural, for example, were described by some youth as people coming together in solidarity to fight for their rights. Building on their critical consciousness, which was informed by their social identities, Latinx youth explored other themes depicted in the murals they visited while touring the campus.

In another area of the campus, at the Mural Moat, one piece that stood out to them was a replica of a Banksy mural. Two child silhouettes standing on top of a pile of what appeared to be guns and handheld weapons were illustrated in the mural. The childlike silhouettes held hands, and above them flew a red heart-shaped balloon that they were holding. Lina interpreted this to be about love because it illustrated unity through the hands holding a heart rising above a mountaintop of weapons. Latinx youth analysis and interpretations of the Oakes Mural's themes, among the other murals they saw, helped shape their critical consciousness about social issues, as well as their hopes and dreams for their communities. Critical consciousness was demonstrated through the multiple interpretations of the murals, which helped them engage in a process of de-ideologizing hegemonic discourses and imagining new ways to engage with history, social issues, and community struggles.

Processes of de-ideologization, denaturalization, and problematization are tied to a critical consciousness.[21] De-ideologization facilitates the capacity to critically analyze social issues through a sociohistorical lens that facilitates people's social analysis and actions to challenge that which is seen as "normal" or reflected in the status quo. Related to the process of de-ideologization is that of denaturalizing hegemonic discourses and ideologies that society presents as ubiquitous, but are actually constructed as common sense at the expense of decolonial, liberatory, and anti-oppressive perspectives that affirm humanity and well-being. The normalization of hegemony is inherently problematic because it creates discourses and perspectives that limit the rights, agency, and determination of communities. Such conditions perpetuate colonial ways of thinking and being that further maintain the inherent oppressive systems of power.

Following the process of de-ideologization and denaturalization, problematization aims to challenge the status quo. Although these processes might be perceived as procedural and formulaic, critical consciousness is an iterative, continuous practice of challenging and deconstructing power to create new knowledge that resonates with and reflects the material and social conditions of people's experiences. Latinx youth developed their critical consciousness as sociopolitical citizens through opportunities for reflection and dialogue, as well as the troubling of histories and perspectives they understood to be disempowering and unjust. Certain themes represented and portrayed through the murals, when followed with opportunities for reflection and dialogue, contributed to the development of their critical consciousness.

Sociopolitical citizenship develops through a critical consciousness rooted in a process of *concientización* to interrupt and deconstruct hegemonic discourses. Without a critical consciousness of social issues, people cannot fully engage politically, nor can they develop the skills needed for collective action to create conditions of well-being, thriving, and justice. As sociopolitical citizens, Latinx youth developed their critical consciousness through experiences that led them to engage with, reflect upon, and discuss, as well as challenge, hegemonic discourses.

By making meaning of their social experiences in relation to the different and complex interpretations of symbols represented in the murals they viewed and interacted with, they resisted and even questioned certain discourses. As they sought to create new meanings that were more grounded in their lives and community stories, Latinx youth developed their critical consciousness.

Socioemotional Awareness

Socioemotional awareness is another domain of sociopolitical citizenship. Developing a critical consciousness in relation to social issues facilitates opportunities for young people to begin to analyze and understand the roots of oppression and explore avenues to create social change. Yet opportunities for such forms of critical consciousness via reflection, dialogue, and social analysis are often laden with feelings and emotions. Learning about histories of injustice and how they manifest in contemporary forms of inequity can unearth difficult emotions, such as anger, indignation, and despair. The literature on sociopolitical development theory, however, has paid little attention to the socioemotional learning and development—or socioemotional awareness—of young people growing up in institutionally marginalized communities. Much of the work on socioemotional learning has taken place with students or youth from white middle- or upper-middle-class families, or groups that are not disproportionately and systemically disenfranchised.[22]

Emotions serve an important role in fostering an understanding of oneself and social circumstances, as well as the development of positive interactions necessary to experience well-being.[23] Positive youth development and socioemotional learning literatures in the field of education suggest that emotions are critical to healthy and positive youth development into adulthood.[24] As salient affective states, emotions function as a barometer to help youth discern and identify circumstances that are difficult because they are unjust, as well as unbearable social conditions needing to be changed. Because these experiences can produce an unsettling emotion or even a physical response, youth can leverage these affective states to catalyze toward action. The types of actions or behaviors youth engage in can be positive and affirming, or detrimental to their own well-being. As Rios documents, Black and Latinx boys who are criminalized and punished in their school, family, and community contexts experience a "youth control complex," which imbues them with a sense of indignation that compels them to engage in troubling behaviors that lead them further down a path of criminality.[25] These behaviors, however, must be understood in a broader structural and sociocultural context of racialized and gendered criminalization, policing, discipline, and punishment.

The capacity for socioemotional awareness, characterized by a critically reflexive understanding of how emotions emerge and their impact, is central to sociopolitical citizenship. Discerning the source of one's affective state and the emotion attached to it, along with the subsequent actions or behaviors that arise, necessitates a critical consciousness that leads to socioemotional awareness. A necessary domain of sociopolitical citizenship and consequently healthy development is the capacity to engage with and attend to social and emotional circumstances. The emotional experiences among Latinx youth suggest the necessity to support their socioemotional awareness in response to intersecting forms of discrimination, exclusion, and othering.

Sociopolitical citizenship recognizes the role of emotions in relation to agency, specifically how emotions are enacted and embodied in the lives of Latinx youth. Some of the emotions they engaged with centered on their experiences with oppression in the context of schooling. Other experiences involved them learning how to develop and maintain their socioemotional awareness, which they saw as necessary to transform difficult, often uncomfortable emotions into positive emotions that could help guide their agency and inform their decision making in more meaningful ways. The transformation of difficult emotions into positive ones can help cultivate a sense of belonging among Latinx youth. Socioemotional awareness is critical to sociopolitical citizenship.

Latinx youth in Change 4 Good were provided with opportunities to engage in emotional work, especially when facilitating focus groups, developing and sharing their mural draft ideas to the group, and speaking publicly at their mural unveiling gathering at their school. Gatherings such as these were often well attended by their school peers, teachers, parents, and community members. Latinx youth developed the skills to work through complex emotions, like nervous excitement, when they were provided with a space where they could reflect and dialogue about their experiences, as nerve-wracking as these could be. In these instances, Change 4 Good program facilitators provided youth with opportunities to confront or work through difficult, often unsettling moments, which could eventually help them engage with other challenging experiences. Providing young people with avenues to engage in emotional work specifically around issues of inequity and injustice can help them develop a socioemotional awareness that will serve their agency and collective action efforts in the long run. The transformation of difficult emotions into action or positive emotions is characterized by a shift, away from the focus of unsettling emotions, toward the development of strategies that are conducive to their agency, participation in decision making, sense of belonging, and even well-being.

Some of the emotional work strategies Latinx youth engaged were the focus of a conversation in one of our Change 4 Good program sessions. In this instance, Latinx youth described how they worked through their emotions to transform them into more sustainable, positive ones.

> Gathered around in a semi-circle, we asked the youth to think about doing focus groups with parents and teachers, instead of doing these just with students as they had done previously. Diego said that he gets nervous when he's talking to parents, so we asked the youth if they had any suggestions for what we could do to address Diego's and other students' nervousness. Santiago said that when he's nervous, someone else will tell him to calm down, and he usually calms down. One of the program facilitators asked him to describe how he actually calms down, and he described it as follows: "Okay, calm down, calm down"—as he spread his arms to the side of his body, lightly closing his eyes and taking deep breaths. Iris added that taking a moment to take a deep breath first might help. Daniela then shared her related experiences of calming down before and during her soccer matches, which would help her score goals. Daniela shared that she would often get nervous, but then her mom or dad would tell her to calm down. She said that they would also tell her to look away and think about something good for a moment, like scoring a goal. The program facilitator then reiterated what Daniela said by sharing that looking away from the situation for a while might help. Joaquín shared that he did the same during his soccer matches; he explained that he would get nervous and his dad would say *"Calm down!"* in a very loud voice, and he would

calm down. We asked him if that worked, and he said, "sometimes," and laughed softly a bit through a shoulder shrug, adding, "I don't know. I just calm down." Daniela offered another suggestion; she said that during her first communion, a relative of hers was nervous about reading a scripture from the bible in front of the congregation so her grandmother told them to just look slightly above the people's heads and avoid looking directly at them. We nodded in agreement and expressed that that's a good tip. Lucia shared that she calms down by thinking about "a happy place." Several of us nodded. We concluded the discussion by adding that one thing that might help reduce their nervousness in facilitating the focus groups with adults, which would include parents, teachers, and community members, would be to make sure that they knew the interview script really well. Some youth nodded their heads, and we elaborated by sharing that if they practiced they would be more confident during the focus groups because they would know what they are doing. The youth seemed to agree with this suggestion and strategy to maintaining the emotional calmness necessary to lead their focus groups.[26]

Latinx youth discerned that speaking before adults made them nervous, yet they recognized that such feelings were possible to overcome. The stories, experiences, and emotional coping strategies shared by Latinx youth may perhaps demonstrate their developing understanding of emotions and how these surfaced to challenge or facilitate certain behaviors, including actions that would allow them to experience wellbeing. The strategies Latinx youth described as behaviors for supporting their attempts to be at ease and calm in stressful situations helped them develop a socioemotional awareness, to some degree. When youth are undertaking or completing a difficult task, this awareness then becomes instrumental for exercising agency, including certain actions that previously might have appeared too difficult.

For instance, Daniela shared how she was able to score a soccer goal under pressure or prevail in a stressful circumstance by shifting her focus away from a negative outcome to a positive one. The rewiring of her emotions or fears into feelings that are less stressful or laden with anxiety over a desired outcome characterized her socioemotional awareness. Joaquín also shared Daniela's experiences with playing sports like soccer. Collectively as a group they associated those difficult emotions and feelings with facilitating focus group discussions with adults. Latinx youth reflections on the value of remaining calm, breathing deeply, not making eye contact with a large audience, and envisioning a positive outcome—or as Lucia described it, "a happy place"—are indicative of their socioemotional awareness, as well as their critical consciousness.

Socioemotional awareness is perhaps best illustrated by Latinx youth capacity to engage with and transcend difficult moments. Latinx youth garnered these skills in socioemotional awareness to move forward with a task and work through difficult, high-stakes activities like participating in sports, speaking in public, and facilitating discussions, like their focus groups. The strategies Latinx youth developed to remain calm under stressful circumstances demonstrate a socioemotional awareness that led them to hold their own. Fostering a sense of emotional stability or strategic emotional endurance in situations that are difficult necessitates overcoming the anguish associated with such challenging experiences. Socioemotional awareness cultivates the emotional strength needed to complete a challenging task, embody agency, and even participate in actions that resist forms of oppression.

Emotions can be a powerful source of motivation to engage meaningfully in opportunities for action and decision making to actualize justice and create social change. In *The Cultural Politics of Emotion*, feminist scholar Sara Ahmed describes emotions as "impressions," markings that leave an emotional and physical impact that manifests or is felt in the body.[27] Emotions are a response to an external output or force that is unsettling because it causes discomfort. As a result, emotions can propel people into action because emotions are a form of energy that is shaped by and, in turn, helps guide behaviors and actions. These emotive "impressions" should not be undermined or perceived as individualized affective states of being, however. The creative and innovative expression of emotion is not static. On the contrary, these are collective as well as relational experiences.

Emotions, when considered as responses to external forces, are fluid and subjectively constructed through a person's perceptions and interpretations of an experience or in anticipation of one. When the emotion attached to the experience or thought is transformed and leveraged in a positive way, emotions can serve a meaningful purpose in directing behavior and action. Among Latinx youth this often led them to harness their agency, as well as to collective action toward creating some form of social change, as Feliz described in her reflections.

> I would describe Change 4 Good as a place to learn about yourself and other people. And it's fun! Every time I went, I would feel very happy, because we learned about different things, important things. I thought the mural was the best part of it because we got to see what was happening around the community, and then show what the community is like with stories and art. The only thing I didn't really like was the fact that some things were forbidden from being put on the mural. I remember that me and Daniela—we saw a photo that we really liked and we presented it to the group to see if we—to recommend it as something we could put in the mural. We all sort of liked the idea, but when it came time to show it to the [school administrators], they said it was too violent, too aggressive I guess, because they thought it might show other students that it's okay to fight, like physically instead of verbally. It made me very frustrated and angry because I didn't think that it was violent. I thought the image was more about, like, what you have to do to make a change in the community. You have to say something, act and stand up for what you want. It made me very sad that we couldn't have that or something like that in the mural. But, in the end, we sort of had something similar, something like it.

Feliz's critical consciousness of the removal of a mural image that the youth felt very passionate about demonstrated her socioemotional awareness. Moreover, Feliz's remarks also made visible her socioemotional awareness, the capacity to discern and identify emotions that were difficult yet rooted in experiences of injustice and silencing. In articulating her emotions in regard to the exclusion of the image, Feliz named emotions like frustration and anger as valid. A righteous feeling of indignation came upon her; this was informed by what she described as adults misunderstanding the image's symbolism and what it was meant to represent. Feliz described how adults mistakenly perceived the image as "violent" and "aggressive," and how this incorrect perception held implications for what they could illustrate in their mural. Nonetheless, Feliz justified the value and significance of the image as having nothing to do with fighting or physical violence, and instead relating it to the importance of speaking up—"say something, act and stand up for what you want." Feliz's process of challenging the school administrators' perspectives pushed against the deficit views about youth agency as apolitical and acritical. Clearly characterizing Feliz's socioemotional awareness as a sociopolitical citizen was the act of speaking back, which perhaps was possible for her to express and articulate because of how she leveraged her emotions to develop a critical consciousness that eventually helped guide her actions. Feliz's understanding of and engagement with her emotions were perhaps emblematic of her developing social identity as a change maker as well.

For Latinx youth growing up in communities that experience multiple forms of disenfranchisement, learning how to productively engage with emotions is critical to helping them discern root causes to social problems and the actions needed to address these conditions. Yet opportunities for young people to learn to discern and engage with their emotions in healthy ways are limited, especially in school settings. Certainly, in the context of schooling, curricula are often structured to emphasize disembodied learning and cognitive rational engagement, instead of developing a socioemotional awareness and critical consciousness among students. Overlooking the role of emotions, specifically the social and emotional development of young people, has consequences for youth development that extend beyond sociopolitical citizenship. Young people who are able to discern and engage with their emotions in supportive, productive, and healthy ways are likely to experience wellness in their lives.[28] The socioemotional awareness that youth develop has significant implications for youth well-being, particularly how they learn to confront, endure, and work through challenging circumstances.

Latinx youth who are politically active in redressing conditions of oppression must develop skills to discern and transform difficult emotions, like nervousness and anger, into action. Working through these difficult emotions does not mean diffusing them or ignoring their impact. On the contrary, it means that Latinx youth must learn to transform troubling emotions into more positive, sustainable ones that will allow them to redirect their physical, mental, and emotional energies into meaningful action. Sociopolitical citizens are not emotive beings acting irrationally. Instead, Latinx youth who are socioemotionally aware are able to leverage their emotions strategically to exercise their agency toward social change. Socioemotional awareness, when paired with a critical consciousness of social issues and the identities these implicate, can be purposefully deployed to address social issues and injustices. Systems of power that produce conditions of oppression can be challenged and changed through practices that involve undertaking actions driven by positive, more sustainable emotions, like hope, as well as love and care for one's communities.

Political Engagement

Political engagement can take various forms, from civic engagement to political activism, to more charitable actions like community service and volunteerism.[29] The range of opportunities provided to young people to engage politically and civically in their communities can help shape their sociopolitical citizenship. Yet it was evident from conversations with Latinx youth that family and community experiences as well as media shaped their understandings of how to engage politically in the public sphere. Joaquín made this clear when he described what people could do to challenge what is presumed to be unjust or to demand certain rights and opportunities, while striving toward social change.

> We can protest. I saw a protest on television. We can protest to have the right to be in different places, to immigrate to countries or go back home. To have papers [legal documentation] and social numbers [social security number], and to work and not be excluded [discriminated] from some work. We can protest to have good jobs and see our family back home [outside the United States].

As Joaquín's interview responses underscore, protesting or collective action was identified as an important, meaningful way to effect social change. His response was not unique among Latinx youth, as several of them shared their thoughts about protests, often in relation to their own lived experiences or in accompanying their parents. Diego's experience attests to this, as he had previously attended a protest with his mother. The critical opportunities youth undertook to participate in social change characterized their political engagement. In *Beyond Resistance! Youth Activism and Community Change*, Shawn Ginwright,

Julio Cammarota, and Pedro Noguera emphasize that when young people are provided with enriching experiences of engaging in collective action, they develop a positive sense of self that helps them garner the political self-efficacy, agency, and determination to see themselves as agents of change.[30] Yet youth-centered opportunities for interrupting systems of power and oppression within education and schooling are often rare or discouraged by adults or stakeholders in such institutionalized spaces like schools.[31] Other settings or opportunities for cultivating youth political engagement, especially their sociopolitical citizenship, are necessary.

In Change 4 Good, Latinx youth were provided with political engagement opportunities via social justice–oriented projects, like the making of a school-based community mural. During one of our program sessions, when we were discerning the connections between community stories and the mural symbols they were drawing, we spent a considerable amount of time unpacking one story that involved students and teachers engaging in a demonstration. Youth described how they supported their teachers in a school protest to challenge the inequitable layoffs of some teachers at their school. Lina, along with other Latinx youth, described the incidents that led up to the protest and its aftermath.

> Relating that [school protest] story to the image of a megaphone, Lina said that she thought the megaphone represented their protesting of teachers being fired from their school. Specifically, about teachers whose funding was getting cut and who were getting fired. The program facilitator then added that the story about the "pink slips" [a pink paper where a layoff notice is written and given to a teacher] was about people coming together and fighting for their rights. Lina agreed and then asked why the "No More Pink Slips" protest sign was taken out of the mural design draft, and the program facilitator said that it had to be taken out because the issue was more complicated, and that having a sign that said "No More Pink Slips" would not be a valid representation of the issue. The program facilitator suggested that they show or represent the themes tied to this story in a different way. . . . Lina questioned this response by explaining that the mural is about and for the community, and "the story about the 'No More Pink Slips' is a real story from the community." She added that the people who were affected were teachers, and this in turn

affected them as students. Lina remarked that several of the teachers at their school received a "pink slip" or a "warning," and she began to list the names of the teachers who were fired because they received a pink slip. Then another student mentioned that Mrs. M was switched to [another elementary school]. . . . Daniela then asked, "Why do people get the pink slips?" and Joaquín responded by saying that "we [students] get pink slips whenever we do something bad, like being late or when we didn't follow the rules." Lina added that they were not talking about "those pink slips," and then clarified by saying that she was talking about "the pink slips that teachers get when they are fired."[32]

Consistent with Lina's reflections, some youth felt that the "No More Pink Slips" caption and associated drawing illustrated an important story that represented their power, agency, and collective action to unite and stand in solidarity with their teachers. The experience of protesting made several Latinx youth feel on par with their teachers. The initial mural draft featured this experience of solidarity through the illustration of a quote about the pink slips. Among Change 4 Good youth, this story, which was shared in the context of the focus group they facilitated, later came to be known as "The Pink Slips Story."

In reflecting upon the themes they sought to represent in their mural, several Latinx youth questioned why certain images or symbols were not being included. One of the most vocal youth was Lina, who articulated that the mural was about and for the community, and should center students' voices and stories. "The Pink Slips Story" was empowering and meaningful for Latinx youth because it provided them with an opportunity to reflect on their political engagement, particularly their collective action and solidarity with their teachers. Latinx youth felt very strongly about the "No More Pink Slips" caption and associated image that featured a megaphone being held in the air by a clenched fist. Through this illustration, Latinx youth sought to represent and make salient their political engagement. Reflections on the significance of that image and corresponding story of solidarity in action were important for them to include in their mural.

Sociopolitical citizenship—embodied and enacted in various ways, as evidenced in Latinx youth experiences—can often manifest through social justice–oriented actions, such as demonstrations, as well as public art, like murals. The mural they created was an example of these efforts, as it involved opportunities for youth to reflect and connect their social identities, critical consciousness, socioemotional awareness, and political engagement with community stories. As a practice of resistance to being silent and passive, sociopolitical citizenship can also surface as a way to challenge experiences of marginalization and othering. The mural provided youth with opportunities to embody and enact sociopolitical citizenship, from collaborating on gathering counter-hegemonic stories about their community to developing, designing, and creating a mural that uplifted them and their school, family, and community.

Political engagement, as observed through "The Pink Slips Story," involved Latinx youth embracing a moment to actively participate in collective action by protesting with their teachers to raise awareness about their concerns. Latinx youth advocated with and perhaps on behalf of their teachers in ways that made them feel seen and heard in school. Collective action exemplified through Latinx youth political engagement involved them pushing back on certain demands or expectations that were incongruent with what they believed was the purpose of the mural. Although the "No More Pink Slips" illustration represented their teachers being laid off, it had a different meaning for Latinx youth. For some youth the pink slips meant "getting in trouble" or being punished. The negative and problematic associations around "pink slips" made the megaphone symbol with the "No More Pink Slips" caption even more significant for them. In striving to represent this story, seemingly pushing back against what school administrators were requesting, Latinx youth social identities as students led them to engage their critical consciousness, socioemotional awareness, and political engagement to advocate for the inclusion of a particular illustration in their mural design.

Latinx youth were adamant about what and how to represent certain themes in the mural, thus demonstrating their agency as sociopolitical citizens. In this regard, political engagement efforts can often help catalyze actions to create social change and address issues of concern among communities. Efforts toward social change must be determined and led by those whose lives are affected by these issues. When enacted through social justice–oriented activities, sociopolitical citizenship unfolds into modes of political engagement. In the context of Change 4 Good, Latinx youth wielded their power by exercising agency and participating in decision making in order to foster social change. These actions demonstrate their political engagement efforts that aligned with and reflected their sociopolitical citizenship. Latinx youth sociopolitical citizenship embodiments, as evidenced in their opportunities and experiences with political engagement, reflected their capacities to claim and enact their agency.

Political engagement among Latinx youth was also characterized by their efforts to take on new leadership roles, as described by Yesenia. During one of our Change 4 Good program sessions, as we worked in small groups to develop a list of people the youth might invite to participate in their focus groups, we were also discussing the school elections.

> We were talking about the upcoming elections at the school when I asked the students if anyone was running for a position. Some raised their hands, and Yesenia looked at me and said, "Me too." She then shared that she was running for the position of "post-master" at the school. I asked her what a post-master did, and she said, "They just send and organize the mail that the school receives." I asked her if her friends were running for any other positions and she said that Lucia was running for vice-president and Lina was running for president. They smiled and nodded in agreement.[33]

Although none of the youth had previously run for a position, they all seemed enthused at the possibility of playing a more active leadership role at their school. Several Latinx youth in Change 4 Good were running for elected positions. Yesenia described the responsibilities of a post-master, a position she appeared to be interested in. Other positions included president and vice-president, which Lina and Lucia were applying for. Although it is unclear whether their desire to participate and take on an active role at their school was connected to their participation in the Change 4 Good program, or whether they were already inclined to participate, this demonstrated their agency and desire to engage meaningfully as leaders by taking an active role at their school. Latinx youth motivations to pursue these leadership positions exemplified their motivation to seek out opportunities for authentic and purposeful engagement. Cultivating and supporting Latinx youth participation in leadership positions, as well as decision making in various contexts, including those that support political engagement, are critical for sustaining their sociopolitical citizenship.

Claiming power required Latinx youth to exercise agency and political engagement in contexts, like schools, that often silence them and position them as subordinate to adults, as well as assimilable into the status quo. Considering that sociopolitical citizenship is a practice of political engagement, often seeking to disrupt systems of power, oppression, and injustice, stories and collective actions such as those Latinx youth engaged demonstrate their modes of resisting. Such counter-hegemonic acts of political engagement are needed to effect social change. Everyday acts of resistance, as described in the writings of decolonial feminist scholar María Lugones, are characterized by an "active subjectivity" that, although subtle, is a meaningful way by which disenfranchised communities can work to undo the oppressive power that structures their lives.[34] Political engagement must be understood as a form of resistance that is inherently tied to an active subjectivity of exercising agency. Political engagement characterized by participation in efforts that involve claiming and taking power in order to better one's circumstances and redress injustices is not an easy task.

Sociopolitical citizenship contends with these social conditions and aims to center the agency of Latinx youth through an affirmation of their voice, which is imperative to their political engagement and collective action. Political engagement must be intentional, collective, and directed at challenging oppression and power. As a domain of sociopolitical citizenship, political engagement is tied to a process and practice of critical consciousness, as well as the capacity to develop a socioemotional awareness of how power unfolds to delegitimize and oppress certain people and experiences. Facilitating opportunities for political engagement, critical consciousness, and socioemotional awareness, which are entwined with and implicate aspects of Latinx youth social identities, is imperative to their embodiment as sociopolitical citizens.

Youth as Active Citizens

As a process, citizenship is entwined with acts, embodiments, identities, and positionalities that afford people a set of protections, rights, and responsibilities that produce or reinforce certain constructions of citizenship. Citizenship, as Latinx youth demonstrate, is and can be an attitude—a social and political subjectivity. Among Latinx youth, whose stories and reflections are featured, citizenship was a way of being, as well as a practice and process of becoming aware of their power and wielding it to create social change while affirming their expressions of agency. Awareness of their circumstances led some Latinx youth to leverage their voices in support of their families and communities.

Sociopolitical citizenship cultivated through the four domains described can help set the foundation for a citizenship embodiment of everyday being and belonging. In conceptualizing the term "sociopolitical citizenship," I bring together Latinx youth social and political subjectivities with perspectives on sociopolitical development theory that emphasize critical consciousness and political engagement, yet also consider the significance of social identities and socioemotional awareness in shaping youth citizenship embodiments. By troubling hegemonic discourses that rendered them silent, invisible, and disenfranchised, Latinx youth embodied sociopolitical citizenship in resistance to constructions of citizenship, legality, and rights.

As a practice, sociopolitical citizenship among Latinx youth was characterized by their claiming of rights, agency, and participation in decision making, as well as having their voices and experiences recognized against a backdrop of ageism and racist nativism. Lina was one of the most outspoken youth in Change 4 Good. After she matriculated from the program, we kept in touch via text messages and Facebook, but we had not seen each other in at least a few months. The summer after sixth grade, Lina and I met for an interview at one of the local *taquerías*. After several minutes of studying the menu, she ordered a plate of nachos and *horchata*. We intended to have our interview inside the *taquería*; however, the sound of music playing through the speakers combined with the cheers of a few young men enthusiastically watching the Chivas v. America soccer game made it a bit too loud for us to have our conversation. I suggested we eat and chat in my car, and Lina agreed. Having settled ourselves in the car, we talked about her transition to middle school, her growing group of friends, and the occasional drama among them. We then swiftly transitioned to talk about how some of her friends were worried about being able to continue to stay in school. When I asked what she meant, she hesitated a bit, but then offered her reflections. Although I had not referred to the contentious political climate and anti-immigrant policies, Lina mentioned the Dream Act, as well as her frustration and disappointment at the poor leadership from the Obama administration, specifically its failure to address the concerns of those whom she described as "immigrant students."

> The Dream Act, I don't know many details about it, but I do know that immigrant—it's about immigrants that are trying to further their education to go to universities, but sometimes they can't because they're limited. . . . Because universities only accept American citizens, people born here [United States], so it's really hard for them to get an education. . . . If I actually had the chance to speak to President Obama, I think, I'd probably be so mad and filled with rage. I would probably just start screaming at him for several reasons, but mostly because of immigration [anti-immigration legislation]. I'd probably talk to him and ask him to think about how it would feel if he couldn't go to college, or was getting separated from his family because his parents didn't have *papeles* [legal documentation]. I think one of the saddest things is when a kid is born here [United States] but their parents don't have any *papeles*, so they're deported and their kids left orphans. It's something you don't forget.

Lina's critique of immigration policies under the Obama administration illustrates her sociopolitical citizenship; her consciousness of existing policies and their impact on undocumented students and families underscored the salience of citizenship, legality, and rights in her life. Informed by their identities as well as their family and community experiences, Latinx youth in Change 4 Good seemed to develop a critical consciousness about the border and border-crossing experiences associated with citizenship, legality, and rights. When given the opportunity to reflect deeply, Lina offered what I describe as a hybrid perspective about her life, which reflects Anzaldúa's notion of the borderlands.[35] Lina's remarks illustrate her understanding of the borderlands, of what Anzaldúa describes as a feeling of being torn between two places, or borders, yet at the same time entwined in both. Lina explained her understanding of the experience of in-betweenness, as she described how families are separated and held apart because of the politics of the border, and more broadly anti-immigrant sentiments rooted in racist nativism.

According to recent scholarship on migration studies examining the impact of anti-immigration discourses on youth in mixed-status families, youth well-being and health, along with perceptions of safety, are negatively and severely compromised by hegemonic discourses, which Lina named.[36] Similar to other youth in mixed-status families, Lina appeared to understand the negative consequences of living in what migration studies scholar Nicholas De Genova characterizes as a state of deportability.[37] Anti-immigration policies, as Lina's statement demonstrates, imbued her with anger, rage, and sadness. Furthermore, her response illustrates her socioemotional awareness of how these circumstances make her feel, and why she is compelled to challenge and question these policies. Her critical consciousness and socioemotional awareness as a sociopolitical citizen reflect her social identities as a Mexican American youth, as well as her political engagement in resistance to anti-immigrant sentiments and policies.

Lina's response also reflects her attempt to make sense of as well as contest the conditions of injustice that she sees—specifically, how the absence of inclusive immigration policies like the Dream Act affects families and young people, particularly undocumented students. Although at times Lina's analysis of such policies is not fully accurate, such as when she stated that "universities only accept American citizens," she offered a critique of the liminal inclusion of undocumented and immigrant people in the United States. Central to Lina's comment was that no student should be denied the opportunity for an education, and no youth should be separated from their parents and family. Policies and ideologies entrenched in hegemonic discourses restrict humane, comprehensive immigration legislation, and lead to deferred or suspended dreams of achieving an education for undocumented youth.

Sociopolitical citizenship is characterized by the social and political subjectivities of Latinx youth like Lina, who through a sociohistorical analysis of social conditions are able to reflect and challenge hegemonic discourses that create conditions of oppression aligned with the status quo. As sociopolitical citizens, Latinx youth forged, wielded, and made claims to citizenship. By doing this, they constituted themselves as agents of change who rightfully belong in a country that often does not value them or their communities. Latinx youth embodied and enacted the four domains of sociopolitical citizenship. As an iterative process of cultivating sociopolitical citizenship, these domains are mutually constitutive, and reflect Latinx youth experiences in their school, family, and community contexts—experiences and contexts where Latinx youth social identities, critical consciousness, socioemotional awareness, and political engagement were affirmed and expressed to support their efforts to create social change in their school. One example was the creation of the mural at their school depicting their community.

The experiences of Latinx youth in Change 4 Good highlight how they embodied sociopolitical citizenship. Together these experiences helped shape Latinx youth sociopolitical citizenship, particularly their embodiments, enactments, and claims to citizenship and rights. Latinx youth sociopolitical citizenship was characterized by the development of four domains that I describe as embodied by Latinx youth in their efforts to have their voices heard and lived experiences acknowledged. Contemporary theories and perspectives of citizenship, including youth rights, all too often reproduce US-based constructions of citizenship as a status, practice, and rights-bearing construct that do not fully account for the ubiquitous ways that youth, and in this case Latinx youth, make meaning of these concepts. Additionally, these perspectives do not reflect how Latinx youth often navigate and resist the hegemony in discourses, relationships, and contexts that disenfranchise them and their communities. Scholars who document how Latinx youth experience, understand, and even question injustices, as they imagine possibilities for social change, must also consider how youth challenge and expand meanings of citizenship, legality, and rights. Conceptualizations of citizenship that reflect the complexities and nuances of feeling and being excluded or on the periphery as citizens—as a consequence of ageist and racist nativist ideologies—were offered by Latinx youth and warrant our attention.

Sociopolitical citizenship is grounded in a valuing of pluralism and difference, as well as an affirmation of Latinx youth agency to give voice to their lived experiences. Described through social identities, critical consciousness, socioemotional awareness, and political participation, Latinx youth sociopolitical citizenship included but was not limited to their actions of speaking up and illustrating community stories depicted in a mural that sought to challenge hegemonic discourses about their school, family, and community. Rooted in their claims to justice and a recognition of themselves, their families, and their communities as deserving of opportunities, rights, and belonging, Latinx youth embodied sociopolitical citizenship through their social and political subjectivities in response to contexts that often rendered them silent. By offering a nuanced view of Latinx youth sociopolitical development beyond the civic and public domain, sociopolitical citizenship presents a critical standpoint for considering and attending to youth subjectivities as they claim citizenship and rights. In other words, sociopolitical citizenship underscores Latinx youth as citizens through their social identities, critical consciousness, emotions, and political engagement.

In this chapter, I discussed interconnected domains associated with sociopolitical citizenship. Sociopolitical citizenship, I argue, is an expansive, more inclusive standpoint to understand and characterize Latinx youth citizenship meaning-making, agency, participation, belonging, and rights. Through Latinx youth reflections and lived experiences, the everyday, ubiquitous embodiments of Latinx youth sociopolitical citizenship were illustrated. In this way, I purport that Latinx youth are sociopolitical citizens troubling and challenging hegemonic discourses associated with citizenship, legality, and rights in school, family, and community contexts that inevitably come to shape their lives as citizens. Characteristics associated with sociopolitical citizenship and how it differs from meanings and practices of citizenship that do not consider Latinx youth as agents of change were also discussed. Latinx youth social and political subjectivities, as embodied and enacted to characterize their sociopolitical citizenship, position them as agents of change with the power to wield their inalienable rights.

5

Claiming Rights beyond State Relations

"Does everyone have equal rights?," asked one of the program facilitators. Lina immediately responded by stating, "No! Having rights is different from actually *having rights*." Lina walked over to the easel with the white piece of paper and pointed to the word "ageism." She added, "Kids aren't treated the same [as adults]. People think that just because we're kids we can't do certain things." Other youth agreed, and began to name some of the rights that youth don't have. Among these were: "students not having rights [in school]," "not being able to vote," "can't go into the hospital," and "not being able to buy certain things." Lina added, "All kids should have a safe community." This remark led youth to talk about the importance of young people being able to care for themselves and their community. Some youth concluded that this could only be possible if adults gave youth the opportunity to be more "independent" and "free."[1]

Rights are predicated on the assumption that a person holds citizenship. The nation-state and its institutions determine and grant or limit people's rights as citizens.[2] Yet citizenship, characterized by a person's relationship to the nation-state, is defined by the attainment of adulthood as determined by age. The processes through which Latinx youth engaged with and understood rights in their lives—especially their troubling of their relationship to rights—fostered their sociopolitical citizenship. These understandings certainly surfaced in the context of Change 4 Good, especially when we discussed issues of concern to their families and community.

Conversations about historic and contemporary struggles to belong, to be seen and heard, were brought up most often in relation to their perceived limited rights and agency as young people. Topics of discussion such as these emerged in relation to their mural project and its themes, especially those reflecting the histories of the civil and labor rights movements and social justice efforts by communities in struggle, for example, when reflecting on the organizing by the United Farm Workers. In Change 4 Good efforts were made by the program facilitators to center and listen to Latinx youth experiences and help them process their reflections about the stories they gathered from their school and community focus groups.

The focus groups Latinx youth facilitated with members of their school and their community featured stories of hope and struggle, of having limited access to opportunities, resources, and rights. After collecting these stories, they engaged in data analysis procedures, which included reflections and dialogues, to help them inform the creation of their mural. Through these experiences and opportunities, the Change 4 Good program facilitators helped Latinx youth discern themes from the focus groups and turn these into images or symbols that could be illustrated in their mural. The mural symbolized their communities' stories, histories, and dreams for their future. It also reflected their hopes for accessing better opportunities for themselves, such as pursuing an education, as well as seeing actualized the well-being of their families and community.

Meanings associated with rights surfaced also in relation to their own lived experiences in school, family, and community contexts, as evidenced by Joaquín's reflection on the significance of rights. For Joaquín, rights were universal, yet differently experienced and accessed, especially as he reflected upon his family's life.

> I think all people have rights. Rights for, like, grown-up people—so they could have their own life. But for kids, I think they have rights—just not the same rights as adults. My brother and my sister have the right to go to school. And my parents have the right to go to work without being told, like, you cannot be here. We kids have different rights. Some people, for example, they can't go—they can't, like, work in certain places 'cause they need a social number [social security number], or they need a driving license to work. But I think that's wrong because everybody should have the [equal] rights that other people have. Equal rights, like having papers so they could be in different places. Like, my parents, they can't go to México. If they go, they can't come back. It should be a right for people to go and come back. I think—yeah, 'cause, my parents should be able to go see their family and country. Like, has it changed? Or how is it now? Is it different or not?

Accounts about their families and community rights, as reflected in Joaquín's response, as well as the opening excerpt featuring Lina's reflections, were nested within a broader structure of power. Furthermore, having rights, as they both clearly describe, does not mean equity, equality, or enfranchisement. For Joaquín's family there are limited opportunities, characterized by their inability to visit family in México, travel across borders, access a social security number and a driver's license, and be able to "have their own life." Rights for young people are different from those afforded to some adults, yet these rights are similarly limited. For instance, youth have the right—indeed, the expectation—to "go to school." Lina's remarks, consistent with Joaquín's, underscored youth differential rights vis-à-vis those of adults.[3]

Joaquín and Lina, like other youth growing up in mixed-status families, developed understandings and experiences with rights associated with constructions of citizenship as well as notions of legality. When combined, these informed their feelings as well as their experiences of belonging. For the most part Latinx youth experienced a moderate degree of rights as freedoms and opportunities; their rights, however, were curtailed by ageist and racist nativist discourses to keep the status quo. Latinx youth were aware of this and acutely unsettled by it. As a result, and from time to time in Change 4 Good, we engaged in group reflections and dialogues to challenge sociocultural constructions of youthhood that limited their agency, as well as the hegemonic discourses that shaped meanings of citizenship, legality, and rights in their own lives and their families.

A Right to a Voice

Voting is how we participate in civic society—be it for president, be it for a municipal election. It's the way we teach our children—in school elections—how to be citizens, and the importance of their voice.
—Loretta Lynch, US Attorney General

Citizenship entails exercising rights and responsibilities. A person in the nation-state has the right to hold and exercise certain privileges, such as voting. Although the Voting Rights Act of 1965 brought about racial and social progress, voting rights are to a degree still reserved for a very select group of people in society. The struggles for equality and freedom must be understood within a broader, centuries-long history of institutional marginalization and the demand by communities for enfranchisement and inclusion. Histories of struggle and resistance, along with associated discourses, helped inform Latinx youth views on voting as a privilege, especially given that they viewed voting as the hallmark of citizenship in the United States because it presumes to give people a voice within democracy. The democratic process of electing representatives and instituting legislation relies upon the responsibilities of a citizen to exercise that right. An individual in the nation-state exercising their right to vote is embodying enfranchisement. Citizenship is the expression of a person reinforcing their ties to and their relationship to the nation-state through the practice of "one person, one vote, one voice."[4] The civic and political actions that characterize citizenship emphasize civic engagement in US institutions and structures that support a thriving society.

Among Latinx youth, voting was viewed as a citizen's right and a privilege that only a select few could exercise. Latinx youth like Joaquín, for instance, equated citizenship with voting: "A citizen is someone that votes." By conceptualizing citizenship as a practice of voting, Joaquín was able to emphasize what he described as a meaningful relationship between an individual and the nation-state. Similarly, Diego stated, "You can't vote if you don't have citizenship. . . . If you're not from here [United States]." Unlike Joaquín, Diego identified citizenship as a prerequisite to voting, and he further explained that citizenship could be associated with nationality and belonging. Joaquín and Diego appeared to equate citizenship, and being a citizen, with the right to vote. Legality and rights, according to Joaquín and Diego, were considered concomitant with being a citizen—these were key privileges and responsibilities of citizenship, and in effect, as Diego notes, associated with a person's ties to a place, namely, the nation-state.

Democratic participation upholds the active practice of voting, yet unsurprisingly, Latinx youth associated voting with residency in the United States, including legality. Although they often inaccurately conceptualized it, some Latinx youth considered legal documentation as necessary for a person to vote. Yesenia, like Joaquín and Diego, equated citizenship with legality, rights, equality, belonging, and voting when she remarked the following in response to my request for her to define citizenship, specifically, what it means to be a citizen in the United States:

> Citizenship is when you're, like, legally allowed to be here [United States] and you have more rights. I think you kind of have equal rights as people that live here, who can vote and have papers.

Papers and voting, along with civic duties, were viewed as fundamental pillars of being a citizen. Yesenia described voting as a practice of citizenship, in relation to a person's immigrant status. As evidenced in her remark, Yesenia echoed the connection between voting and citizenship consistent with those offered previously by other Latinx youth. Three significant connections were salient in Yesenia's remarks, which could be interpreted as the trinity of citizenship: enfranchisement should involve full legal and social recognition as a citizen; sense of belonging to the nation-state; and rights, specifically voting. Yesenia's meaning-making about citizenship was associated with and informed by the significance of being able to act and exercise one's right to vote. Enfranchisement was linked with political engagement experiences that furthered one's sense of belonging.

US-based constructions of citizenship that informed Latinx youth meaning-making are consistent to a degree with research on youth general views on citizenship.[5] Although most studies have been conducted predominantly with youth from white middle- or upper-middle-class status families, results indicate that voting is considered an important marker of citizenship. A possible explanation for this is that in the United States, young people under the age of eighteen do not have the right to vote. Hence, voting is associated with being a citizen and being engaged as a voter. Latinx youth nonetheless described citizenship as a practice associated with voting and the right to participate in the democratic decision-making process of the nation-state. Feliz's response emphasized the importance of citizenship as an action that involved voting, along with other civic duties and practices. To illustrate this, in the context of an interview, Feliz appeared to unpack the construction of citizenship by juxtaposing the material resources and privileges associated with birthright citizenship.

> Undocumented people are like regular people [legal permanent residents]. But these people can't vote. I think what they could do is rent a house and work in specific places, like maybe in the farmland [agriculture] or something like that. They could put their children in public schools. They could have, I think, a bank—like, a banking account. They could have cell phones. They could have almost everything that a regular citizen has, except they don't have the right to vote, I think, or to buy properties, and have better—or more opportunities, like go to college, work better jobs, and other things.

Feliz highlighted voting as a right that undocumented people and legal permanent residents do not have. Moreover, she made visible some of the material resources that legal permanent residents can access. Her response described how permanent residents and to a degree undocumented people could live their lives as "regular citizens," yet they experience limited access to resources, opportunities, and rights with implications upon their lives. Certain privileges and opportunities, such as access to an education and better jobs, could be limited because of their immigrant status.

Voting constitutes an important symbolic and performative act of not only citizenship, but also modes of belonging and civic engagement. Through voting, and even claiming the right to do so, people can wield power and influence in society. In Change 4 Good Latinx youth occasionally discussed this, especially the right to vote, which appeared to be heavily curtailed for young people. Latinx youth, as a result, described voting as a responsibility of a citizen, either birthright or naturalized. These themes were the focus of one significant conversation where we engaged youth in a reflection about the history and significance of rights, such as voting in the United States.

Unlike other sessions where we would often break up into smaller groups and have more hands-on activities that included collaging, drawing, and analyzing stories and reflecting on their mural themes, this time we engaged as a larger group because the topic of rights was part of several previous Change 4 Good program sessions. Worth noting is Latinx youth understandings of their rights, with keen emphasis on voting.

The program facilitator continued to explain that women couldn't always vote. She said that at one point, the only people who could vote were white men. She asked, "Who can vote now?" One student said, "Everybody," and she said that not everyone could vote, and asked if the students in the classroom could vote. The students shook their heads with a "No." . . . . We asked the students if young people could vote, "Do kids have a right to vote?" All the students exclaimed, "No." One of the students asked, "At what age can people vote?" and another student said, "Eighteen." Lina said that the reason youth cannot vote is because "They are not adults." We asked why this was the case, and Lucia said, "Because they're mean?" And Celine stated, "The government." Feliz then expressed that she felt that youth do not vote because "They [youth] might make the wrong decision." Feliz felt that people might vote for certain people because they are "pretty." We asked the youth why they thought Lucia speculated that. Some students said that some people feel that youth don't know how to learn about who they are voting about. We asked, "Could they [youth] learn?" Lucia then replied that they could not because teachers don't talk about voting or how and who to vote for.[6]

Latinx youth identified voting as an important practice that reinforced people's relationship to the nation-state. The connections to voting Latinx youth made were related to constructions of citizenship as a status, a practice, and a right, specifically a label associated with being privileged or recognized as a voter. A person who is recognized as a voter is afforded the opportunity to practice or exercise the privilege to participate in a democracy. Voting, for instance, was described as a marker of being an adult. Moreover, voting was associated with discernment or knowledge about the voting process, such as whom to vote for, how to vote, and why voting is important, especially for those whose values or views align with the common good. Lina, for example, expressed that young people are neither prepared nor familiar with the voting process. Furthermore, she added that youth often know very little about the possible candidates who may run for election. Her remark implied that it was very likely that youth would be making ill-informed decisions that she believed would be influenced by superficial or objective markers associated with certain candidates based on their perceived appearance, or assumptions of who they are and the interests they might represent.

Consistent with US-based constructions of citizenship is the notion that citizenship is a label where the boundaries of citizenship are determined by those in positions of power with the intent of disenfranchising members of subordinate social groups.[7] To give an example, in the United States, a formerly incarcerated person can possess the label or juridical status of a citizen; however, in some states the person cannot exercise their right to vote in some elections and/or jurisdictions because of their criminal record. In this case, the practice of citizenship is severely restricted and determined by a set of sociolegal conditions or criteria set forth by the nation-state, which, as history demonstrates, continues to criminalize and disenfranchise certain groups, among them Latinx and immigrant communities.

Voting is a civic and political act that implicates the nation-state and its members, as well as a person's privileges and responsibilities in relation to the communities that constitute society. Latinx youth viewed voting as a marker and, most importantly, a practice of citizenship. Although at times Latinx youth drew inaccurate or false equivalencies between voting and legal residency, particularly an authorized immigration status, their discussions reflected US-based constructions of legality through the practice of voting. Conceptualizations of citizenship that define it solely as the act of voting are limiting because these do not consider the sociohistorical, political, and economic challenges of obtaining legal documentation or an authorized immigration status, as well as access to resources to facilitate voting, such as a voting ballot or the polls. The emergence of voting in relation to citizenship highlights the value and significance Latinx youth associate with voting rights. Research demonstrates that young people living in Latinx immigrant and mixed-status families are exposed to discourses that view citizenship as the possession of legal documents and the right to vote, and this appears consistent with the meanings offered by Latinx youth.[8]

Youth Claims to Full Citizenship

Youth studies literature typically purports that young people's understandings about rights are rather too abstract or irrelevant in their meaning. The abstractions of youth citizenship do not capture the nuances of their meaning-making and experiences as citizens in full, however. When asked to define rights, young people in general often characterize these as privileges and responsibilities that are determined or defined by the "government" or "the president," entities tied to the nation-state. Rights are perceived as being related to and formed by meanings of legality, an authorized immigration status, as well as a sense of belonging. Latinx youth also described rights in relation to an individual's access to material, social, and legal resources that could support their agency.

As we facilitated conversations with Latinx youth about the inability of young people to vote because of their age, discussions of historic events, contemporary social problems, community stories, and student experiences surfaced. When these did, topics associated with youth agency, as either supported or constrained, were consequently a part of them. These emerged during conversations in Change 4 Good where Latinx youth would occasionally engage in discussions about rights that troubled the term's sociolegal associations.

> Consistent with our prior discussions on the history of rights in the United States, the program facilitator asked youth whether they could vote. There was a brief moment of silence and youth shook their heads indicating "No." Jackie remarked, "We can't vote." Diego asked why youth couldn't vote, but no one provided an answer. The youth seemed thoughtful and perplexed by the question. After a few minutes, however, Santiago claimed that it was because "The government is mean." Celine shared that it was because they were not the voting age, which is eighteen. Diego challenged this by asking why youth had to be eighteen, and what was so special about that number. Lina tried to respond, cautiously pausing between her words, and eventually stating, "Because then you're an adult. You're an adult when you're eighteen. It's the law." We pressed youth critical reflection further by asking why you had to be an adult. One youth said, "Because when you're an adult you know more about the people you're voting for." In response to that we asked if youth thought that was always true. Another program facilitator rephrased the question, "Sometimes adults might vote without really knowing whom they're voting for." A couple youth nodded in agreement. . . . The facilitator asked if youth could vote

in school, and they all agreed indicating that yes they could vote on school elections. Then a program facilitator asked, open-endedly, whether youth could also vote in national elections, given that this was, in some ways, similar to their voting inside their school. Some youth slowly nodded their heads, while others remained thoughtful and uncertain of where they stood in response to this question. Joaquín broke the silence when he stated, "If kids have more information about the people they're voting for, they could maybe vote?"[9]

Latinx youth considered voting a hallmark of democracy and citizenship. Yet they also saw voting as being restricted to and practiced by a select group of people. The age requirement for voting was the most salient restriction for Latinx youth. When asked whether young people could vote, most Latinx youth stated that they could not because they were under the voting age. Some Latinx youth, such as Joaquín, for example, stated that if youth were given a chance to vote, which included opportunities to engage with the US electoral and political process, as well as information for them to discern, they could likely vote with confidence. Latinx youth conceptualizing of rights, informed by their lived experiences, underscored their claims to belong and participate in decision making in matters that concern them, as well as in creating conditions to better their lives.

When pressed further and asked to elaborate on these associations, Latinx youth remarked that government institutions, as well as adults—specifically, teachers—were accountable for their limited or rather possibly uninformed decision making, if they were granted the right to vote as youth. To further illustrate Latinx youth reflections on this topic, Diego challenged this construction to a degree by questioning why a person had to be eighteen to vote. Facetiously, Santiago stated that it was because the government was mean. Underlying Santiago's remark on the meanness of the US government was a reflection of a past experience of differential treatment, one of perhaps several, where Santiago felt disparaged by certain institutions, and therefore disenfranchised. Unable to provide an explanation for the perceived arbitrariness of the voting age, Latinx youth questioned people's capacity to actually engage in voting. Some youth argued that adults were capable of making better decisions than youth.

Voting age is a significant and salient issue for youth. Claims to rights by Latinx youth differed from those of adults, especially when they demanded recognition as citizens even though they were well under adult age. Eighteen is currently the legal voting age in the United States; however, this was not always the case. In 1971 the voting age was lowered from twenty-one, largely in response to young adults being drafted into war efforts at the age of eighteen, yet still being denied the right to vote. Voting rights were premised on young adults' claims to full enfranchisement, as reflected in the slogan "Old enough to fight, old enough to vote." The legislative change in voting age became a fundamental statute of the Twenty-Sixth Amendment of the US Constitution.

To some degree, Latinx youth subscribed to US-based constructions of youthhood associated with perceived youth incompetence and naïveté about social issues or matters that concern the nation-state. When pressed to further conceptualize the meaning of rights in their lives, some youth were able to provide more nuanced explanations. Feliz's meaning-making about rights illustrates this.

> I know that rights are something that you are given. Like, it depends, like, sometimes—'cause you may have the right at school to use the computers and other privileges at school. At your house you may have, like, the right to watch TV whenever you want or not. I don't know, but there are different types of rights. But my citizen rights might be, like, to have the right to vote, have the right to, umm, I don't know, have a house, I guess, and the right to adopt kids. . . . Rights are mostly like a privilege. Like something you could do or you don't have to do.

Feliz characterized rights as involving agency in decision making, specifically privileges that people are able to access to pursue opportunities or certain intentions, such as adopting children. As Feliz's one-year-old brother crawled freely around the living room of her home, I observed her struggle to keep focus on her remarks, often equating rights with free will, but also privileges and opportunities. Feliz offered a few examples, such as a young person choosing to use a computer or other resources at school without consequence. During her explanations Feliz referenced "citizens' rights," such as voting, to describe how a person's immigrant status, specifically their documented status, facilitates their access to rights and opportunities. When pressed further, Feliz equated rights with privileges and the freedom to act, to choose, and, above all, to have free will. To a degree, Feliz's response underscored Latinx youth general understanding that "there are different types of rights." This implied that rights vary in application and distribution, and ultimately are earned through legal mechanisms.

Conceptualizing rights as "something you could do or you don't have to do," according to Feliz, emphasizes the importance of agency beyond self-determination. Discussions on the differential rights of young people were part of Latinx youth reflections and meaning-making about rights. For instance, some Change 4 Good youth were familiar with the Bill of Rights and related discourses.

> The stories and anecdotes that we debriefed from the community stories [focus groups] led us to discuss themes and young people's relationship to rights, or as stated in a focus group story: "Kids fighting for their rights." This particular theme related to changes they wanted to see happen at their school. I intervened to remind the youth about the comment Lina made about youth fighting for their rights and working together to create change. I told them, "Some of you shared that youth should be their own advocates." The youth then began to advocate for themselves, and what they wanted to see happen at school. I added that this was all related to their school, and to equity and equality in education. Celine then brought up the importance of the civil rights movement. Jackie said that was related to "the Bill of Rights," and added a funny remark, "The rights of a guy named Bill." Some of the youth responded by stating, "Not all people have the same rights." Lina stated, "Not everyone has the same rights. Kids don't have the same rights as adults." The youth then shared several experiences when their opinion or decision making is not considered or encouraged. Some youth claimed, "Kids should have an opinion or a say on what happens in the country." Feliz raised her hand and said that her cousin's "fairy godmother" was sick. Some of the youth laughed because what Feliz meant to say was just "godmother." Disregarding these comments, she explained that her cousin's [godmother] had brain cancer, and he wanted to see her at the hospital but could not because they would only allow people over the age of eighteen to go in. Feliz explained feeling sad for him because he wanted to see her, but he didn't have the right of adults to go into certain hospital

areas. Lina said that she was really sad for him too, and that it was not fair. Feliz added that her cousin was afraid that his godmother might die, and he would not be able to see her and say goodbye.[10]

The implications of these rights underscored for Latinx youth that the nation-state upheld unalienable rights for some people but not equally for others. Latinx youth understood that being told or knowing that one has certain rights does not necessarily mean that such rights are accessible to all. The stories that Feliz shared and discussed demonstrated how having rights does not mean that people's rights will be protected. On the contrary, certain rights are meant to curtail the agency of some in the name of safety and care. The story of Feliz's cousin being denied a hospital visit to his godmother was meant to illustrate how adults sought to protect youth and keep them safe. At the same time, however, it made Feliz's cousin feel excluded because he was being denied a right he believed he had. The inability to be with a loved family member seemed to go against youth rights to self-determination.

For Latinx youth, the complicated and often contradictory meanings associated with rights surfaced in relation to those experiences where they felt excluded. Additionally, their accounts showed how nurturance and self-determination rights are not mutually inclusive or complementary. On the contrary, some rights are restrictive, limiting youth participation and, most importantly, their agency. Sociolegal constructions of rights for young people also constrained and challenged youth participation in decision making and their sense of belonging.

Described in various ways, rights implied a direct relationship to citizenship, including the entitlements that citizenship as a status and practice grants to certain people. As entitlements to citizenship, legal rights were characterized by the procedural and civil rights that the nation-state bestows to individuals and groups who possess the lawful authorization to reside in a given country. In most cases this is associated with birthright citizenship or naturalization, as well as legal permanent residency or an authorized immigration status. Citizenship as a rights-bearing construct consequently affords people privileges and responsibilities, which are mutually reinforcing as these represent a person's status and practice in relationship to the nation-state. Legal rights symbolize power because these ascribe certain privileges, responsibilities, and opportunities for some people.[11] Unlike legal rights, social rights are constructed by hegemonic discourses that determine who is to be included in the collective "we." Social rights operate in relation to structures of power that determine people's access to resources, and the conditions through which people can exercise their rights, including opportunities.[12] Under this sociolegal construction of rights, the agency that some people have or are denied reflects the hegemonic discourses that uphold the status quo.[13]

In conceptualizing rights and discussing how she sees them being experienced in her community, Jackie mentioned that when some people arrive in a new country as immigrants their rights, as well as access to resources and opportunities, are limited. The circumstances of their immigrant status, as either authorized or undocumented immigrants, severely hamper their economic, health, and social well-being. Seated cross-legged in one of the rundown playgrounds in a local, dry grassy park near her home, Jackie described to me her understanding about rights and their significance in her family, and her concerns about her brother's immigrant status.

> JACKIE: Everybody has rights. Wherever you come from, you have rights, but some people, like my brother, cannot have equal rights, like, some people can't get their, uhhh, driver's license. All people should have equal rights, they should be able to drive, they should be able to get their license like everybody else. I think we're all the same. I think they—
>
> JESICA: Who?
>
> JACKIE: Latins—
>
> JESICA: Latinos?
>
> JACKIE: Yeah, *Latinos*. The government doesn't let Latinos or undocumented people get their license and they're not allowed to come over to America. Like, they—
>
> JESICA: Latinos?
>
> JACKIE: Yes, Latinos. Like if they're here in the US they're not . . . they don't get the equal rights as people in the US that are citizens supposedly. But I believe we're all citizens *here*. I think that Latinos are citizens. Like, if you're a member of a community you have rights, so citizenship and rights are kinda connected.

Jackie explained that Latinx, regardless of their legal status, should be considered citizens of the United States because they are members and active participants who contribute to the thriving of the nation-state. In fact, Jackie claimed that all people should have equal rights and citizenship. Drawing on her community experiences, Jackie shared how undocumented people cannot access equal opportunities in the United States.

Undocumented people, for instance, cannot have access to a driver's license in certain states, and in some cases the process for acquiring one can be significantly bureaucratic. California's Safe and Responsible Driver Act, established through California Assembly Bill 60, as an example, grants eligible undocumented people the ability to apply for a driver's license; however, this requires a person entrusting the state with personal information, which many might hesitate to provide for fear or concerns over their own and their family's safety. Legislation aligned with AB 60 contributed to the development of Deferred Action for Childhood Arrivals (DACA). Under the Trump administration, however, DACA has been challenged time and time again. Despite efforts since 2017 to have DACA terminated, as of this writing in 2020 DACA is still in effect and youth are able to apply for DACA renewal only.

The Trump administration's efforts to rescind DACA have limited access to some eligible youth. According to Jackie's witnessing of her brother's experience, specifically not being able to obtain a driver's license, opportunities are still severely limited for most undocumented people. Even in California, presumably the most "immigrant-friendly" region of the country, resources and opportunities for undocumented people are restricted. Jackie's response highlighted the dichotomous relationship between belonging and rights for Latinx. Evidently, Jackie recognized that in a US context some Latinx are not legitimately seen or treated as first-class citizens with rights; they are not equally included or seen as members of the nation-state.

Belonging as an Inalienable Right

Contesting the dispossession of rights is a characteristic of sociopolitical citizenship. In line with sociopolitical citizenship, Latinx youth meaning-making about rights was informed by their social identities, critical consciousness, and socioemotional awareness of the implications of having or not having rights, as well as their political engagement. Rather than waiting for rights to be given or granted, Latinx youth saw their rights as constrained by certain structures, like schooling, and needing to be claimed.

As an embodiment of citizenship, not a passive complacent process, sociopolitical citizenship reflects aspects of what cultural anthropologist Renato Rosaldo termed cultural citizenship.[14] Characterized by the relational experiences of sociocultural belonging, cultural citizenship is defined by the political forms of engagement that center community cultural resources as assets for empowerment and collective action.[15] Sociopolitical citizenship relates to cultural citizenship or associated sociocultural and political constructions of belonging, collective action, and agency, also reflected in terms such as dissenting citizenship[16] and flexible citizenship,[17] but there are key differences. Unlike cultural citizenship, sociopolitical citizenship among Latinx youth is characterized by the subjectivities that inform the development of a critical consciousness, the importance of social identities and forming a socioemotional awareness, as well as accessing opportunities for political engagement.

Regardless of the structures set forth by the nation-state, citizenship demands that people stake claims to rights, especially the right to belong, and be treated with dignity and respect. Sociopolitical citizenship is a critique of US-based constructions of citizenship under the nation-state that do not affirm the dignity and well-being of Latinx youth, their families, and their communities. Reflecting on Latinx people's rights and enfranchisement in the United States, Jackie, among other youth, drew a link between citizenship and rights, arguing that these are interconnected. Rights and citizenship are mutually constitutive; the struggle for rights often becomes the catalyst for movements to de-center the power of the nation-state in determining who is or can become a citizen. Challenging the structures of power by demanding rights is an act of sociopolitical citizenship, which Latinx youth occasionally exemplified in the context of Change 4 Good. Rights to full citizenship reserved only for adults were often challenged and juxtaposed, to a degree, with Latinx youth rights and lived experiences. Latinx youth agreed that rights, in theory, were accorded to all people or members of US society. The distribution and application of such rights in practice, however, were much more nuanced and complex.

Troubling the sociolegal meaning of rights in their lives was at the crux of Latinx youth conceptualizations of rights and, relatedly, citizenship and legality. Latinx youth described rights in relation to how they experienced these in their everyday lives. Given that rights are socially constructed, and young people view rights in relation to the systems of power that influence their lives, Latinx youth meaning-making about rights extended beyond individual self-determination toward a discussion of rights associated with the community, a sense of belonging, and a recognition of youth as full citizens. Some Latinx youth considered conceptualizing rights in relation to sociolegal meanings. Others, however, saw this as too narrow of a definition because rights can be—and, for some communities, must be—claimed.

Latinx youth reflections on rights often positioned them as contributors to their communities, and they occasionally expressed and claimed their rights with their fullest sense of agency. Lucia, for instance, tried to explain her point in between burger bites as we caught up with each other several months after she moved on from elementary school. When I picked her up from her home I asked her where she wanted to go for our interview, and she enthusiastically exclaimed, "Bob Burgers," a retro burger joint that both locals and tourists visit. Halfway through the interview, I asked about rights, to which she replied,

> I think children might not have all the same rights as adults do, but I know that children have rights too. Like, you have the right to, hmm, I'm kinda stuck on that one. . . . Well, everyone has, like, the right to, hmm, I remember we learned this in school, teachers were telling us about human rights. Like, you—you have the right to speak your mind, you can—I think there's thirty rights that we learned about. Can't remember all of them. Everyone should have rights. Like, everyone should have the right to say and do what they want. I have rights. Yeah, I think so. I think I'm different, I know I'm not going—not going to be the same as everyone else but I believe I do have rights. I feel like I should have the right to be listened to. I mean, just because you are different doesn't mean you can't have the same things as others. Many people are different. No one is going to be the same. I think everyone should have rights.

According to Lucia, all people should have rights regardless of their social status differences. Lucia explained that despite being a young person, differently positioned in comparison to adults, she still had rights—particularly the right to be heard. Claims to agency and the capacity to wield power, including the right to participate and engage in decision making, were central to Lucia's response. Lucia claimed that young people have a right to be heard and be taken seriously by adults regardless of their age. Demanding to be heard, seen, and included could be described as a form of resistance to sociocultural constructions of youth as passive; this stance underscores an embodiment of sociopolitical citizenship.

Latinx youth reflected and troubled their positionalities within US society. In particular, they were unsettled by the discourses on rights, which purported to uphold their nurturance and self-determination, yet what they experienced was at odds with these claims. How could youth claim a stake to full citizenship in a society that willfully ignores them and denies their right to full participation in decision making? This was a key question that permeated Latinx youth meaning-making about rights. When asked to determine whether all people have equal human rights, Lucia stated that all people have rights, yet she highlighted the importance of belonging in order to experience full citizenship. Meanings such as these translated to experiences of agency and collective action, which reflected their sense of social responsibility and solidarity.

Learning about human rights, including the right to freedom of speech, was consistent with Lucia's conceptualization, and reflected Daniela's understanding of rights. Daniela, however, drew from her own experiences to explain her meaning.

> Rights don't tell you, you have to be, like, you have to be, like, a certain gender, a certain skin color, to be in this country, they like . . . you don't have to wear this, like, a specific type of clothing. Like me, I like jeans, I don't really like skirts or dresses, I like shorts and jeans, it's more comfortable for me, I think that's why I like soccer, 'cause I like shorts. If I don't like dresses and skirts and they make me wear that, then I'm not gonna feel comfortable. If there's a type of food you eat and all of the sudden you're not allowed to eat that and you're allergic to it, you basically lose your rights, and you start to have a different culture. It's not what it used

to be. Like me, if I like to play soccer and all of the sudden they say girls can't play anymore then I'd start crying and then I would try to get *my right back*.

While I was interviewing Daniela, her father was seated across from the dining table in the living room watching sports updates on the Spanish media channel, and when he heard Daniela remark that she was not comfortable wearing dresses and skirts, he turned around and confirmed, "¡Solo quiere andar en chores!" (She only wants to wear shorts!). Confirming her father's remarks, Daniela understood rights as having the freedom to be who she is and engage in activities that she is passionate about.

Daniela's response echoed the UN-CRC's definitions of self-determination rights as youth having a choice. Furthermore, she viewed rights in relation to her social identities, specifically her age and gender. Through this reflection and response, Daniela demonstrated a recognition of the significance of identities in informing the value one attaches to rights, including the capacity to fully embody and act upon these. When hypothetically asked what she would do if her rights were denied, she claimed, "I would try to get *my right back*." Daniela's claims are important to note, given that political engagement often characterized by making demands to rights is an important expression of sociopolitical citizenship. It is crucial to act upon and claim rights that may be limited by the social structures that maintain hegemonic discourses—especially when people's rights, and ultimately their agency, are curtailed by the status quo. Exercising one's rights constitute an embodiment of sociopolitical citizenship.

With our backs leaning against the mural wall, having relocated from under the scorching heat of the picnic tables at the elementary school, I asked Yesenia to share with me her understanding and perspectives about rights. Yesenia was quick to share what she knew.

> YESENIA: Well, I know there's, like, human rights, and there are rights as in stuff you have the right to do and there's stuff that you shouldn't do. Human rights . . . I was just learning something about this. Okay, so human rights are the rights that we humans have no matter what. We have the right to our opinion, I think, to speak free in this coun-

try. We also have the right to, uhh—oh yeah, we're—we have a right to not be discriminated. We're not allowed to discriminate people because of their religion or sexual thingy.

JESICA: Sexual orientation?

YESENIA: Yeah, *sexual orientation*. You can't just go and judge somebody because of what they like or who they like. Oh, and you're not allowed to discriminate people because of their race. You can't just go and judge somebody because of their skin color or because of where they were born.

Yesenia described human rights as privileges that all people are afforded regardless of their age, race, ethnicity, and immigrant status, among other markers of identity. Like Lucia's statement, Yesenia's definition emphasized people's right to do good by others, emphasizing the importance of not inflicting harm or abuse upon other people. Yesenia claimed that race, ethnicity, and sexuality should not limit a person's human rights. The critical consciousness that informed Yesenia's meaning-making, as exemplified in her response, demonstrated the ways rights cannot and must not be denied to anyone because of their identities. Additionally, Yesenia described how discrimination functioned in oppressive ways to curtail people's access to resources and opportunities. Race and gender were identified as categories that are deployed to marginalize people and limit their citizenship, including their sense of belonging. For Latinx youth, age intersected with race, ethnicity, and immigrant status to shape their citizen experiences and claims to rights. Through a reflection of their own identities, Latinx youth made compelling connections between rights and citizenship.

Discrimination was an explanation offered in relation to Latinx youth conceptualizing of rights. Feliz, for example, echoed Yesenia's reference to people's violent behavior toward those who are perceived as foreign or different, at times questioning how society constructs and criminalizes certain "good" and "bad" behaviors. As our conversation continued I noticed Feliz carefully craft a response.

> I think everyone should have equal rights even if they're different, but I think sometimes it depends if that person did good or bad, you know. What I think isn't bad is, like, getting caught coming from your home

place [country] to come here [United States] and then getting put into prison 'cause you came here without permission [legal documents]. I think that's not very crimeable [unlawful], if you came here to do a good thing for your family and yourself. It's not very fair [to be criminalized] because some people that have rights, and don't take the opportunity and people that don't have that right want that opportunity and say, "Wow, these people are very lucky and they are not taking the opportunity," and they start thinking what if I had the opportunity to do that and they probably will never be able to do that 'cause they don't have the right.

Feliz emphasized that everyone should have rights despite differences in immigrant experiences and status. Yet according to current policies and practices, behaviors are viewed as important determinants in constructing who is perceived as deserving of rights and therefore citizenship. Immigrant people ineligible for legal status are framed through anti-immigrant sentiments and policies as undeserving of rights, respect, and dignity, and are even positioned as criminals to be excluded from society. Hegemonic discourses via these characterizations position certain immigrants as unworthy of being and becoming citizens, or full-fledged human beings before the eyes of the nation-state.

Feliz qualified border crossing without legal documents as good, or noncriminal, because those who crossed the border did so to provide for a better life and future for their family, and meant to do good by others. As other Latinx youth had claimed, and as explicitly stated by Feliz, undocumented people are not criminals. Feliz advocated that instead of being criminalized, undocumented immigrants should be granted rights, protected, and provided with resources and opportunities for a better life. Remarks like these point to a conceptualization of citizenship and rights as pluriversal qualities that allow people the freedom to move within and beyond borders.[18] In this regard, the right to immigrate for the betterment, safety, and well-being of one's family should not be considered a crime, but instead a necessity for their thriving and well-being. In Feliz's view immigration should not be condemned or viewed as a threat. Immigration is a response to the systemic and systematic social, economic, and political inequalities and inequities that cause people to leave their homeland, or country of origin.

Despite that vast range of meanings and perspectives offered by Latinx youth, rights were often described as equal access to opportunities. Yet not all responses or reflections focused on the material and institutional resources afforded through the possession of rights. Diego, for example, emphasized the importance of being treated with dignity and respect.

> Everyone should have the same amount of respect, 'cause we're all human, we're all the same. I mean, if we didn't have rights, we wouldn't have freedom.

Diego assumed that because all people are human, they are also citizens and deserving of rights. By explicitly referring to human rights and their claims to sociolegal rights, Diego problematized the role of the nation-state in conferring rights. While Diego made claims to universal citizenship and rights, he equated rights with freedom, particularly in the latter part of his response: "If we didn't have rights, we wouldn't have freedom." In this statement, he conceptualized rights as a precursor to freedom. Diego described rights as necessary for people's freedom. Latinx youth responses illustrated their claims to rights in line with a sociopolitical citizenship standpoint that centered their voices alongside their social and political subjectivities to belong. Latinx youth agency, including opportunities for active participation in decision making, must be supported and cultivated to facilitate youth thriving, well-being, and enfranchisement as citizens in the present.

Conclusion

Reimagining Citizenship, Legality, and Rights

Juan Felipe Herrera's poem "Everyday We Get More Illegal" is a reminder of the Latinx immigrant experience, especially Latinx resistance to being othered, and the importance of affirming the humanity of Latinx immigrants. According to Herrera, the first Chicano US Poet Laureate to receive such recognition, there is complexity in living and existing as an immigrant in the United States. Is it possible to imagine a society where every day, instead of getting "more illegal," we become more humane in our values, words, and actions? Can we cultivate settings where Latinx youth can thrive? Hegemonic discourses in US society perceive Latinx as "illegal," or foreign, and youth as powerless, acritical, and politically apathetic, yet the realities are far from this. The voices, reflections, and experiences of Latinx youth featured in *Growing Up Latinx* challenge the ageism and racist nativism that permeate these hegemonic discourses. Latinx youth stories attest to the complexity and diversity among Latinx immigrant experiences. The social and political subjectivities Latinx youth embody and describe demonstrate how their meaning-making about citizenship, legality, and rights simultaneously limited *and* emboldened their agency and their claims to be understood, as well as to be heard, to be seen, and to belong.

Latinx immigrant communities, despite being positioned by hegemonic discourses as "illegal," continued to harness the fortitude to strive for a better life. For the young and future Latinx generations, a better life is one teeming with access to opportunities, resources, and conditions that affirm their dignity, well-being, and thriving. At a time when Latinx youth existence is viewed as a threat to the status quo, and Latinx families are constructed as un-American and foreign, US society contends with questions of who belongs and who does not. Who is a citizen and who is "illegal"? As the nation-state grapples with these questions, Herrera's poem, like *Growing Up Latinx*, invites us to challenge the hegemonic discourses that reproduce the "illegality" of the other—Latinx youth, who are young people, Latinx, American, and, most of all, citizens.

The Latinx youth whose stories, reflections, and experiences are featured here embodied and enacted an expression of citizenship that was grounded in their social and political subjectivities—experiences that were rooted in their positionalities as the children of Latinx immigrants in the United States. Latinx youth meaning-making about citizenship, legality, and rights—in relation to their school, family, and community experiences in a heightened anti-immigrant climate—was largely shaped by hegemonic discourses and contexts that marginalized them or positioned them as second-class citizens. Latinx youth grow up being never fully recognized as citizens or Americans. Race and ethnicity, along with culture and language, and most importantly age, intersect to render them noncitizens and un-American even when some may very well *be* citizens—born and raised in the United States.

As Latinx immigrant families continue to live, work, and struggle to attain rightful inclusion and a fullest sense of belonging in the United States, scholarship must challenge the hegemonic discourses that reproduce their marginalization. *Growing Up Latinx* is a contribution in that direction. In effect, people—foreign or US-born—are not "illegal." Rather, laws, practices, and discourses position them as such, and it these constructions that we, as a society, must challenge and render unlawful. The pursuit of a better life should not be criminalized, as Latinx youth coming of age in the United States claim. We must strive to challenge hegemonic discourses that curtail and limit Latinx youth rights, dignity, humanity, and, most importantly, their agency as sociopolitical citizens.

Coming of Age in the United States

Democracy lies in the current and future contributions of the country's young people. History shows that young people—especially from communities of color—have led US liberation struggles and social movements. Latinx youth constitute a significant and growing demographic that can contribute to the sustainment and fulfillment of these struggles for social change, justice, and the upholding of democracy. As Black Panther Party member and leading founder Huey Newton stated, "The revolution has always been in the hands of the young. The young always inherit the revolution. . . . They are the activists. They are the real vanguard of change because they haven't been indoctrinated and they haven't submitted. They haven't been beaten into line as some of the older people have."[1] Social change lies in the hearts and fists of young people, who are at the intersections of multiple forms of oppression and institutional marginalization, yet also hold the radical hope to imagine and work to actualize transformative change. Youth are at the front lines charging these efforts against the hegemonic discourses that continue to reify deficit views about then, given their positionalities. Latinx youth capacities for developing and engaging their social identities, critical consciousness, socioemotional awareness, and political engagement that emboldens their agency attest to their power to work toward social justice.

The demographics of young people in the United States are changing. These are indicating a shift in the nation-state's population becoming predominantly Latinx, or of Latinx descent. Latinx youth experiences illustrate the complexities of growing up in a nation-state that limits and challenges their capacities and efforts toward becoming active participants and contributors to society. The limitations Latinx youth experience, however, are attempts to continue their disenfranchisement as a means to maintain the status quo. Democratic values and practices that are inclusive of Latinx youth must begin with structural, sociocultural, and political shifts in how society and its institutions engage with and perceive Latinx youth. Through an ethnographic analysis of Latinx youth reflections of their lived experiences in school, family, and community contexts, especially the Change 4 Good program, I described Latinx youth meaning-making about citizenship, legality, and rights as these manifested in their lives. Along with their social and political subjectivities, the voices of Latinx youth in the United States were discussed in relation to their social identities, critical consciousness, socioemotional awareness, and political engagement.

A public example of sociopolitical citizenship is youth activist Sophie Cruz's statement underscoring the importance of being fearless, holding onto hope, forming coalitions, and continuing to "fight for the rights."

> I also want to tell the children not to be afraid because we are not alone. . . . There are still many people that have their hearts filled with

love and tenderness to struggle in this path of life. Let's keep together and fight for the rights.

Sophie's words embody domains of sociopolitical citizenship. Like Sophie, Latinx youth in Change 4 Good, despite their age, race, ethnicity, and immigrant status, made legitimate claims to citizenship and rights. Acts of sociopolitical citizenship like these must be understood as an expression of citizenship. Amid the failure of US society and its institutions to recognize youth from Latinx immigrant families as full citizens with rights, young people often must find, even build, ways to claim their voice and place in settings, like school, that do not authentically include them. As the stories herein illustrate, Latinx youth reframed and claimed citizenship and made demands to belong and be recognized as citizens with agency. They challenged and reconceptualized citizenship by developing and expressing their social identities, critical consciousness, socioemotional awareness, and political engagement with the social conditions and circumstances affecting their lives.

US anti-Latinx and anti-immigrant sentiments, which continue to marginalize and vilify Latinx communities, are further amplified by the ageism that significantly disenfranchises Latinx youth. Since the sheer presence of Latinx immigrant communities in the United States is constructed as "illegal," the nation-state continues to maintain hegemonic discourses, policies, practices, and ideologies, like racist nativism, that deem them unlawful. Consequently, the lived experiences of Latinx youth exist within the social structures set by their school, family, and community contexts. While it is improbable that Latinx youth growing up in the United States will be unconstrained by constructions of citizenship, legality, and rights, they will manage to resist some of these discourses in ways that may parallel or differ from the youth in Change 4 Good.

As these social conditions and systems of power contribute to Latinx youth experiences of precarity, questions on their development and sense of belonging within the nation-state become imperative. Latinx youth growing up in a changing society can help inform the contemporary theorizing on youth citizenship, rights, positive youth development, and civic engagement. How US institutions such as education and immigration engage with and simultaneously position Latinx youth holds implications for their individual and collective sociopolitical development, as well as their well-being. Relegating Latinx youth to a subordinate, second-class status as future citizens will have long-term consequences for the thriving of US democracy. And yet Latinx youth growing up in Latinx immigrant and mixed-status families *do* find ways to challenge these hegemonic discourses and deficit perspectives, at the same time as they strive to exercise their agency and demand rights.

Cultivating Youth Sociopolitical Citizenship

As trespassers of borders and border walls that are constructed to "protect" the nation-state, Latinx immigrants face the challenging task to affirm their humanity against ongoing anti-immigrant sentiments, hegemonic discourses, and policies fueled by racist nativism. The physical borders that set Latinx immigrant communities apart are among the many barriers they must confront as they strive for a better life for themselves and their families, especially their children. Through laws, policies, practices, and hegemonic discourses, the nation-state forecloses opportunities for Latinx immigrant communities to thrive. The absence of supportive contexts of reception reinforces the disenfranchisement of Latinx immigrant families who are deemed and treated as "illegal." Relatedly, Latinx youth described often being positioned by adults, especially teachers, as second-class citizens in the context of schooling. Experiences of second-class citizenship led Latinx youth to consider themselves as citizens *to be*, thereby aligning with a future citizen perspective of young people. From time to time they also sought out opportunities to claim rights. As noted in their reflections, some rights are given to people, but others must be claimed through collective action and political engagement that simultaneously challenges hegemonic discourses.

As a collaborative youth-centered program, Change 4 Good engaged youth voices, perspectives, and experiences in the development of the curriculum and the particular projects youth pursued, from focus groups to a school-based mural. The Change 4 Good team implemented meaningful opportunities for youth participation in decision making, encouraging youth to contribute to the development of their focus groups and research process, and take ownership of what was produced and created, especially the mural. By (1) identifying a social problem or issue affecting their lives, (2) collecting and analyzing data to learn more about the problem, (3) developing and implementing an action to address the issue, and (4) then evaluating the impact of the action and whether it addressed the problem, young people harnessed their agency. Additionally, through these activities, Latinx youth developed their social identities, critical consciousness, socioemotional awareness, and opportunities for political engagement, thereby cultivating their social and political subjectivities as sociopolitical citizens.

Latinx youth in Change 4 Good often reflected upon and challenged discourses about citizenship, as well as legality and rights, that surfaced in relation to their school, family, and community contexts. Fostering opportunities for Latinx youth to engage in these active ways led them to develop a critical understanding of systems of power associated with social issues, which they engaged with through reflections and dialogues in Change 4 Good activities. Outcomes from Latinx youth experiences, as illustrated in the statements they offered, emphasize the importance of cultivating spaces that support youth sociopolitical citizenship. Joaquín, for instance, expressed feeling "proud" because he "was doing something in [and about] the community." Similarly, Jackie reported feeling "happy" and cheerful in the Change 4 Good program because she was interviewing members of her community; she was engaged in a fun and purposeful activity that had direct relevance to her life because it was rooted in her family and community experiences. Opportunities to engage agency in decision making and collective action, as well as being included, were critical to Latinx youth because they could position themselves as active participants in helping improve or resist hegemonic discourses about their communities.

Social justice–oriented, youth-centered, youth-driven, community-engaged activities cultivated Latinx youth sociopolitical citizenship, characterized by their engagement in projects and actions toward creating change in their school and communities. An important project Latinx youth engaged in was the creation of a school-based mural to raise awareness about their community's needs and strengths, while telling an affirming story about their community. Community stories like these reflect their struggles and challenges, as well as hopes and dreams. In sharing these accounts from the Change 4 Good program, we can see that Latinx youth embodied sociopolitical citizenship in relation to their meaning-making about citizenship, legality, and rights.

Latinx youth voices and experiences require the interrogation of the contexts, curricula, frameworks, and relationships that support or hinder their agency and participation. Indeed, this begs the following questions: What would it take for society to consider the agency and social and political subjectivities of Latinx youth as meaningful expressions of citizenship? How would this shape the nation-state's perspectives and structures of support for Latinx youth, especially as they become a prominent demographic in the United States? Surely it would require a paradigm shift in how society approaches, views, and engages with young people, particularly Latinx youth. Additionally, it would necessitate youth-centered and strengths-based frameworks, as well as counterhegemonic discourses grounded in stories and actions that challenge deficit views of Latinx youth as foreign, naïve, or even criminality-prone youth who must be disciplined and assimilated into the status quo determined by the nation-state. The socialization of Latinx immigrants, especially youth, is undeniably characterized by racist nativist logics tied to Americanization and assimilationist efforts into US culture, values, and ideologies. An attempt to assimilate and Americanize immigrants seems prevalent in US education institutions; this insidious pattern must change, as it stifles the voices and agency of immigrant and nonwhite communities, such as Latinx youth whose ways of being, belonging, and engaging differ from those of other young people. *Growing Up Latinx* contends with these questions and dilemmas rooted in hegemonic discourses, racist nativism, and sociocultural constructions of youthhood that limit youth agency, including perspectives of Latinx youth as citizens. Sociopolitical citizenship aims to incite action and a rejection of Latinx youth disenfranchisement by centering the voices, lived experiences, and social and political subjectivities of Change 4 Good Latinx youth coming of age in the United States.

Concluding Reflections

Growing Up Latinx invites scholars, educators, youth advocates, and allies, as well as readers, to consider what research, theory, and practice developed *with* and *through* the lived experiences of young people can look like. By understanding the positionalities and lived experiences of Latinx youth coming of age in the United States, policy makers can develop more humane legislation to support youth and Latinx. Centering Latinx youth experiences and the diversity in their meaning-making about citizenship, legality, and rights is the guiding intention and motivation of this book. Yet despite this intention and these efforts to deconstruct and reconceptualize citizenship by describing Latinx youth perspectives on citizenship, legality, and rights, there are a few limitations worth noting.

Significant challenges to examining citizenship through the lens of young people arise precisely because there are protections and parameters set in place to safeguard them from possible conditions that could compromise their well-being and safety. Maintaining and upholding the safety of young people is of foremost importance and priority. In protecting young people from the possible negative consequences of research, Institutional Review Boards to an extent get to determine what and how research is done. Considering these conditions, I discuss some challenges and insights in relation to this work in order to invite scholars to engage in future research with Latinx youth on topics of citizenship, legality, and rights, as well as the development of sociopolitical citizenship.

The voices and experiences of thirteen Latinx youth in the context of the Change 4 Good afterschool program were featured in this book. Although this is a relatively small sample, given the unique location and characteristics of the setting, the outcomes and experiences of Latinx youth offer an in-depth and nuanced perspective of youth meaning-making about citizenship. As such, these experiences cannot be generalized to other contexts or groups of young people, yet important patterns can be observed, such as the importance of school, family, and community in shaping youth meanings of citizenship, legality, and rights. Furthermore, because this ethnography took place in the context of Change 4 Good and fieldnotes are limited to this specific setting, important insights can be gained about ways to support youth sociopolitical development in afterschool settings, youth-centered programs, or learning contexts beyond or outside the school or classroom setting. Latinx youth reflected on their school, family, and community experiences, and their reflections constitute part of the data, which are specific to the Change 4

Good program. The high-inference fieldnotes and interpretations based on observations and statements made by the youth in Change 4 Good, as presented and analyzed in this work, offer valuable insights. Where appropriate, these are presented and discussed as Latinx youth reflections on their lives. At other times, limited analyses of their statements were offered to center and amplify Latinx youth voices.

Ethnographic fieldwork took place during what most in the United States would consider the "post-racial" era. Color-blind characterizations such as these were marked by the consecutive presidential elections of Barack Obama in 2008 and 2012. Latinx youth came of age under the presidencies of Obama, which were characterized by less explicitly racialized anti-immigrant discourses and policies, which become significantly palpable under the Trump administration. Under the Obama administration, families were being separated, detained, and deported at a disproportionate rate. Racist nativism and other forms of discrimination, injustice, and inequity, then and now, mark the lives of many Latinx immigrant communities across the United States. Conditions of institutional marginalization impact the lives of young people in both direct and indirect ways. While there were certain visible differences between the Obama and Trump administrations, anti-immigration policies, economic precarity, racialized forms of violence, and political and social exclusions continue to significantly target Latinx youth and their families. Given these factors, an additional limitation is the inability to examine the social and political subjectivities of Latinx youth across time and in broader contexts. Despite these limitations, this work is significant and important because it provides an in-depth portrait of thirteen Latinx youth troubling, nuancing, and reimagining meanings of citizenship beyond a status, practice, and rights-bearing construct.

Latinx youth reflections offer us a critical understanding of the experiences of young people in a very specific and unique location: the Central Coast of California. In the public and popular media, this region is characterized by its diversity, inclusion, and economic thriving, as well as political liberalism, yet what was stated and shared by Latinx youth in Change 4 Good was not consistent with these narratives. Furthermore, it was not consonant with the very real fears and uncertainties that were experienced by Latinx immigrant communities in the surrounding regions where Latinx youth and their families resided. Immigration and

Customs Enforcement (ICE) raids have continued to take place time and time again over the past ten years in the area, especially Santa Cruz County.

The stories of Latinx youth growing up in immigrant working-class and low-income families are left untold or overshadowed by discourses that exclude them and their communities. Such experiences are further reinforced by the lip service of the promising California Golden State, where diverse, inclusive, and liberal politics reign. Yet Latinx youth in Change 4 Good shared how their families and communities struggled firsthand with racist nativism and intersecting forms of discrimination. Latinx youth offered stories of exclusion that reflected their experiences, as well as demands for rights, dignity, and respect. I humbly propose that the limitations described, which might be interpreted as compromising the potential generalizability, replicability, and impact of this research, should instead be considered as elements that make this work unique, significant, and of relevance and value to contemporary critical studies in youth development, education, citizenship, and immigration.

An important goal of this book is to call attention to the need for more research that centers the voices of Latinx youth. The counter-hegemonic stories Latinx youth produced in relation to their experiences and reflections in Change 4 Good challenged their silencing and invisibility. Latinx youth troubled discourses on the presumably declining civic engagement and political apathy among young people as well. For example, they engaged agency in pursuing and developing activities such as the creation of a school-based mural to tell their own story, and thus challenge the status quo maintained by the hegemonic discourses that were associated with them, their families, and their community. Latinx youth produced and engaged their reflections of the varied forms of resistance, agency, and collective action.

Sociopolitical citizenship describes Latinx youth social identities, critical consciousness, socioemotional awareness, and political engagement toward social change through the creation of a mural. The mural-making process, along with the focus groups, involved them thinking through US-based constructions of citizenship, legality, and rights that have excluded them and their communities. The lived experiences that informed the social and political subjectivities of Latinx youth constituted their embodiments and enactments as citizens with rights to wield. The stories, reflections, and experiences offered by Latinx youth strive to demonstrate that Latinx youth raised and immersed in US society and its institutions can and do embody and enact citizenship in unique and meaningful ways. *Growing Up Latinx* affirms Latinx youth agency, participation, and belonging in contexts, like school, where they are treated as second-class citizens.

Summary

In part 1 of the book I featured Latinx youth efforts at making meaning of citizenship, while part 2 centered on illustrating their sociopolitical citizenship along four domains, as well as their understandings of rights. Chapter 1 described Latinx youth meaning-making about citizenship, including its associations with legality, particularly how these are constructed through the possession of documents, or *papeles*, as well as the right to vote. One key theme involved Latinx youth constructions of citizenship as a status, which surfaced in relation to reflections on belonging, birthright, and naturalized citizenship, as well as immigrant experiences. Expanding upon these claims, chapters 2 and 3 focused on describing Latinx youth views on citizenship as a practice and a right, such as equating voting and law-abidingness with citizenship and legality. Given that youth are under the US voting age, I described Latinx youth reflections on what it means to practice citizenship in the context of schooling. Latinx youth understandings of citizenship, which they equated with being a "good" student, reified the structures of power, especially the hidden curriculum, as well as disciplinary norms in the classroom. Being perceived as a "good" student held implications for them in the classroom and their presumed development as future "good" citizens. The hidden curriculum and Character Education were discussed as examples of schooling practices instituted and purported to consequently shape Latinx youth citizenship. These curricula and schooling practices, however, offered youth limited opportunities to exercise agency.

Part 2 of the book focused on Latinx youth claims to citizenship as related to the development of their social and political subjectivities, including their rights. Chapter 4 expanded upon the critical perspectives presented in part 1 to offer a standpoint for understanding Latinx youth agency via what I conceptualized as sociopolitical citizenship. Latinx youth reflected upon their positionalities to make sense of how age, race, ethnicity, and immigrant status seeped through their lived experiences, most notably their meanings of citizenship, legality, and rights. In chapter 5, Latinx youth rights were questioned, specifically as these were presented in relation to the United Nations Convention on the Rights of the Child (UN-CRC). Troubling these constructions, I discussed how Latinx youth conceptualized their rights beyond US-based and UN-CRC definitions of citizenship specific to young people. While these statutes aim to protect and uphold the rights and well-being of youth, nurturance rights and self-determination rights pose significant limitations to youth agency and collective action. Thus, Latinx youth challenged the individualized construction of rights and how the United States' disavowal of the UN-CRC structures discourses, social contexts, and youth-adult relationships in rather limiting ways. In turn, these experiences inform Latinx youth understandings of their rights and perceptions of themselves as agents of change. These understandings also emphasize the necessity to expand the meaning of rights to include the social, communal, and collective responsibilities for care and solidarity with others, as Latinx youth described.

Gathering from the evidence provided in parts 1 and 2, I offer some closing reflections. First, Latinx youth meaning-making troubled US-based constructions of citizenship, legality, and rights—Latinx youth embodiments and enactments as citizens reflected their social and political subjectivities. Second, sociopolitical citizenship is a standpoint for describing Latinx youth agency, participation in decision making, and belonging. Additionally, it informs how some youth made claims to rights that underscored the pluriversality of citizenship. Third, reflections on the meanings of citizenship and rights, as offered by Latinx youth, nuanced contemporary theorizing and empirical views on Latinx youth development. At times, Latinx youth social and political subjectivities emerged precisely in the context of the Change 4 Good program's activities. At other times, these unfolded in their school, family, and community contexts. Fourth, deficit views on Latinx youth development are challenged by their reflections of their experiences, as well as the activities and opportunities facilitated through Change 4 Good, which rendered visible their agency. Latinx youth as sociopolitical citizens at times reproduced, yet most often challenged, hegemonic discourses associated with US-based constructions of citizenship, legality, and rights.

In *Growing Up Latinx*, dynamic perspectives on youth studies, Latinx identities, and varied forms of citizenship were brought together to present a nuanced analysis of Latinx youth sociopolitical development. Latinx youth meaning-making about citizenship, legality, and rights was informed by the intersections of their age, race, ethnicity, and immigrant status. In general, how Latinx youth experience citizenship in their lives, including school, family, and community contexts, remains absent from scholarly and public discourses, as well as sociocultural theories on youth development. As scholars and educators, as well as youth advocates and allies, we must emphasize and render visible Latinx youth agency. We can do so by cultivating opportunities that uplift Latinx youth voices and acts of everyday citizenship within and outside the context of schooling. We must also expand the literatures on critical youth and Latinx studies, as well as youth development, to make space for their experiences. Latinx youth sociopolitical citizenship—as embodied in their school, family, and community contexts—constitutes an important intervention across multiple disciplines and fields of study focused on youth of Latinx descent.

By threading together Latinx youth experiences with a range of literatures, I have shown how Latinx youth questioned US-based constructions of citizenship through the centering of their experiences as both youth and Latinx. Furthermore, Latinx youth meaning-making about citizenship, legality, and rights was grounded in their social and political subjectivities, which reflected their lived experiences and those of their families. At times, Latinx youth meaning-making about citizenship echoed hegemonic discourses. Yet, when cultivated in their social identities, critical consciousness, socioemotional awareness, and political engagement, they articulated and embodied new meanings of citizenship—meanings that revealed a more capacious notion of citizenship that sought to trouble the status quo of *who is* and *what it means to be* a citizen. Constructions of citizenship that intersect with perspectives of youthhood that rendered them second-class or future citizens, or noncitizens in the present, must be challenged and resisted. Latinx youth coming of age in the United States in a time of contested citizenship troubled the hegemonic discourses on citizenship, legality, and rights in their lives through their capacity to engage agency as sociopolitical citizens. Recognizing Latinx youth as citizens is possible when we as adults garner the will to listen to young people, and when we commit to supporting and cultivating the power of youth.

ACKNOWLEDGMENTS

Growing Up Latinx was shepherded by the support, resources, and encouragement of many people: mentors who became colleagues, colleagues who are now friends, and friends who are like family—a family that has accompanied me along my academic journey from the PhD to the tenure-track. This work has been blessed by their *ánimo, consejos, y fe* (encouragement, advice, and faith) in my efforts to make this book a reality. Thank you.

I thank the New York University Press editorial team, especially Ilene Kalish, who saw potential and a vision for my book early on. Thanks to Sonia Tsuruoka for her transparency, advocacy, and assistance along the book development process. I am grateful and appreciative of the anonymous reviewers and writing mentors, Dra. Aurora Chang and Jordan Beltran Gonzales (Academic Mechanic), for providing their critical insights, feedback, and comments on earlier and developing manuscript drafts. The creation of this book could not have been possible without their guidance and stewardship.

Many mentors supported me through my scholarly projects, and eventually this book, beginning in undergraduate studies, and then the social psychology graduate program at the University of California, Santa Cruz. Campbell Leaper, the first to offer me a research assistantship as an undergraduate student, and Regina (Gina) D. Langhout, my PhD advisor and mentor, both supported my research interests and dissertation. Gina's mentoring helped me cultivate a community-social psychology practice that is fundamental to my formation as a community-engaged researcher. I am indebted to Gina for her guidance and belief in my academic pursuits. I hold much gratitude as well for the Community Psychology Research and Action Team (CPRAT), where many of my research ideas and interests were developed, challenged, and valued. At the time of this work, members of CPRAT included Gina, Danielle Kohfeldt, Sarah Grace, Erin Ellison, Bob Majzler, Angela

Nguyen, and David Gordon. Thanks to Danielle, David, and Angela, and the student researchers, especially Diana Yip and Alex Bowen, in the Change 4 Good afterschool program who helped support Latinx youth empowerment, critical literacy development, and leadership, some of which is featured in this work. Thanks to artist "Shile" Cifuentes for her commitment to Change 4 Good, especially her help throughout the mural-making process. Through these shared experiences, I formed a meaningful bond with Angela, whose friendship and validation helped me get through the PhD and the writing of this book.

Thank you to the Maplewood Elementary School students and their families, who welcomed me into their lives, homes, and celebrations. I am grateful as well to the teachers and administrators at Maplewood Elementary who were present over the course of my fieldwork. I also thank the Maplewood communities that welcomed me into their neighborhood and social activities.

To my mentors affiliated with the Latin American and Latinx Studies Department at UC Santa Cruz, Sylvanna M. Falcón, Patricia Zavella, Adrián Félix (now at UC Riverside), Jonathan Fox (now at American University), and Cindy Cruz (now at University of Arizona)—thank you! I am especially beholden to Jessica Taft, whose unwavering support during the PhD and over the years has helped this book project materialize. Jessica edited a special issue in a journal that featured my first publication. Now, a decade later, I come full circle, publishing my first book thanks to Jessica's guidance.

I am grateful as well for the UC Santa Cruz Women of Color Writing Cluster and the Dissertating Latinidades Collective for holding space *en comunidad* (in community) to reflect, share, and heal our wounds while navigating academia. Thanks to my *compañeras* (comrades) Elizabeth Gonzalez, Graciela Solís, Lucia Alcala, and Xóchitl C. Chávez—together, we shared company while dissertating and creating *sabiduría* (knowledge, wisdom).

Several friends and colleagues encouraged the development of this book project, from holding space for conversations, reflections, and frustrations, to offering feedback on working ideas, book proposals, and chapter drafts, to the minutiae of references and formatting challenges. I name those whose words and actions have been foundational to getting me to this moment. Without them, I could not have mended my relationship to writing—a healing process of writing in practice that has allowed me to craft this book word by word. Thanks to Kara Hisatake, Janelle Silva, Urmitapa Dutta, Deanne Bell, Bianca L. Guzmán, Ireri Bernal, Yvette G. Flores, and Christopher Sonn for their friendship, accompaniment, and support. Kara was the first to read through my book proposal, including several drafts. Because of her generous feedback and guidance, the book proposal unfolded into something worthy of dissemination to publishers.

To the International Youth Organizing Study team, Roderick J. Watts, Ben Kirshner, and Rashida Govan, thank you for supporting my work and interests in graduate school and embracing me as an equal contributor on the research team. By welcoming me as a research associate and collaborator, they allowed me to develop confidence in my ideas, writing, and research praxis. Ben's encouragement and generous resourcefulness throughout the book development process helped move this project forward.

At Santa Clara University, where I am currently an Assistant Professor in the Ethnic Studies Department, I feel grounded and supported as a teacher-scholar due to the care, encouragement, and resourceful guidance of the Ethnic Studies *familia* (family). I am thankful to Anna Sampaio, James Lai, Anthony Q. Hazard Jr., Allia I. Griffin, and Pauline Nguyen, as well as our students—Alejandra Magaña Gamero, Jennifer Gonzalez, Isaac D'Amore Nieblas, Areli Hernández, Kimberly Fernández-Pedraza, Rhyann Robinson, Alma Orozco, Chloe Gentile-Montgomery, Meghan Adams, Andrea Peña, Daisy Luna, Khiely Jackson, Sydney Thompson, and so many others who are now alumni. As a department, they welcomed me initially as a lecturer, then a postdoctoral fellow, and now a faculty member. I am profoundly grateful for the department's unwavering encouragement and validation of my research, and development as a teacher-scholar. Similarly, I appreciate the support from the College of Arts and Sciences (CAS), as well as the Provost's Office, which provided a Summer Faculty Research Grant to help me make progress on the book project.

Many other admirable and kindhearted SCU members have also embraced me and supported my work. Among them are Provost Lisa Kloppenberg, CAS Dean Daniel Press, Senior Assistant Dean Kathleen Schneider, and dear colleagues Laura Nichols, Sharmila Lodhia, Eileen

Elrod, Linda Garber, Brett Solomon, Claudia Rodriguez-Mojica, Alma Garcia, Francisco Jiménez, Marco Bravo, Erick Ramirez, Chad Raphael, Irene Cermeño, Ray Plaza, Danielle Aguilar, Jennifer Merritt, Erin Kimura-Walsh, Gail Gradowski, Lorenzo Gamboa, Josue R. Fuentes, and Karen Hernandez. The Culture, Power, Difference (CPD) Working Group, established by Christina Zanfagna, Courtney Mohler (now at Butler University), and Anthony Q. Hazard Jr., and joined by colleagues Allia I. Griffin, Danielle Fuentes Morgan, Cruz Medina, and Mythri Jegathesan, provided a critical space for ideas and works-in-progress to flourish. With enthusiasm and promise of sustained grounding toward my academic thriving, I look forward to deepening my roots at Santa Clara University.

I am thankful to Dr. Teresa Lively for her accompaniment, compassion, and guidance toward self-kindness and healing. And to the Breathe Together and Santa Cruz Yoga communities, which offered a refuge for reflection, renewal, and restorative well-being.

The connections, friendships, and communities I formed over the years carried this book project forward, to the same extent as the family blessings, encouragements, and inquiries that followed some version of the question "¿Cómo vas con el libro?" (How is the book coming along?). *Mil gracias* (many thanks) to my families in Huandacareo (Michoacán, México), Chicago (IL, USA), and Esfahan (Iran) for their support and understanding, and for forgiving my absences at family gatherings and celebrations. *Mi más profundo agradecimiento a mis padres, Yolanda y Rogelio Fernández, por sus sacrificios y oraciones, y por brindarme oportunidades para sobresalir y poner en practica los valores que me inculcaron—de vivir con humildad y dignidad, y servir con voluntad y compromiso.* I thank my brothers, Rogelio Jr. and Saúl, my sister-in-law, Emily, and *sobrinxs*—Sofía, Thalía, and Julián—for giving me joy with their *travesuras*. They will grow up Latinx in the United States, and I look forward to bearing witness to their story.

Lastly, but of no less importance, I am grateful to Hossein, for reminding me to breathe and be mindful, for helping me strike a rhythm of harmony between my personal and professional endeavors, and for uplifting me in my falls, grounding me in moments of uncertainty, and affirming for me the bigger picture when I lose sight of it. May we continue to embrace our ways of loving, learning, and growing in mutual acceptance, compassion, and well-being.

APPENDIX

TABLE A.1. Demographics of Latinx Youth in Change 4 Good Afterschool Program

Youth Name	Age	Gender Expression	Ethnoracial Identification	Country of Birth	Family Status
Andrés	9	Boy	Mexican, American	United States	Mixed-status
Joaquín	11	Boy	Mexican, American	México	Mixed-status
Celine	10	Girl	Salvadorean, American	United States	Non-mixed-status
Daniela	10	Girl	Mexican, American	United States	Mixed-status
David	10	Boy	Salvadorean, American	El Salvador	Mixed-status
Diego	10	Boy	Mexican, American	United States	Mixed-status
Feliz	10	Boy	Mexican, American	United States	Mixed-status
Iris	10	Girl	Mexican, American	United States	Mixed-status
Jackie	10	Girl	Mexican, American	United States	Mixed-status
Lina	10	Girl	Mexican, American	United States	Mixed-status
Lucia	10	Girl	Mexican, American	United States	Non-mixed-status
Santiago	9	Boy	Mexican, African American	United States	Non-mixed-status
Yesenia	11	Girl	Guatemalan, American	Guatemala	Mixed-status

NOTES

PREFACE

1 Consistent with the complexities of the terms "youth" and "child" is the use of the *x* in "Latinx." Although the limitations and critiques of the use of "Latinx" to describe Latinas and Latinos are warranted, throughout this book I am intentional in my use of the *x* to denote gender expansiveness, thereby making the term more inclusive of differing gender identities that may not fall along the female and male binaries that are prevalent in gendered languages like Spanish. According to some Latinx scholars, such as Catalina M. de Onís, "Latinx" is a gender-expansive term to refer to people of Latin American descent who do not conform to linguistic gender binaries associated with the terms "Latino" or "Latina/o." Afro-Indigenous poet Alan Pelaez Lopez writes that the *x* in "Latinx" "is a wound as opposed to a trend that speaks to the collective history. The 'X' is attempting to speak to the violence of colonization, slavery, against women and femmes, and the fact that many of us experience such an intense displacement and silence that we have no language in which to articulate who we are." Pelaez Lopez, "X in Latinx."

2 "Mixed-status family" is a term used to characterize families with members of varying legal status. Often it is used to describe families with citizen and noncitizen parents and children who are foreign-born. A common situation is one where at least one parent is a noncitizen, either undocumented, legal permanent resident, or some other status, and the children are citizens by virtue of being born in the United States.

3 Ageism is a form of discrimination and oppression that operates to systematically and systemically maintain hierarchies of adult power over young people. This arrangement of power functions to reproduce and legitimate the social, cultural, and institutional marginalization as well as disenfranchisement of young people in society. In most industrialized Western-centric societies, this is particularly the case. See Gordon, "Allies Within and Without"; and Taft and Gordon, "Youth Activists, Youth Councils."

4 See Pérez Huber et al., "Getting beyond the 'Symptom'"; and Pérez Huber, "Using Latina/o Critical Race Theory." According to education scholar Lindsay Pérez Huber, racist nativism is defined as "the assigning of values to real or imagined differences in order to justify the superiority of the native, who is perceived to be white, over that of the non-native, who is perceived to be people and immigrants

of color, and thereby defend the native's right to dominance" (Pérez Huber, "Using Latina/o Critical Race Theory," 81). Racist nativism is a conceptual frame that helps researchers understand how "the historical racialization of immigrants of color has shaped the contemporary experiences of Latinx undocumented immigrants" (79).
5 González Rey, "Affectivity"; González Rey, "Subjetividad."
6 Schmidt Camacho, *Migrant Imaginaries*.
7 Hegemony is characterized by the ideologies, practices, and structures that reinforce the imposition of forms of power, domination, influence, or control over others, such that it structures, in systematic and iterative ways, the social organization and worldview or perspectives of people and societies, such that they come to see themselves and their hierarchical organizations as normal, static, and unchangeable.

INTRODUCTION

1 Fieldnote, November 11, 2012.
2 In using the phrasing "immigrant status," I am referring to the experience of immigration, as well as the sociolegal, documented, or undocumented status of a person.
3 Vink, "Comparing Citizenship Regimes," 221.
4 "Transmigrant" is a term used to describe an immigrant person whose daily experiences depend on multiple and constant interconnections across international borders, and whose social and cultural identities are configured in relationship to more than one nation-state. See Basch, Schiller, and Szanton Blanc, *Nations Unbound*; and Schiller, Basch, and Szanton Blanc, "Transnationalism." Transnational migration is the process by which immigrants forge and sustain simultaneous multi-stranded social as well as cultural, political, and economic relations that link together their countries of origin with their place(s) of settlement (Basch, Schiller, and Szanton Blanc, *Nations Unbound*, 6).
5 Estrada, *Kids at Work*; Gonzales, *Lives in Limbo*.
6 Migration studies scholar Nicholas De Genova writes that "migrant 'illegality' is lived through a palpable sense of deportability, which is to say, the possibility of deportation, the possibility of being removed from the space of the nation-state." Thus, deportability is the positioning of undocumented immigrants as trespassers who, at the will of the nation-state, are likely to be removed and deported; the condition of living under this fear and threat, however, has implications for the lived realities of immigrant communities. De Genova, "Migrant 'Illegality.'" See also Abrego, *Sacrificing Families*; and Dreby, "Burden of Deportation."
7 Flores, Lopez, and Krogstad, "US Hispanic Population."
8 Patten, "Nation's Latino Population."
9 Schink and Hayes-Bautista, "Latino Gross Domestic Product."
10 Manning, "Membership of the 116th Congress."
11 NALEO Educational Fund, "Policymakers"; Krogstad, "Key Facts."

12 Introduced by sociologist Felix Padilla, the term *Latinidad* is a theoretical concept used to describe the pan-ethnic identity, sociocultural expressions, traditions, and customs, as well as political repertories of communities of Latin American descent in the United States. *Latinidad* is characterized by the specific geographic and political experiences of Latin American origin communities in the United States. Yet, as a social construct, *Latinidad* also references the complexities of immigration, colonialism, racism, colorism, nationality, language, and the politics of identity and belonging. See Aparicio, "(Re)constructing Latinidad"; Caminero-Santangelo, *On Latinidad*; and Padilla, *Latino Ethnic Consciousness*.
13 Political scholar Iris Young posits that whatever the legal citizenship status of Latinx, and regardless of their generational presence and contributions to US society, Latinx as members of an ethnic minority are likely to be seen and treated as "other," and therefore as foreigners. Building on this argument, Raymond Rocco, a Latinx studies political scientist, suggests that Latinx are likely treated as non-members of society, as not belonging to their communities in the fullest sense; thus Latinx "are uniquely positioned as permanently foreign immigrants in the imagination of Anglo Americans." Rocco, "Transforming Citizenship," 9. See Young, *Inclusion and Democracy*.
14 Human Rights Watch, "US/California."
15 Kohli, Markowitz, and Chavez, "Secure Communities."
16 Juárez, Gómez-Aguiñaga, and Bettez, "Twenty Years after IIRIRA."
17 Taylor et al., "Unauthorized Immigrants."
18 Del Mar Farina, *White Nativism*.
19 Zayas, *Forgotten Citizens*.
20 Gulbas and Zayas, "Children of Undocumented Immigrants."
21 Brabeck and Xu, "Impact of Detention"; Dreby, "Burden of Deportation."
22 Isin and Wood, *Citizenship and Identity*; Lister, "Inclusive Citizenship."
23 Young, "Polity and Group Difference."
24 Field, *Struggle for Equal Adulthood*.
25 Pérez Huber, "Using Latina/o Critical Race Theory."
26 Almaguer, "Race, Racialization, and Latino Populations"; Menchaca, "Latinas/os and the Mestizo Racial Heritage"; Molina, *How Race Is Made*.
27 According to Raymond Rocco, exclusionary inclusion describes the pattern of differential incorporation, belonging, and inclusion of minority social groups in the nation-state, thereby shaping patterns of membership and belonging. Rocco, "Transforming Citizenship."
28 Building on the work of Latin American and Latinx studies scholar Suzanne Oboler, education scholar Genevieve Negrón-Gonzales asserts that the term "tolerated illegality" describes the idea that "undocumented workers are welcome as long as they are compliant and fulfill their role as subjugated workers who are neither seen nor heard." Indeed, the experience of tolerated illegality structures the lives, contexts, and opportunities of undocumented communities, subjecting them to a

disenfranchised, marginalized status. Negrón-Gonzales, "Undocumented Youth Activism."
29 Rocco, "Transforming Citizenship."
30 Molina, *How Race Is Made.*
31 Oboler, *Latinos and Citizenship*; Rocco, "Transforming Citizenship"; Rocco, *Transforming Citizenship.*
32 Lister, "Investing in the Citizen-Workers"; Lockyer, "Education for Citizenship"; Invernizzi and Williams, *Children and Citizenship.*
33 Cox, "Scholarship and Activism"; Field, *Struggle for Equal Adulthood.*
34 Cohen, "Neither Seen nor Heard"; Moosa-Mitha, "Difference-Centred Alternative."
35 Gutiérrez and Rogoff, "Cultural Ways of Learning"; Orellana, "Work Kids Do"; Ramírez Sánchez, "'Helping at Home.'"
36 Estrada, *Kids at Work*; Invernizzi and Williams, *Children and Citizenship*; Taft, *Kids Are in Charge.*
37 Corona Caraveo and Pérez-Zavala, "Participación infantil"; Pallares, *Family Activism*; Taft, *Rebel Girls.*
38 Lister, "Why Citizenship."
39 Lister, "Why Citizenship"; Mayall, "Sociology of Childhood"; Moosa-Mitha, "Difference-Centered Alternative"; Smith at al., "Young People as Real Citizens."
40 Invernizzi and Williams, *Children and Citizenship*; Jans, "Children as Citizens."
41 See UNICEF, "Convention on the Rights of the Child." The United Nations Convention on the Rights of the Child (UN-CRC) is a human rights treaty that outlines the social, cultural, political, economic, and health rights of children, or young people under the age of eighteen. The treaty is upheld by several industrialized and developing nations, as well as nations tied to the United Nations' affairs. Underscoring its commitment to serving and protecting children, the UN-CRC states that "childhood is separate from adulthood, and lasts until 18; it is a special, protected time, in which children must be allowed to grow, learn, play, develop and flourish with dignity." Although highly praised for its commitment to the care and well-being of young people, the treaty has been met with strong critiques that underscore the document's neocolonial views on youthhood and family structures.
42 Ruck, Abramovitch, and Keating, "Children's and Adolescents' Understanding"; Mayall, "Sociology of Childhood"; Mayall, *Towards a Sociology for Childhood.*
43 Cammarota and Romero, "Critically Compassionate Intellectualism"; Noguera, "Latino Youth."
44 The term "status quo" is used to describe or refer to the existing state of affairs, or the ways things exist, are organized, and are structured as they are. It is the way things are now, or have been set and maintained by those in positions of power and influence to determine and organize the institutions, norms, and cultural practices of a given society or social context.
45 The word "sociohistorical" describes the ways social and historical factors or perspectives operate to inform people's subjective understandings of their experiences in the present. This also includes a social and historical understanding of

the past to explain and make sense of present circumstances and existing structures, and thus how these organize their lives.
46 See Crenshaw, "Demarginalizing the Intersection"; Crenshaw, "Mapping the Margins"; and Nash, "Re-thinking Intersectionality." Coined by legal scholar Kimberlé Crenshaw, the term "intersectionality" underscores the "multidimensionality" of marginalized subjects' lived experiences ("Demarginalizing the Intersection," 139). The study of intersectionality emerged in the late 1980s and early 1990s from critical race studies, a scholarly movement born in the legal academy committed to problematizing the law's purported color-blindness, neutrality, and objectivity. From its inception, intersectionality has focused on a specific intersection: race and gender. Intersectionality rejects the "single-axis framework" often embraced by feminist and anti-racist scholars, and instead focuses on "the various ways in which race and gender interact to shape the multiple dimensions of Black women's . . . experiences" (Crenshaw "Mapping the Margins," 1244, as cited in Nash, "Re-thinking Intersectionality," 2). Intersectionality serves as a theoretical, methodological, and political framework to describe the interconnections of oppression, inequity, and injustice often invisibilized by one-dimensional paradigms.
47 Watts at al., "Powerful Youth."
48 Watts, Griffith, and Abdul-Adil, "Sociopolitical Development"; Watts, Williams, and Jagers, "Sociopolitical Development."
49 Hope and Jagers, "Role of Sociopolitical Attitudes"; Watts, Williams, and Jagers, "Sociopolitical Development."
50 Wong, Zimmerman, and Parker, "Typology of Youth Participation."
51 Delgado and Staples, "Youth-Led Organizing."
52 Diemer, "Pathways to Occupational Attainment."
53 Ginwright, Noguera, and Cammarota, *Beyond Resistance!*
54 Ginwright and Cammarota, "New Terrain"; Watts et al., "Powerful Youth."
55 Christens and Dolan, "Interweaving Youth Development"; Diemer, "Pathways to Occupational Attainment."
56 Fox et al., "Critical Youth Engagement"; Kirshner, Hipolito-Delgado, and Zion, "Sociopolitical Development"; Kornbluh et al., "Youth Participatory Action Research"; Watts and Hipolito-Delgado, "Thinking Ourselves to Liberation?"
57 Fernández and Langhout, "Living on the Margins"; Langhout et al., "Photovoice and House Meetings."
58 Fernández and Langhout, "Community with Diversity."
59 Abrego, *Sacrificing Families*; Fox and Rivera-Salgado, *Indigenous Mexican Migrants*, 171–201.
60 Fernández and Langhout, "Living on the Margins."
61 Freedberg, "Despite Progress."
62 Research/scholarship featuring the Change 4 Good afterschool program: Kohfeldt et al., "Youth Empowerment"; Kohfeldt and Langhout, "Five Whys Method"; Langhout, Kohfeldt, and Ellison, "How We Became the Schmams"; Kohfeldt,

Bowen, and Langhout, "'They Think Kids Are Stupid'"; Kohfeldt, "Children as Activist Artists"; Dutt and Kohfeldt, "Towards a Liberatory Ethics of Care"; Fernández, Nguyen, and Langhout, "'It's a Puzzle!'"; Fernández, "Latina/o Youth Cultural Citizenship."
63. Langhout and Thomas, "Imagining Participatory Action Research."
64. Cammarota and Fine, *Revolutionizing Education*; Clark, "Young Children as Protagonists"; Fox et al., "Critical Youth Engagement"; Jacquez, Vaughn, and Wagner, "Youth as Partners."
65. Kornbluh et al., "Youth Participatory Action Research."
66. Foster-Fishman et al., "Youth ReACT."
67. Kornbluh et al., "Youth Participatory Action Research."
68. Chen, Weiss, and Nicholson, "Girls Study Girls Inc."
69. Foster-Fishman et al., "Youth ReACT."
70. Clark, "Young Children as Protagonists."
71. Fine, "Postcards from Metro America," 2.
72. Yosso, *Critical Race Counterstories*.
73. The term "sociolegal" is used to refer to the interdisciplinary analysis of the ways legal phenomena, or the law, inform and are informed by society and social dynamics.
74. Prieto, "Conciencia con compromiso."
75. According to John Bell, "The word adultism refers to behaviors and attitudes based on the assumption that adults are better than young people, and entitled to act upon young people without their agreement. This mistreatment is reinforced by social institutions, laws, customs, and attitudes. . . . The essence of adultism is disrespect of the young. . . . The identification of adultism is further complicated by differing cultural, ethnic, gender, class, or religious approaches to these developmental stages. The concept of adultism, the systematic mistreatment and disrespect of young people, is relatively new and has not been widely accepted." Bell, "Understanding Adultism."
76. Invernizzi and Williams, *Children and Citizenship*.
77. James and Prout, "New Paradigm."

PART 1. MAKING MEANING OF CITIZENSHIP

1. Yuval-Davis, "Women, Citizenship and Difference"; Yuval-Davis, "Some Reflections"; Lister, "Why Citizenship"; Lister, "Unpacking Children's Citizenship"; Lister et al., "Young People Talk about Citizenship"; Smith et al., "Young People as Real Citizens."
2. Hall and Held, "Citizens and Citizenship"; Isin and Wood, *Citizenship and Identity*; Isin and Turner, "Investigating Citizenship."
3. Cockburn, "Children and the Feminist Ethic"; Moosa-Mitha, "Difference-Centered Alternative."
4. Jans, "Children as Citizens"; Lister, "Inclusive Citizenship"; Roche, "Children."
5. Fieldnote, March 8, 2012.

6 According to American historian Mae Ngai, the alien citizen is a construct to describe the sociolegal and racial formation of Asian and Latinx groups in the United States. Thus, an alien citizen is an "American citizen by virtue of her birth in the United States but whose citizenship is suspect, if not denied, on account of the racialized identity of her immigrant ancestry. In this construction, the foreignness of non-European peoples is deemed unalterable, making nationality a kind of racial trait." Ngai, "Birthright Citizenship."
7 Kosher and Ben-Arieh, "What Children Think"; Lister et al., "Young People Talk about Citizenship"; Ruck and Horn, *Young People's Perspectives*; Ruck, Peterson-Badali, and Helwig, "Children's Perspectives."
8 Marshall, "Citizenship and Social Class."
9 Ramakrishnan and Bloemraad, *Civic Hopes*; Delanty, "Citizenship as a Learning Process"; Isin and Turner, *Handbook of Citizenship Studies*; Yuval-Davis, "Belonging."
10 Isin and Wood, *Citizenship and Identity*; Lister, "Why Citizenship."

CHAPTER 1. LEGALITY AS HAVING *PAPELES*
1 Mayall, "Sociology of Childhood."
2 Menjívar and Kanstroom, *Constructing Immigrant "Illegality"*; Zayas, *Forgotten Citizens*.
3 Hoppock, "Operation Janus"; Taxin, "US Launches Bid."
4 De Genova, "Migrant 'Illegality.'"
5 Flores-González, *Citizens but Not Americans*.
6 Chavez, *Latino Threat*; Rocco, "Transforming Citizenship."
7 Menjívar and Kanstroom, *Constructing Immigrant "Illegality."*
8 Dreby, *Everyday Illegal*.
9 Mathema, "Keeping Families Together."
10 Capps, Fix, and Zong, *Profile of US Children*.
11 Dreby, *Everyday Illegal*; Romero, *Living Together*; Zayas, *Forgotten Citizens*.
12 Fieldnote, July 28, 2010.
13 Theriault, "More Than 1,100 Arrested."
14 Squire, *Contested Politics*.
15 Menjívar and Kanstroom, *Constructing Immigrant "Illegality."*
16 Zayas, *Forgotten Citizens*.
17 Fieldnote, April 26, 2012.
18 American Immigration Council, "US Citizen Children."
19 Lind, "Trump Administration's Separation."
20 Heidbrink, *Migrant Youth*; Zayas, *Forgotten Citizens*.
21 Fieldnote, November 10, 2011.
22 Heidbrink, *Migrant Youth*.
23 Berger Cardoso et al., "Integration of Unaccompanied Migrant Youth."
24 Abrego, *Sacrificing Families*; Heidbrink, *Migrant Youth*.
25 Heidbrink, *Migrant Youth*; Zayas, *Forgotten Citizens*.

26 Gonzales, *Lives in Limbo*; Suárez-Orozco and Suárez-Orozco, *Children of Immigration*.
27 Del Mar Farina, *White Nativism*.
28 Bloemraad, *Becoming a Citizen*; De Genova, "Migrant 'Illegality'"; Félix, *Specters of Belonging*.
29 De Genova, "Migrant 'Illegality'"; De Genova, *Working the Boundaries*.
30 Menjívar and Kanstroom, *Constructing Immigrant "Illegality"*; Nyers, "Migrant Citizenships"; Sassen, "Incompleteness."
31 De Genova, *Working the Boundaries*; Sampaio, *Terrorizing Latina/o Immigrants*.
32 Passel and Lopez, "Up to 1.7 Million Unauthorized Immigrant Youth."
33 Gonzales, *Lives in Limbo*.
34 Valdivia and Valdivia, "My Un(DACA)mented Life."
35 Delanty, *Citizenship in a Global Age*.
36 Lister, "Why Citizenship."
37 Lister, "Investing in the Citizen-Workers."
38 Cohen, "Neither Seen nor Heard"; Estrada, *Kids at Work*; Jans, "Children as Citizens"; Roche, "Children"; Taft, *Kids Are in Charge*.
39 Abrego, *Sacrificing Families*; Heidbrink, *Migrant Youth*.
40 Estrada, *Kids at Work*.
41 Fieldnote, July 27, 2011.

CHAPTER 2. SOCIALIZING FUTURE CITIZENS

1 Bloemraad, Korteweg, and Yurdakul, "Citizenship and Immigration"; Yuval-Davis, "Belonging."
2 Aronowitz and Giroux, *Education Still under Siege*; Gramsci, *Gramsci Reader*.
3 Gatto, *Dumbing Us Down*; Giroux and Penna, "Social Education"; Giroux, "Education and the Crisis of Youth"; Jay, "Critical Race Theory."
4 Suad Nasir and Kirshner, "Cultural Construction"; Delpit and Dowdy, *Skin That We Speak*; Westheimer and Kahne, "Educating the 'Good' Citizen."
5 Arce, "Latino Bilingual Teachers"; Darder and Torres, *Latinos and Education*; Giroux and Penna, "Social Education"; hooks, *Teaching to Transgress*; Delpit, *Other People's Children*.
6 De Lissovoy, "Education and Violation."
7 Monroe, "Why Are 'Bad Boys' Always Black?"; Skiba, Michael, et al., "Color of Discipline."
8 Langhout and Mitchell, "Engaging Contexts."
9 Rios, *Punished*; Skiba, Horner, et al., "Race Is Not Neutral."
10 Fieldnote, March 15, 2012. Rosa and Ruth are not the real names of the adults being discussed. I have changed their names to protect their privacy.
11 Fieldnote, July 2, 2012.
12 Langhout, "Acts of Resistance"; Thornberg, "Moral Construction of the Good Pupil."
13 Langhout and Mitchell, "Engaging Contexts."

14 Brooks and Goble, *Case for Character Education*; Revell, "Religious Education"; Rowe, "Taking Responsibility."
15 Lickona, "Eleven Principles."
16 Noddings, *Educating Moral People*; Price, review of *Educating Moral People*.
17 Robinson-Lee, "Framework for Understanding Character Education."
18 Kohn, "How Not to Teach Values"; Revell and Arthur, "Character Education."
19 Revell, "Religious Education."
20 Chang, *Struggles of Identity*; Flores-González, *Citizens but Not Americans*; Getrich, *Border Brokers*.
21 Bloemraad, Sarabia, and Fillingim, "'Staying Out of Trouble'"; Estrada, *Kids at Work*; France, "'Why Should We Care?'"; Terriquez and Kwon, "Intergenerational Family Relations"; Westheimer and Kahne, "What Kind of Citizen?"; Sherrod, Flanagan, and Youniss, "Dimensions of Citizenship."
22 Fieldnote, July 7, 2011.
23 Aronowitz and Giroux, *Education Still under Siege*; Giroux and McLaren, "Introduction."
24 Langhout and Mitchell, "Engaging Contexts"; Thornberg, "Moral Construction."
25 Chang, *Struggles of Identity*; Flores-González, *Citizens but Not Americans*; Noguera, "Latino Youth"; Orellana, *Translating Childhoods*.
26 Sandoval, *Methodology of the Oppressed*.
27 Fieldnote, April 19, 2012.
28 Levine, *Future of Democracy*.
29 Fieldnote, March 15, 2012.
30 Fieldnote, March 1, 2012.
31 Morris, *Pushout*.
32 Fieldnote, March 3, 2011.
33 Dewey, *School and Society*; Haupt, "School as a Microcosm"; Nollet, "Schools as Microcosms."

CHAPTER 3. RIGHTS AS A PRIVILEGE
1 Qvortrup, Corsaro, and Honig, "Why Social Studies"; Ruck et al., "Development of Children's Knowledge."
2 Lee, "Child's Voice"; Levesque, "Internationalization of Children's Human Rights."
3 Ruck, Abramovitch, and Keating, "Children's and Adolescents' Understanding"; Ruck et al., "Development of Children's Knowledge."
4 Arches and Fleming, "Young People and Social Action"; Munro et al., "Contribution of the United Nations Convention"; Smith, "Children and Young People's Participation."
5 Fieldnote, May 12, 2011.
6 Neoliberalism is an ideology with implications for social, political, and economic structuring that prioritizes the value of free market competition over government regulation, investment in the common good, and public ownership and decision making in democratic economic affairs. Neoliberalism, like capitalism, empha-

sizes profit, production, and privatization over distribution of resources, access to services and opportunities, and rights.
7 Fieldnote, May 12, 2011.
8 Fieldnote, July 27, 2011. I have changed the yard-duty adult's name to Gloria here to protect her privacy.
9 Fieldnote, July 27, 2011.
10 Rios, *Punished*.
11 Helwig, "Adolescents' and Young Adults' Conceptions"; Melton, "Children's Concepts"; Melton and Limber, *What Children's Rights Mean*.
12 Fieldnote, May 12, 2011.
13 Hart and Hart, "Children's Rights."
14 Pallares, *Family Activism*.
15 Fieldnote, April 14, 2011.
16 Fieldnote, July 27, 2011.
17 Fieldnote, March 1, 2012.
18 Dewey, *School and Society*.
19 Aronowitz and Giroux, *Education Still under Siege*; Giroux and McLaren, "Introduction."

PART 2. EMBODYING CITIZENSHIP
1 Melton, "Children's Concepts."
2 Cherney and Perry, "Children's Attitudes."
3 Cherney and Perry, "Children's Attitudes"; Lister, "Why Citizenship"; Morrow, "We Are People Too"; Ruck and Horn, "Charting the Landscape"; Ruck et al., "Development of Children's Knowledge"; Ruck, Abramovitch, and Keating, "Children's and Adolescents' Understanding."
4 For exceptions, see Solís, Fernández, and Alcalá, "Mexican Immigrant Children"; and Taft, *Rebel Girls*.
5 Solís, "Re-thinking Illegality"; Solís, Fernández, and Alcalá, "Mexican Immigrant Children."

CHAPTER 4. CITIZENSHIP AS A SOCIOPOLITICAL PROCESS
1 Watts, Griffith, and Abdul-Adil, "Sociopolitical Development."
2 Kirshner, "Introduction"; Watts and Guessous, "Sociopolitical Development."
3 Christens and Peterson, "Role of Empowerment"; Ginwright, Noguera, and Cammarota, *Beyond Resistance!*
4 Watts and Flanagan, "Pushing the Envelope"; Watts, Griffith, and Abdul-Adil, "Sociopolitical Development."
5 Pallares, *Family Activism*.
6 Bernal and Knight, "Ethnic Identity"; Torres and Magolda, "Reconstructing Latino Identity"; Hurtado and Silva, "Creating New Social Identities."
7 Hurtado, "Understanding Multiple Group Identities."
8 Deaux, "Reconstructing Social Identity"; Deaux, "Social Identification."

9   Tajfel, "Social Identity."
10 Hurtado, Gurin, and Peng, "Social Identities"; Hurtado and Gurin, *Chicana/o Identity*.
11 Turner, "Some Current Issues."
12 Hurtado and Silva, "Creating New Social Identities."
13 Hurtado, "Understanding Multiple Group Identities"; Hurtado and Gurin, *Chicana/o Identity*.
14 Hurtado, Gurin, and Peng, "Social Identities."
15 Deaux, "Reconstructing Social Identity"; Deaux, "Social Identification"; Hurtado, "Understanding Multiple Group Identities."
16 Freire, *Pedagogy of the Oppressed*.
17 Fieldnote, April 26, 2012.
18 Martín-Baró, *Writings*; Montero, "Political Psychology."
19 Juana Alicia, a San Francisco–based muralist, worked with Oakes College students at UC Santa Cruz to plan and paint the mural over the course of one academic year. The creation of the mural was a response to the colonial messages and representations of other artwork on campus. The mural, titled *La promesa de Loma Prieta: Que no se repita la historia* (The promise of Loma Prieta: That history not repeat itself), sought to reflect the liberation struggles and social movements that were important to the students of Oakes College. More information about the mural is accessible at https://iascollectivemuseum.com.
20 Fieldnote, October 12, 2011.
21 Martín-Baró, *Writings*; Montero, "Political Psychology"; Montero, "De la realidad."
22 Rubio-Hernandez and Ayón, "'Pobrecitos los niños'"; Weissberg et al., "Social and Emotional Learning."
23 Durlak et al., *Handbook of Social and Emotional Learning*.
24 Hamedani and Darling-Hammond, *Social Emotional Learning*.
25 Rios, *Punished*.
26 Fieldnote, February 2, 2012.
27 Ahmed, *Cultural Politics of Emotion*.
28 Greenberg et al., "Enhancing School-Based Prevention"; Payton et al., "Social and Emotional Learning."
29 Diemer and Li, "Critical Consciousness Development"; Fisher, "Youth Political Participation"; Flanagan and Sherrod, "Youth Political Development"; Sherrod, Torney-Purta, and Flanagan, *Handbook of Research on Civic Engagement*.
30 Ginwright, Noguera, and Cammarota, *Beyond Resistance!*
31 Ginwright and Cammarota, "New Terrain."
32 Fieldnote, July 3, 2012.
33 Fieldnote, October 13, 2011.
34 Lugones, *Pilgrimages/peregrinajes*.
35 See Anzaldúa, *Borderlands/La Frontera*. According to Anzaldúa, *borderlands* or borderland theory is the process of personal and social identity deconstruction and reconstruction that aims to interrogate and confront systems of power and

oppression that were forced upon specific communities with histories of institutional marginalization and systemic subordination. In naming the borderlands, Anzaldúa is also describing those in-between spaces where the colonial and decolonial possibilities coalesce to invite a reimagining of possibilities and new visions for a transformation of being that aligns with a critical consciousness of and for liberation.

36 Das Gupta, "'Don't Deport Our Daddies'"; Dreby, "Burden of Deportation"; Enriquez, "Multigenerational Punishment"; Rodriguez, "Experiencing 'Illegality'"; Warikoo and Bloemraad, "Economic Americanness."
37 De Genova, "Migrant 'Illegality.'"

CHAPTER 5. CLAIMING RIGHTS BEYOND STATE RELATIONS

1 Fieldnote, July 27, 2011.
2 Lister, "Why Citizenship."
3 Moosa-Mitha, "Difference-Centered Alternative."
4 Epps, "Who Gets to Be Represented."
5 Lister, "Why Citizenship"; Morrow, "We Are People Too"; Ruck et al., "Development of Children's Knowledge"; Sherrod, Flanagan, and Youniss, "Dimensions of Citizenship"; Sherrod, "Adolescents' Perceptions."
6 Fieldnote, Spring, May 12, 2011.
7 Isin, *Recasting the Social in Citizenship*.
8 Solís, Fernández, and Alcalá, "Mexican Immigrant Children."
9 Fieldnote, May 12, 2011.
10 Fieldnote, July 27, 2011.
11 Bloemraad, Korteweg, and Yurdakul, "Citizenship and Immigration"; Yuval-Davis, "Intersectionality."
12 Flores, "New Citizens."
13 Moosa-Mitha, "Difference-Centered Alternative."
14 According to anthropologist Renato Rosaldo, cultural citizenship refers to "the right to be different and to belong in a participatory democratic sense. It claims that, in a democracy, social justice calls for equity among all citizens, even when such differences as race, religion, class, gender, or sexual orientation potentially could be used to make certain people less equal or inferior to others. The notion of belonging means full membership in a group and the ability to influence one's destiny by having a significant voice in basic decisions." Rosaldo, "Cultural Citizenship," 402.
15 Flores and Benmayor, *Latino Cultural Citizenship*; Rosaldo, "Cultural Citizenship."
16 Coined by Asian American studies scholar Sunaina Marr Maira, dissenting citizenship describes a specific form of expression and embodiment of citizenship that is resistant or noncompliant with the existing order of things, and as such it is enacted through modes of dissent and rejection of what is perceived as oppressive and compromising to a healthy democracy and the common good. Furthermore, in writing about South Asian youth in the United States, Maira writes, "Dissent-

ing citizenship is still a form of citizenship, and engages with the role and responsibility of the nation-state and the question of belonging and rights for subjects, however marginalized, so it encapsulates the contradictions of challenging the state while seeking inclusion within it." Maira, *Missing*, 35.

17 Unlike other notions of citizenship, "flexible citizenship" is used by anthropologist Aihwa Ong to describe the underlying economic incentives for people to choose to obtain, embody, and express modes of citizenship that do not center on notions of community, belonging, and rights, but instead focus on the fulfillment of economic stability and opportunities. Unlike Rosaldo, Ong argues that people choose citizenship based on economic reasons instead of political ones. See Ong, "Flexible Citizenship."

18 Dahlin and Hironaka, "Citizenship beyond Borders."

CONCLUSION

1 Newton, "Huey Newton Talks to the Movement."

BIBLIOGRAPHY

Abrego, Leisy J. *Sacrificing Families: Navigating Laws, Labor, and Love across Borders*. Palo Alto: Stanford University Press, 2014.
Ahmed, Sara. *The Cultural Politics of Emotion*. 2nd ed. Edinburgh: Edinburgh University Press, 2014.
Almaguer, Tomás. "Race, Racialization, and Latino Populations in the United States." In *Racial Formation in the Twenty-First Century*, edited by Daniel Martinez HoSang, Oneka LaBennett, and Laura Pulido, 143–61. Berkeley: University of California Press, 2012.
American Immigration Council. "US Citizen Children Impacted by Immigration Enforcement." November 2019. www.americanimmigrationcouncil.org.
Anzaldúa, Gloria. *Borderlands/La Frontera: The New Mestiza*. San Francisco: Aunt Lute, 1987.
Aparicio, Frances R. "(Re)constructing Latinidad: The Challenge of Latina/o Studies." In *A Companion to Latina/o Studies*, edited by Juan Flores and Renato Rosaldo, 39–48. Malden, MA: Wiley-Blackwell, 2008.
Arce, Josephine. "Latino Bilingual Teachers: The Struggle to Sustain an Emancipatory Pedagogy in Public Schools." *International Journal of Qualitative Studies in Education* 17, no. 2 (2004): 227–46.
Arches, Joan, and Jennie Fleming. "Young People and Social Action: Youth Participation in the United Kingdom and United States." *New Directions for Youth Development* 2006, no. 111: 81–90.
Aronowitz, Stanley, and Henry A. Giroux. *Education Still under Siege*. Westport: Greenwood, 1993.
Basch, Linda, Nina Glick Schiller, and Cristina Szanton Blanc. *Nations Unbound: Transnational Projects, Postcolonial Predicaments and Deterritorialized Nation-States*. Langhorne: Gordon and Breach, 1994.
Bell, John. "Understanding Adultism: A Major Obstacle to Developing Positive Youth-Adult Partnerships." Youth Build, USA, 1995. https://actioncivics.scoe.net.
Berger Cardoso, Jodi, Kalina Brabeck, Dennis Stinchcomb, Lauren Heidbrink, Olga Acosta Price, Óscar F. Gil-García, Thomas M. Crea, and Luis H. Zayas. "Integration of Unaccompanied Migrant Youth in the United States: A Call for Research." *Journal of Ethnic and Migration Studies* 45, no. 2 (2019): 273–92.
Bernal, Martha E., and George P. Knight. "Ethnic Identity of Latino Children." In *Psychological Interventions and Research with Latino Populations*, edited by Jorge Garcia and Maria C. Zea, 15–38. Newton: Allyn and Bacon, 1997.

Bloemraad, Irene. *Becoming a Citizen: Incorporating Immigrants and Refugees in the United States and Canada*. Berkeley: University of California Press, 2006.

Bloemraad, Irene, Anna Korteweg, and Gökçe Yurdakul. "Citizenship and Immigration: Multiculturalism, Assimilation, and Challenges to the Nation-State." *Annual Review of Sociology* 34 (2008): 153–79.

Bloemraad, Irene, Heidy Sarabia, and Angela E. Fillingim. "'Staying Out of Trouble' and Doing What Is 'Right': Citizenship Acts, Citizenship Ideals, and the Effects of Legal Status on Second-Generation Youth." *American Behavioral Scientist* 60, no. 13 (2016): 1534–52.

Brabeck, Kalina, and Qingwen Xu. "The Impact of Detention and Deportation on Latino Immigrant Children and Families: A Quantitative Exploration." *Hispanic Journal of Behavioral Sciences* 32, no. 3 (2010): 341–61.

Brooks, B. David, and Frank G. Goble. *The Case for Character Education: The Role of the School in Teaching Values and Virtue*. New York: Quick, 1997.

Caminero-Santangelo, Marta. *On Latinidad: US Latino Literature and the Construction of Ethnicity*. Gainesville: University Press of Florida, 2007.

Cammarota, Julio, and Michelle Fine, eds. *Revolutionizing Education: Youth Participatory Action Research in Motion*. New York: Routledge, 2010.

Cammarota, Julio, and Augustine Romero. "A Critically Compassionate Intellectualism for Latina/o Students: Raising Voices above the Silencing in Our Schools." *Multicultural Education* 14, no. 2 (2006): 16–23.

Capps, Randy, Michael Fix, and Jie Zong. *A Profile of US Children with Unauthorized Immigrant Parents*. Washington: Migration Policy Institute, 2016.

Chang, Aurora. *The Struggles of Identity, Education, and Agency in the Lives of Undocumented Students: The Burden of Hyperdocumentation*. New York: Springer, 2017.

Chavez, Leo. *The Latino Threat: Constructing Immigrants, Citizens, and the Nation*. Stanford: Stanford University Press, 2013.

Chen, PeiYao, Faedra Lazar Weiss, and Heather Johnston Nicholson. "Girls Study Girls Inc.: Engaging Girls in Evaluation through Participatory Action Research." *American Journal of Community Psychology* 46, nos. 1–2 (2010): 228–37.

Cherney, Isabelle, and Nancy Walker Perry. "Children's Attitudes toward Their Rights: An International Perspective." In *Monitoring Children's Rights*, edited by E. Verhellen, 241–50. Netherlands: Kluwer Law International, 1996.

Christens, Brian D., and Tom Dolan. "Interweaving Youth Development, Community Development, and Social Change through Youth Organizing." *Youth & Society* 43, no. 2 (2011): 528–48.

Christens, Brian D., and N. Andrew Peterson. "The Role of Empowerment in Youth Development: A Study of Sociopolitical Control as Mediator of Ecological Systems' Influence on Developmental Outcomes." *Journal of Youth and Adolescence* 41, no. 5 (2012): 623–35.

Clark, Alison. "Young Children as Protagonists and the Role of Participatory, Visual Methods in Engaging Multiple Perspectives." *American Journal of Community Psychology* 46, nos. 1–2 (2010): 115–23.

Cockburn, Tom. "Children and the Feminist Ethic of Care." *Childhood* 12, no. 1 (2005): 71–89.
Cohen, Elizabeth F. "Neither Seen nor Heard: Children's Citizenship in Contemporary Democracies." *Citizenship Studies* 9, no. 2 (2005): 221–40.
Corona Caraveo, Yolanda, and Carlos Pérez-Zavala. "Participación infantil en un movimiento de resistencia." In *Infancia, Legislación y Política*, edited by Yolanda Corona Caraveo, 79–93. México: UAM, 2000.
Cox, Laurence. "Scholarship and Activism: A Social Movements Perspective." *Studies in Social Justice* 9, no. 1 (2015): 34–53.
Crenshaw, Kimberlé. "Demarginalizing the Intersection of Race and Sex: A Black Feminist Critique of Antidiscrimination Doctrine, Feminist Theory and Antiracist Politics." *University of Chicago Legal Forum* 1989: 139–68. https://philpapers.org.
———. "Mapping the Margins: Identity Politics, Intersectionality, and Violence against Women." *Stanford Law Review* 43, no. 6 (1991): 1241–99.
Dahlin, Eric C., and Ann Hironaka. "Citizenship beyond Borders: A Cross-National Study of Dual Citizenship." *Sociological Inquiry* 78, no. 1 (2008): 54–73.
Darder, Antonia, and Rodolfo D. Torres. *Latinos and Education: A Critical Reader*. New York: Routledge, 1997.
Das Gupta, Monisha. "'Don't Deport Our Daddies': Gendering State Deportation Practices and Immigrant Organizing." *Gender & Society* 28, no. 1 (2014): 83–109.
Deaux, Kay. "Reconstructing Social Identity." *Personality and Social Psychology Bulletin* 19, no. 1 (1993): 4–12.
———. "Social Identification." In *Social Psychology: Handbook of Basic Principles*, edited by Edward T. Higgins and Arie W. Kruglanski, 777–98. New York: Guilford, 1996.
De Genova, Nicholas P. "Migrant 'Illegality' and Deportability in Everyday Life." *Annual Review of Anthropology* 31, no. 1 (2002): 419–47.
———. *Working the Boundaries: Race, Space, and "Illegality" in Mexican Chicago*. Durham: Duke University Press, 2005.
Delanty, Gerard. "Citizenship as a Learning Process: Disciplinary Citizenship versus Cultural Citizenship." *International Journal of Lifelong Education* 22, no. 6 (2003): 597–605.
———. *Citizenship in a Global Age: Society, Culture, Politics*. Philadelphia: Open University Press, 2000.
Delgado, Melvin, and Lee Staples. "Youth-Led Organizing, Community Engagement, and Opportunity Creation." In *Handbook of Community Practice*, 2nd ed., edited by Marie Weil, Michael Reisch, and Mary L. Ohmer, 547–65. Los Angeles: Sage, 2012.
De Lissovoy, Noah. "Education and Violence: Conceptualizing Power, Domination, and Agency in the Hidden Curriculum." *Race, Ethnicity and Education* 15, no. 4 (2012): 463–84.
del Mar Farina, Maria. *White Nativism, Ethnic Identity and US Immigration Policy Reforms: American Citizenship and Children in Mixed Status, Hispanic Families*. New York: Routledge, 2017.

Delpit, Lisa. *Other People's Children: Cultural Conflict in the Classroom.* New York: New Press, 1995.
Delpit, Lisa, and Joanne Kilgour Dowdy, eds. *The Skin That We Speak: Thoughts on Language and Culture in the Classroom.* New York: New Press, 2008.
Dewey, John. *The School and Society and The Child and the Curriculum.* Chicago: University of Chicago Press, 2013.
Diemer, Matthew A. "Pathways to Occupational Attainment among Poor Youth of Color: The Role of Sociopolitical Development." *Counseling Psychologist* 37, no. 1 (2009): 6–35.
Diemer, Matthew A., and Cheng-Hsien Li. "Critical Consciousness Development and Political Participation among Marginalized Youth." *Child Development* 82, no. 6 (2011): 1815–33.
Dreby, Joanna. "The Burden of Deportation on Children in Mexican Immigrant Families." *Journal of Marriage and Family* 74, no. 4 (2012): 829–45.
———. *Everyday Illegal: When Policies Undermine Immigrant Families.* Berkeley: University of California Press, 2015.
Durlak, Joseph A., Celene E. Domitrovich, Roger P. Weissberg, and Thomas P. Gullotta, eds. *Handbook of Social and Emotional Learning: Research and Practice.* New York: Guilford, 2015.
Dutt, Anjali, and Danielle Kohfeldt. "Towards a Liberatory Ethics of Care Framework for Organizing Social Change." *Journal of Social and Political Psychology* 6, no. 2 (2018): 575–90.
Enriquez, Laura E. "Multigenerational Punishment: Shared Experiences of Undocumented Immigration Status within Mixed-Status Families." *Journal of Marriage and Family* 77, no. 4 (2015): 939–53.
Epps, Garrett. "Who Gets to Be Represented in Congress?" *Atlantic,* December 2015. www.theatlantic.com.
Estrada, Emir. *Kids at Work: Latinx Families Selling Food on the Streets of Los Angeles.* New York: New York University Press, 2019.
Félix, Adrián. *Specters of Belonging: The Political Life Cycle of Mexican Migrants.* New York: Oxford University Press, 2019.
Fernández, Jesica Siham. "Latina/o Youth Cultural Citizenship: Re-Conceptualizing Dominant Constructions of Citizenship through Membership, Sense of Belonging, Claiming Space and Rights." PhD diss., University of California, Santa Cruz, 2015.
Fernández, Jesica Siham, and Regina Day Langhout. "A Community with Diversity of Culture, Wealth, Resources, and Living Experiences: Defining Neighborhood in an Unincorporated Community." *American Journal of Community Psychology* 53, nos. 1–2 (2014): 122–33.
———. "Living on the Margins of Democratic Representation: Socially Connected Community Responsibility as Civic Engagement in an Unincorporated Area." *American Journal of Community Psychology* 62, nos. 1–2 (2018): 75–86.
Fernández, Jesica Siham, Angela Nguyen, and Regina Day Langhout. "'It's a Puzzle!': Elementary School-Aged Youth Concept-Mapping the Intersections of Community

Narratives." *International Journal for Research on Extended Education* 3, no. 1 (2015): 24–39.
Field, Corinne T. *The Struggle for Equal Adulthood: Gender, Race, Age, and the Fight for Citizenship in Antebellum America*. Chapel Hill: University of North Carolina Press, 2014.
Fine, Michelle. "Postcards from Metro America: Reflections on Youth Participatory Action Research for Urban Justice." *Urban Review* 41, no. 1 (2009): 1–6.
Fisher, Dana R. "Youth Political Participation: Bridging Activism and Electoral Politics." *Annual Review of Sociology* 38 (2012): 119–37.
Flanagan, Constance A., and Lonnie R. Sherrod. "Youth Political Development: An Introduction." *Journal of Social Issues* 54, no. 3 (1998): 447–56.
Flores, Antonio, Mark Hugo Lopez, and Jens Manuel Krogstad. "US Hispanic Population Reached New High in 2018, but Growth Has Slowed." Pew Research Center, July 8, 2019. www.pewresearch.org.
Flores, William Vincent. "New Citizens, New Rights: Undocumented Immigrants and Latino Cultural Citizenship." *Latin American Perspectives* 30, no. 2 (2003): 295–308.
Flores, William Vincent, and Rina Benmayor, eds. *Latino Cultural Citizenship: Claiming Identity, Space, and Rights*. Boston: Beacon, 1997.
Flores-González, Nilda. *Citizens but Not Americans: Race and Belonging among Latino Millennials*. New York: New York University Press, 2017.
Foster-Fishman, Pennie G., Kristen M. Law, Lauren F. Lichty, and Christina Aoun. "Youth ReACT for Social Change: A Method for Youth Participatory Action Research." *American Journal of Community Psychology* 46, nos. 1–2 (2010): 67–83.
Fox, Jonathan, and Gaspar Rivera-Salgado, eds. *Indigenous Mexican Migrants in the United States*. San Diego: UCSD Center for US-Mexican Studies, 2004.
Fox, Madeline, Kavitha Mediratta, Jessica Ruglis, Brett Stoudt, Seema Shah, and Michelle Fine. "Critical Youth Engagement: Participatory Action Research and Organizing." In *Handbook of Research on Civic Engagement in Youth*, edited by Lonnie R. Sherrod, Judith Torney-Purta, and Constance A. Flanagan, 621–49. New York: Wiley, 2010.
France, Alan. "'Why Should We Care?': Young People, Citizenship and Questions of Social Responsibility." *Journal of Youth Studies* 1, no. 1 (1998): 97–111.
Freedberg, Louis. "Despite Progress, California's Teaching Force Far from Reflecting Diversity of Students." *EdSource*, April 25, 2018. https://edsource.org.
Freire, Paulo. *Pedagogy of the Oppressed*. New York: Bloomsbury, 2018.
Gatto, John Taylor. *Dumbing Us Down: The Hidden Curriculum of Compulsory Schooling*. Gabriola Island, British Columbia: New Society, 2002.
Getrich, Christina. *Border Brokers: Children of Mexican Immigrants Navigating US Society, Laws, and Politics*. Tucson: University of Arizona Press, 2019.
Ginwright, Shawn, and Julio Cammarota. "New Terrain in Youth Development: The Promise of a Social Justice Approach." *Social Justice* 29, no. 4 (90) (2002): 82–95.

Ginwright, Shawn, Pedro Noguera, and Julio Cammarota. *Beyond Resistance! Youth Activism and Community Change: New Democratic Possibilities for Practice and Policy for America's Youth*. New York: Routledge Taylor & Francis Group, 2006.

Giroux, Henry A. "Education and the Crisis of Youth: Schooling and the Promise of Democracy." *Educational Forum* 73, no. 1 (December 2008): 8–18.

Giroux, Henry A., and Peter McLaren. "Introduction: Schooling, Cultural Politics, and the Struggle for Democracy." In *Critical Pedagogy, the State, and Cultural Struggle*, edited by Henry A. Giroux and Peter McLaren, xi–xxxv. Albany: State University of New York Press, 1989.

Giroux, Henry A., and Anthony N. Penna. "Social Education in the Classroom: The Dynamics of the Hidden Curriculum." *Theory & Research in Social Education* 7, no. 1 (1979): 21–42.

Gonzales, Roberto G. *Lives in Limbo: Undocumented and Coming of Age in America*. Berkeley: University of California Press, 2016.

González Rey, Fernando L. "Affectivity from a Perspective of Subjectivity." *Psicología: Teoria e Pesquisa* 15, no. 2 (1999): 127–34.

———. "Subjetividad, cultura e investigación cualitativa en psicología: La ciencia como producción culturalmente situada." *Revista Liminales, Chile* 1, no. 4 (2013): 13–36.

Gordon, Hava Rachel. "Allies Within and Without: How Adolescent Activists Conceptualize Ageism and Navigate Adult Power in Youth Social Movements." *Journal of Contemporary Ethnography* 36, no. 6 (2007): 631–68.

Gramsci, Antonio. *The Gramsci Reader: Selected Writings, 1916–1935*. New York: New York University Press, 2000.

Greenberg, Mark T., Roger P. Weissberg, Mary Utne O'Brien, Joseph E. Zins, Linda Fredericks, Hank Resnik, and Maurice J. Elias. "Enhancing School-Based Prevention and Youth Development through Coordinated Social, Emotional, and Academic Learning." *American Psychologist* 58, nos. 6–7 (2003): 466–74.

Gulbas, Lauren E., and Luis H. Zayas. "Children of Undocumented Immigrants: Imperiled Developmental Trajectories." In *Race, Ethnicity and Self: Identity in Multicultural Perspective*, edited by D. P. Salett and E. R. Koslow. Washington: NASW Press, 2015.

Gutiérrez, Kris D., and Barbara Rogoff. "Cultural Ways of Learning: Individual Traits or Repertoires of Practice." *Educational Researcher* 32, no. 5 (2003): 19–25.

Hall, Stuart, and David Held. "Citizens and Citizenship." In *New Times: The Changing Face of Politics in the 1990s*, edited by Stuart Hall and Martin Jacques, 173–90. London: Lawrence and Wishart, 1989.

Hamedani, Maryam G., and Linda Darling-Hammond. *Social Emotional Learning in High School: How Three Urban High Schools Engage, Educate, and Empower Youth*. Stanford: Stanford Center for Opportunity Policy in Education. https://edpolicy.dstanford.edu.

Hart, Stuart N., and Brannon W. Hart. "Children's Rights in Education: An Historical Perspective." *School Psychology Review* 20, no. 3 (1991): 345–58.

Haupt, Paul M. "The School as a Microcosm of Communities and Their Heritage and the Need to Encapsulate This in the Writing of School Histories." *Yesterday and Today* 5 (2010): 15–21.
Heidbrink, Lauren. *Migrant Youth, Transnational Families, and the State: Care and Contested Interests.* Philadelphia: University of Pennsylvania Press, 2014.
Helwig, Charles C. "Adolescents' and Young Adults' Conceptions of Civil Liberties: Freedom of Speech and Religion." *Child Development* 66, no. 1 (1995): 152–66.
hooks, bell. *Teaching to Transgress: Education as the Practice of Freedom.* New York: Routledge, 1994.
Hope, Elan C., and Robert J. Jagers. "The Role of Sociopolitical Attitudes and Civic Education in the Civic Engagement of Black Youth." *Journal of Research on Adolescence* 24, no. 3 (2014): 460–70.
Hoppock, Matthew. "Operation Janus and Operation Second Look: Denaturalization of Citizens with Removal Orders." Hoppock Law Firm, March 4, 2018. www.hoppocklawfirm.com.
Human Rights Watch. "US/California: Thousands of Immigrant Parents Detained." May 15, 2017. www.hrw.org.
Hurtado, Aída. "Understanding Multiple Group Identities: Inserting Women into Cultural Transformations." *Journal of Social Issues* 53, no. 2 (1997): 299–327.
Hurtado, Aída, and Patricia Gurin. *Chicana/o Identity in a Changing US Society: ¿Quién soy? ¿Quiénes somos?* Tucson: University of Arizona Press, 2004.
Hurtado, Aída, Patricia Gurin, and Timothy Peng. "Social Identities—A Framework for Studying the Adaptations of Immigrants and Ethnics: The Adaptations of Mexicans in the United States." *Social Problems* 41, no. 1 (1994): 129–51.
Hurtado, Aída, and Janelle M. Silva. "Creating New Social Identities in Children through Critical Multicultural Media: The Case of Little Bill." *New Directions for Child and Adolescent Development* 2008, no. 120: 17–30.
Invernizzi, Antonella, and Jane Williams, eds. *Children and Citizenship.* Thousand Oaks: Sage, 2008.
Isin, Engin F., ed. *Recasting the Social in Citizenship.* Toronto: University of Toronto Press, 2008.
Isin, Engin F., and Bryan S. Turner, eds. *Handbook of Citizenship Studies.* Thousand Oaks: Sage, 2002.
———. "Investigating Citizenship: An Agenda for Citizenship Studies." *Citizenship Studies* 11, no. 1 (2007): 5–17.
Isin, Engin F., and Patricia K. Wood. *Citizenship and Identity.* Thousand Oaks: Sage, 1999.
Jacquez, Farrah, Lisa M. Vaughn, and Erin Wagner. "Youth as Partners, Participants or Passive Recipients: A Review of Children and Adolescents in Community-Based Participatory Research (CBPR)." *American Journal of Community Psychology* 51, no. 1 (2013): 176–89.
James, Allison, and Alan Prout. "A New Paradigm for the Sociology of Childhood? Provenance, Promise and Problems." In *Constructing and Reconstructing Childhood:*

Contemporary Issues in the Sociological Study of Childhood, edited by Allison James and Alan Prout, 7–33. New York: Routledge, 2015.

Jans, Marc. "Children as Citizens: Towards a Contemporary Notion of Child Participation." *Childhood* 11, no. 1 (2004): 27–44.

Jay, Michelle. "Critical Race Theory, Multicultural Education, and the Hidden Curriculum of Hegemony." *Multicultural Perspectives: An Official Journal of the National Association for Multicultural Education* 5, no. 4 (2003): 3–9.

Juárez, Melina, Bárbara Gómez-Aguiñaga, and Sonia P. Bettez. "Twenty Years after IIRIRA: The Rise of Immigrant Detention and Its Effects on Latinx Communities across the Nation." *Journal on Migration and Human Security* 6, no. 1 (2018): 74–96.

Kirshner, Ben. "Introduction: Youth Activism as a Context for Learning and Development." *American Behavioral Scientist* 51, no. 3 (2007): 367–79.

Kirshner, Ben, Carlos Hipolito-Delgado, and Shelley Zion. "Sociopolitical Development in Educational Systems: From Margins to Center." *Urban Review* 47, no. 5 (2015): 803–8.

Kohfeldt, Danielle Marie. "Children as Activist Artists: Constructing Citizenship through Social Justice Arts-Based Participatory Action Research." PhD diss., University of California, Santa Cruz, 2014.

Kohfeldt, Danielle, Alexandra Rae Bowen, and Regina Day Langhout. "'They Think Kids Are Stupid': yPAR and Confrontations with Institutionalized Power as Contexts for Children's Identity Work." *Revista Puertorriqueña de Psicología* 27, no. 2 (2016): 276–91.

Kohfeldt, Danielle, Lina Chhun, Sarah Grace, and Regina Day Langhout. "Youth Empowerment in Context: Exploring Tensions in School-Based yPAR." *American Journal of Community Psychology* 47, nos. 1–2 (2011): 28–45.

Kohfeldt, Danielle, and Regina Day Langhout. "The Five Whys Method: A Tool for Developing Problem Definitions in Collaboration with Children." *Journal of Community & Applied Social Psychology* 22, no. 4 (2012): 316–29.

Kohli, Aarti, P. Markowitz, and Lisa Chavez. "Secure Communities by the Numbers: An Analysis of Demographics and Due Process." Research Report. Chief Justice Earl Warren Institute on Law and Social Policy, University of California, Berkeley Law School, 2011. www.law.berkeley.edu.

Kohn, Alfie. "How Not to Teach Values: A Critical Look at Character Education." *Phi Delta Kappan* 78 (1997): 428–39.

Kornbluh, Mariah, Emily J. Ozer, Carrie D. Allen, and Ben Kirshner. "Youth Participatory Action Research as an Approach to Sociopolitical Development and the New Academic Standards: Considerations for Educators." *Urban Review* 47, no. 5 (2015): 868–92.

Kosher, Hanita, and Asher Ben-Arieh. "What Children Think about Their Rights and Their Well-Being: A Cross-National Comparison." *American Journal of Orthopsychiatry* 87, no. 3 (2017): 256–73.

Krogstad, Jens Manuel. "Key Facts about the Latino Vote in 2016." Pew Research Center, October 14, 2016. www.pewresearch.org.

Langhout, Regina Day. "Acts of Resistance: Student (In)visibility." *Culture & Psychology* 11, no. 2 (2005): 123–58.
Langhout, Regina Day, Jesica Siham Fernández, Denise Wyldebore, and Jorge Savala. "Photovoice and House Meetings as Tools within Participatory Action Research." In *Handbook of Methodological Approaches to Community-Based Research: Qualitative, Quantitative, and Mixed Methods*, edited by Leonard A. Jason and David S. Glenwick, 81–91. New York: Oxford University Press, 2016.
Langhout, Regina Day, Danielle M. Kohfeldt, and Erin Rose Ellison. "How We Became the Schmams: Conceptualizations of Fairness in the Decision-Making Process for Latina/o Children." *American Journal of Community Psychology* 48, nos. 3–4 (2011): 296–308.
Langhout, Regina Day, and Cecily A. Mitchell. "Engaging Contexts: Drawing the Link between Student and Teacher Experiences of the Hidden Curriculum." *Journal of Community & Applied Social Psychology* 18, no. 6 (2008): 593–614.
Langhout, Regina Day, and Elizabeth Thomas. "Imagining Participatory Action Research in Collaboration with Children: An Introduction." *American Journal of Community Psychology* 46, nos. 1–2 (2010): 60–66.
Lee, Soo Jee. "A Child's Voice vs. a Parent's Control: Resolving a Tension between the Convention on the Rights of the Child and US Law." *Columbia Law Review* 117, no. 3 (2017): 687–727.
Levesque, Roger, Jr. "The Internationalization of Children's Human Rights: Too Radical for American Adolescents." *Connecticut Journal of International Law* 9, no. 2 (1993): 237–93.
Levine, Peter. *The Future of Democracy: Developing the Next Generation of American Citizens*. Hanover: University Press of New England, 2007.
Lickona, Thomas. "Eleven Principles of Effective Character Education." *Journal of Moral Education* 25, no. 1 (1996): 93–100.
Lind, Dara. "The Trump Administration's Separation of Families at the Border Explained." *Vox*, August 14, 2018. www.vox.com.
Lister, Ruth. "Inclusive Citizenship: Realizing the Potential." *Citizenship Studies* 11, no. 1 (1997): 49–61.
———. "Investing in the Citizen-Workers of the Future: Transformations in Citizenship and the State under New Labour." *Social Policy & Administration* 37, no. 5 (2003): 427–43.
———. "Unpacking Children's Citizenship." In *Children and Citizenship*, edited by Antonella Invernizzi and Jane Williams, 9–19. Thousand Oaks: Sage, 2008.
———. "Why Citizenship: Where, When and How Children?" *Theoretical Inquiries in Law* 8, no. 2 (2007): 693–718.
Lister, Ruth, Noel Smith, Sue M. Middleton, and Lynne Cagle Cox. "Young People Talk about Citizenship: Empirical Perspectives on Theoretical and Political Debates." *Citizenship Studies* 7, no. 2 (2003): 235–53.
Lockyer, Andrew. "Education for Citizenship: Children as Citizens and Political Literacy." In *Children and Citizenship*, edited by Antonella Invernizzi and Jane Williams, 20–31. Thousand Oaks: Sage, 2008.

Lugones, María. *Pilgrimages/peregrinajes: Theorizing Coalition against Multiple Oppressions*. Lanham: Rowman and Littlefield, 2003.

Maira, Sunaina Marr. *Missing: Youth, Citizenship and Empire after 9/11*. Durham: Duke University Press, 2009.

Manning, Jennifer E. "Membership of the 116th Congress: A Profile." *Congressional Research Service*, June 1, 2020. https://fas.org.

Marshall, Thomas H. "Citizenship and Social Class, 1950." In *The Anthropology of Citizenship: A Reader*, edited by Sian Lazar, 52–59. Malden: Wiley Blackwell, 2013.

Martín-Baró, Ignacio. *Writings for a Liberation Psychology*. Cambridge: Harvard University Press, 1994.

Mathema, Silva. "Keeping Families Together: Why All Americans Should Care about What Happens to Unauthorized Immigrants." Center for American Progress, March 16, 2017. www.americanprogress.org.

Mayall, Berry. "The Sociology of Childhood in Relation to Children's Rights." *International Journal of Children's Rights* 8, no. 3 (2000): 243–59.

———. *Towards a Sociology for Childhood: Thinking from Children's Lives*. Buckingham: Open University Press, 2002.

Melton, Gary B. "Children's Concepts of Their Rights." *Journal of Clinical Child & Adolescent Psychology* 9, no. 3 (1980): 186–90.

Melton, Gary B., and Susan P. Limber. *What Children's Rights Mean to Children: Children's Own Views*. Lincoln: University of Nebraska Press, 1992.

Menchaca, Martha. "Latinas/os and the Mestizo Racial Heritage of Mexican Americans." In *A Companion to Latina/o Studies*, edited by Juan Flores and Renato Rosaldo, 313–24. New York: Blackwell, 2011.

Menjívar, Cecilia, and Daniel Kanstroom, eds. *Constructing Immigrant "Illegality": Critiques, Experiences, and Responses*. New York: Cambridge University Press, 2013.

Molina, Natalia. *How Race Is Made in America: Immigration, Citizenship, and the Historical Power of Racial Scripts*. Berkeley: University of California Press, 2014.

Monroe, Carla R. "Why Are 'Bad Boys' Always Black? Causes of Disproportionality in School Discipline and Recommendations for Change." *Clearing House: A Journal of Educational Strategies* 79, no. 1 (2005): 45–50.

Montero, Maritza. "De la realidad, la verdad y otras ilusiones concretas: Para una epistemología de la psicología social comunitaria." *Psykhe* 8, no. 1 (2011): 9–18.

———. "The Political Psychology of Liberation: From Politics to Ethics and Back." *Political Psychology* 28, no. 5 (2007): 517–33.

Moosa-Mitha, Mehmoona. "A Difference-Centred Alternative to Theorization of Children's Citizenship Rights." *Citizenship Studies* 9, no. 4 (2005): 369–88.

Morris, Monique. *Pushout: The Criminalization of Black Girls in Schools*. New York: New Press, 2016.

Morrow, Virginia. "We Are People Too: Children's and Young People's Perspectives on Children's Rights and Decision-Making in England." *International Journal of Children's Rights* 7, no. 2 (1999): 149–70.

Munro, Emily R., John Pinkerton, Philip Mendes, Georgia Hyde-Dryden, Maria Herczog, and Rami Benbenishty. "The Contribution of the United Nations Convention on the Rights of the Child to Understanding and Promoting the Interests of Young People Making the Transition from Care to Adulthood." *Children and Youth Services Review* 33, no. 12 (2011): 2417–23.

NALEO Educational Fund. "Policymakers: Resources for Latino School Board Members, Municipal and County Officials, State Legislators and Federal Elected and Appointed Officials." 2017. https://naleo.org.

Nash, Jennifer C. "Re-thinking Intersectionality." *Feminist Review* 89, no. 1 (2008): 1–15.

Negrón-Gonzales, Genevieve. "Undocumented Youth Activism as Counter-Spectacle: Civil Disobedience and Testimonio in the Battle around Immigration Reform." *Aztlán: A Journal of Chicano Studies* 40, no. 1 (2015): 87–112.

Newton, Huey. "Huey Newton Talks to the Movement about the Black Panther Party, Cultural Nationalism, SNCC Liberals, and White Revolutionaries." *Movement*, August 1968. https://archive.lib.msu.edu.

Ngai, Mae. "Birthright Citizenship and the Alien Citizen." *Fordham Law Review* 75 (2007): 2521–30.

Noddings, Nel. *Educating Moral People: A Caring Alternative to Character Education*. New York: Teachers College Press, 2002.

Noguera, Pedro A. "Latino Youth: Immigration, Education, and the Future." *Latino Studies* 4, no. 3 (2006): 313–20.

Nollet, Jean Marc. "Schools as Microcosms of Society." In *Violence in Schools—A Challenge for the Local Community*, 15–17. Strasbourg, France: Council of Europe Publishing, 2003.

Nyers, Peter. "Migrant Citizenships and Autonomous Mobilities." *Migration, Mobility, & Displacement* 1, no. 1 (2015): 23–39.

Oboler, Suzanne, ed. *Latinos and Citizenship: The Dilemma of Belonging*. New York: Palgrave Macmillan, 2006.

Ong, Aihwa. "Flexible Citizenship among Chinese Cosmopolitans." *Cultural Politics* 14 (1998): 134–62.

Orellana, Marjorie Faulstich. *Translating Childhoods: Immigrant Youth, Language, and Culture*. New Brunswick: Rutgers University Press, 2009.

———. "The Work Kids Do: Mexican and Central American Immigrant Children's Contributions to Households and Schools in California." *Harvard Educational Review* 71, no. 3 (2001): 366–90.

Padilla, Felix M. *Latino Ethnic Consciousness: The Case of Mexican Americans and Puerto Ricans in Chicago*. Chicago: University of Notre Dame Press, 1985.

Pallares, Amalia. *Family Activism: Immigrant Struggles and the Politics of Noncitizenship*. New Brunswick: Rutgers University Press, 2014.

Passel, Jeffrey S., and Mark Hugo Lopez. "Up to 1.7 Million Unauthorized Immigrant Youth May Benefit from New Deportation Rules." Pew Hispanic Center, August 14, 2012.

Patten, Eileen. "The Nation's Latino Population Is Defined by Its Youth: Nearly Half of US-Born Latinos Are Younger Than 18." Pew Research Center, April 20, 2016. www.pewresearch.org.

Payton, John W., Dana M. Wardlaw, Patricia A. Graczyk, Michelle R. Bloodworth, Carolyn J. Tompsett, and Roger P. Weissberg. "Social and Emotional Learning: A Framework for Promoting Mental Health and Reducing Risk Behavior in Children and Youth." *Journal of School Health* 70, no. 5 (2000): 179–85.

Pelaez Lopez, Alan. "The X in Latinx Is a Wound, Not a Trend." Color Bloq, n.d. www.colorbloq.org.

Pérez Huber, Lindsay. "Using Latina/o Critical Race Theory (LatCrit) and Racist Nativism to Explore Intersectionality in the Educational Experiences of Undocumented Chicana College Students." *Educational Foundations* 24, nos. 1–2 (2010): 77–96.

Pérez Huber, Lindsay, Corina Benavides Lopez, Maria C. Malagon, Veronica Velez, and Daniel G. Solorzano. "Getting beyond the 'Symptom,' Acknowledging the 'Disease': Theorizing Racist Nativism." *Contemporary Justice Review* 11, no. 1 (2008): 39–51.

Price, Margaret. Review of *Educating Moral People: A Caring Alternative to Character Education*, by Nel Noddings. *Christian Higher Education* 4, no. 1 (2005): 71–73.

Prieto, Linda. "Conciencia con compromiso: Maestra perspectives on teaching in bilingual education classrooms." PhD diss., University of Texas at Austin, 2009.

Qvortrup, Jens, William A. Corsaro, and Michael-Sebastian Honig. "Why Social Studies of Childhood? An Introduction to the Handbook." In *The Palgrave Handbook of Childhood Studies*, 1–18. London: Palgrave Macmillan, 2009.

Ramakrishnan, S. Karthick, and Irene Bloemraad, eds. *Civic Hopes and Political Realities: Immigrants, Community Organizations, and Political Engagement*. New York: Russell Sage Foundation, 2008.

Ramírez Sánchez, Martha A. "'Helping at Home': The Concept of Childhood and Work among the Nahuas of Tlaxcala, México." In *Working to Be Someone: Child Focused Research and Practice with Working Children*, edited by Beatrice Hungerland, Manfred Liebel, Brian Milne, and Anne Wihstutz, 87–95. London: Jessica Kingsley, 2007.

Revell, Lynn. "Religious Education, Conflict and Diversity: An Exploration of Young Children's Perceptions of Islam." *Educational Studies* 36, no. 2 (2010): 207–15.

Revell, Lynn, and James Arthur. "Character Education in Schools and the Education of Teachers." *Journal of Moral Education* 36, no. 1 (2007): 79–92.

Rios, Victor M. *Punished: Policing the Lives of Black and Latino Boys*. New York: New York University Press, 2011.

Robinson-Lee, Wanda. "A Framework for Understanding Character Education in Middle Schools." PhD diss., Walden University, 2008.

Rocco, Raymond A. *Transforming Citizenship: Democracy, Membership, and Belonging in Latino Communities*. East Lansing: Michigan State University Press, 2014.

———. "Transforming Citizenship: Membership, Strategies of Containment, and the Public Sphere in Latino Communities." *Latino Studies* 2, no. 1 (2004): 4–25.

Roche, Jeremy. "Children: Rights, Participation and Citizenship." *Childhood* 6, no. 4 (1999): 475–93.

Rodriguez, Cassaundra. "Experiencing 'Illegality' as a Family? Immigration Enforcement, Social Policies, and Discourses Targeting Mexican Mixed-Status Families." *Sociology Compass* 10, no. 8 (2016): 706–17.
Romero, Mary. *Living Together, Living Apart: Mixed Status Families and US Immigration Policy*. Seattle: University of Washington Press, 2015.
Rosaldo, Renato. "Cultural Citizenship and Educational Democracy." *Cultural Anthropology* 9, no. 3 (1994): 402–11.
Rowe, Don. "Taking Responsibility: School Behaviour Policies in England, Moral Development and Implications for Citizenship Education." *Journal of Moral Education* 35, no. 4 (2006): 519–31.
Rubio-Hernandez, Sandy P., and Cecilia Ayón. "'Pobrecitos los niños': The Emotional Impact of Anti-Immigration Policies on Latino Children." *Children and Youth Services Review* 60 (2016): 20–26.
Ruck, Martin D., Rona Abramovitch, and Daniel P. Keating. "Children's and Adolescents' Understanding of Rights: Balancing Nurturance and Self-Determination." *Child Development* 69, no. 2 (1998): 404–17.
Ruck, Martin D., and Stacey S. Horn. "Charting the Landscape of Children's Rights." *Journal of Social Issues* 64, no. 4 (2008): 685–99.
———. *Young People's Perspectives on the Rights of the Child: Implications for Theory, Research and Practice*. Hoboken: Wiley-Blackwell, 2008.
Ruck, Martin D., Daniel P. Keating, Rona Abramovitch, and Christopher J. Koegl. "The Development of Children's Knowledge about Rights: Some Evidence for How Young People View Rights in Their Own Lives." *Journal of Adolescence* 21, no. 3 (1998): 275–89.
Ruck, Martin D., Michele Peterson-Badali, and Charles C. Helwig. "Children's Perspectives on Nurturance and Self-Determination Rights: Implications for Development and Well-Being." In *Handbook of Child Well-Being: Theories, Methods and Policies in Global Perspective*, edited by Asher Ben-Arieh, Ferran Casas, Ivar Frones, and Jill E. Korbin, 2537–59. New York: Springer, 2014.
Sampaio, Anna. *Terrorizing Latina/o Immigrants: Race, Gender, and Immigration Politics in the Age of Security*. Philadelphia: Temple University Press, 2015.
Sandoval, Chela. *Methodology of the Oppressed*. Minneapolis: University of Minnesota Press, 2013.
Sassen, Saskia. "Incompleteness and the Possibility of Making: Towards Denationalized Citizenship?" *Cultural Dynamics* 21, no. 3 (2009): 227–54.
Schiller, Nina Glick, Linda Basch, and Cristina Szanton Blanc. "Transnationalism: A New Analytic Framework for Understanding Migration." *Annals of the New York Academy of Sciences* 645, no. 1 (1992): 1–24.
Schink, Werner, and David Hayes-Bautista. "Latino Gross Domestic Product (GDP) Report: Quantifying the Impact of American Hispanic Economic Growth." Latino Futures Research, June 2017. http://accf.org.
Schmidt Camacho, Alicia. *Migrant Imaginaries: Latino Cultural Politics in the US-México Borderlands*. New York: New York University Press, 2008.

Sherrod, Lonnie R. "Adolescents' Perceptions of Rights as Reflected in Their Views of Citizenship." *Journal of Social Issues* 64, no. 4 (2008): 771–90.

Sherrod, Lonnie R., Constance A. Flanagan, and James Youniss. "Dimensions of Citizenship and Opportunities for Youth Development: The What, Why, When, Where, and Who of Citizenship Development." *Applied Developmental Science* 6, no. 4 (2002): 264–72.

Sherrod, Lonnie R., Judith Torney-Purta, and Constance A. Flanagan, eds. *Handbook of Research on Civic Engagement in Youth*. New York: Wiley, 2010.

Skiba, Russell J., Robert H. Horner, Choong-Geun Chung, M. Karega Rausch, Seth L. May, and Tary Tobin. "Race Is Not Neutral: A National Investigation of African American and Latino Disproportionality in School Discipline." *School Psychology Review* 40, no. 1 (2011): 85–107.

Skiba, Russell J., Robert S. Michael, Abra Carroll Nardo, and Reece L. Peterson. "The Color of Discipline: Sources of Racial and Gender Disproportionality in School Punishment." *Urban Review* 34, no. 4 (2002): 317–42.

Smith, Anne. "Children and Young People's Participation Rights in Education." *International Journal of Children's Rights* 15, no. 1 (2007): 147–64.

Smith, Noel, Ruth Lister, Sue Middleton, and Lynne Cox. "Young People as Real Citizens: Towards an Inclusionary Understanding of Citizenship." *Journal of Youth Studies* 8, no. 4 (2005): 425–43.

Solís, Jocelyn. "Re-thinking Illegality as a Violence against, Not by Mexican Immigrants, Children, and Youth." *Journal of Social Issues* 59, no. 1 (2003): 15–31.

Solís, Jocelyn, Jesica Siham Fernández, and Lucia Alcalá. "Mexican Immigrant Children and Youth's Contributions to a Community Centro: Exploring Civic Engagement and Citizen Constructions." In *Youth Engagement: The Civic-Political Lives of Children and Youth*, edited by Sandi Kawecka Nenga and Jessica K. Taft, 177–200. Bingley: Emerald Group. https://doi.org/10.1108/S1537-4661(2013)0000016012.

Squire, Vicki, ed. *The Contested Politics of Mobility: Borderzones and Irregularity*. New York: Routledge, 2010.

Suad Nasir, Na'ilah, and Ben Kirshner. "The Cultural Construction of Moral and Civic Identities." *Applied Developmental Science* 7, no. 3 (2003): 138–47.

Suárez-Orozco, Carola, and Marcelo M. Suárez-Orozco. *Children of Immigration*. Cambridge: Harvard University Press, 2009.

Taft, Jessica K. *The Kids Are in Charge: Activism and Power in Peru's Movement of Working Children*. New York: New York University Press, 2019.

———. *Rebel Girls: Youth Activism and Social Change across the Americas*. New York: New York University Press, 2010.

Taft, Jessica K., and Hava R. Gordon. "Youth Activists, Youth Councils, and Constrained Democracy." *Education, Citizenship and Social Justice* 8, no. 1 (2013): 87–100.

Tajfel, Henry. "Social Identity and Intergroup Behaviour." *Social Sciences Information* 13, no. 2 (1974): 65–93.

Taxin, Amy. "US Launches Bid to Find Citizenship Cheaters." Associated Press, June 11, 2018. https://apnews.com.

Taylor, Paul, Mark Hugo Lopez, Jeffrey S. Passel, and Seth Motel. "Unauthorized Immigrants: Length of Residency, Patterns of Parenthood." Pew Hispanic Center, 2011. http://assets.pewresearch.org.

Terriquez, Veronica, and Hyeyoung Kwon. "Intergenerational Family Relations, Civic Organizations, and the Political Socialization of Second-Generation Immigrant Youth." *Journal of Ethnic and Migration Studies* 41, no. 3 (2015): 425–47.

Theriault, Denis C. "More Than 1,100 Arrested throughout California in Immigration Raids." *San Jose Mercury News*, September 29, 2008. www.mercurynews.com.

Thornberg, Robert. "The Moral Construction of the Good Pupil Embedded in School Rules." *Education, Citizenship and Social Justice* 4, no. 3 (2009): 245–61.

Torres, Vasti, and Marcia B. Baxter Magolda. "Reconstructing Latino Identity: The Influence of Cognitive Development on the Ethnic Identity Process of Latino Students." *Journal of College Student Development* 45, no. 3 (2004): 333–47.

Turner, John C. "Some Current Issues in Research on Social Identity and Self-Categorization Theories." *Social Identity: Context, Commitment, Content* 3, no. 1 (1999): 6–34.

UNICEF. "Convention on the Rights of the Child." 2020. www.unicef.org.

Valdivia, Carolina, and Diana Valdivia. "My Un(DACA)mented Life: Experiences of Undocumented Immigrant Young Adults Growing Up and Resisting through Activism." *Journal of Transborder Studies* 2 (Summer 2014): 1–18.

Van Sluys, Katie. "Trying On and Trying Out: Participatory Action Research as a Tool for Literacy and Identity Work in Middle Grades Classrooms." *American Journal of Community Psychology* 46, nos. 1–2 (2010): 139–51.

Vink, Maarten. "Comparing Citizenship Regimes." In *The Oxford Handbook of Citizenship*, edited by Ayelet Shachar, Rainer Bauböck, Irene Bloemraad, and Maarten Vink. New York: Oxford University Press, 2017.

Warikoo, Natasha, and Irene Bloemraad. "Economic Americanness and Defensive Inclusion: Social Location and Young Citizens' Conceptions of National Identity." *Journal of Ethnic and Migration Studies* 44, no. 5 (2018): 736–53.

Watts, Roderick J., and Constance A. Flanagan. "Pushing the Envelope on Youth Civic Engagement: A Developmental and Liberation Psychology Perspective." *Journal of Community Psychology* 35, no. 6 (2007): 779–92.

Watts, Roderick J., Derek M. Griffith, and Jaleel Abdul-Adil. "Sociopolitical Development as an Antidote for Oppression—Theory and Action." *American Journal of Community Psychology* 27, no. 2 (1999): 255–71.

Watts, Roderick J., and Omar Guessous. "Sociopolitical Development: The Missing Link in Research and Policy on Adolescents." In *Beyond Resistance! Youth Activism and Community Change*, edited by Shawn Ginwright, Pedro Noguera, and Julio Cammarota, 59–80. New York: Routledge Taylor & Francis Group, 2006.

Watts, Roderick J., and Carlos P. Hipolito-Delgado. "Thinking Ourselves to Liberation? Advancing Sociopolitical Action in Critical Consciousness." *Urban Review* 47, no. 5 (2015): 847–67.

Watts, Roderick J., Ben Kirshner, Rashida Govan, and Jesica S. Fernández. "Powerful Youth, Powerful Communities: An International Study of Youth Organizing." Unpublished report, 2018. www.research2action.net.

Watts, Roderick J., Nat Chioke Williams, and Robert J. Jagers. "Sociopolitical Development." *American Journal of Community Psychology* 31, nos. 1–2 (2003): 185–94.

Weissberg, Roger P., Joseph A. Durlak, Celene E. Domitrovich, and Thomas P. Gullotta. "Social and Emotional Learning: Past, Present, and Future." In *Handbook of Social and Emotional Learning: Research and Practice*, edited by Joseph A. Durlak, Celene E. Domitrovich, Roger P. Weissberg, and Thomas P. Gullotta, 3–19. New York: Guilford, 2015.

Westheimer, Joel, and Joseph Kahne. "Educating the 'Good' Citizen: Political Choices and Pedagogical Goals." *PS: Political Science & Politics* 37, no. 2 (2004): 241–47.

———. "What Kind of Citizen? The Politics of Educating for Democracy." *American Educational Research Journal* 41, no. 2 (2004): 237–69.

Wong, Naima T., Marc A. Zimmerman, and Edith A. Parker. "A Typology of Youth Participation and Empowerment for Child and Adolescent Health Promotion." *American Journal of Community Psychology* 46, nos. 1–2 (2010): 100–114.

Yosso, Tara. *Critical Race Counterstories along the Chicana/Chicano Educational Pipeline*. New York: Routledge, 2005.

Young, Iris Marion. *Inclusion and Democracy*. New York: Oxford University Press, 2000.

———. "Polity and Group Difference: A Critique of the Ideal of Universal Citizenship." *Ethics* 99, no. 2 (1989): 250–74.

Yuval-Davis, Nira. "Belonging and the Politics of Belonging." *Patterns of Prejudice* 40, no. 3 (2006): 197–214.

———. "Intersectionality and Feminist Politics." *European Journal of Women's Studies* 13, no. 3 (2006): 193–209.

———. "Some Reflections on the Questions of Citizenship and Anti-Racism." In *Rethinking Anti-Racisms*, edited by Floya Anthiaas and Cathie Lloyd, 52–67. New York: Routledge, 2005.

———. "Women, Citizenship and Difference." *Feminist Review* 57, no. 1 (1997): 4–27.

Zayas, Luis H. *Forgotten Citizens: Deportation, Children, and the Making of American Exiles and Orphans*. New York: Oxford University Press, 2015.

INDEX

active subjectivity, 141–142
adultism: defined as, 24; ideology of, 194n75
ageism, 189n3; analysis by Santiago, 88; Latinx youth subjectivities, 14, 124; and racist nativism, 3, 12–13, 27, 30, 172; student activism, 142; students' heightened fears, 72. *See also* future citizens; racist nativism
Alicia, Juana, 199n19; Oakes Mural, 125–127
alien citizen: Mae Ngai, 195n6; as perpetual foreigner, 31, 36
Andrés, 40; adoption and familial deportation, 41–44; rights, 100

Bell, John, 194n75
belonging: belongingness, 72; Change 4 Good, 61, 63; and citizenship, 29, 48, 67, 107; cultural citizenship, 200n14; enfranchisement, 151–152; exclusionary inclusion, 191n27; gang-affiliated groups, 101–102; hegemonic discourse, 28, 30, 113; as an inalienable right, 161–163; having *papeles*, 33, 36, 54; racist nativism, 39, 111, 166; schooling experiences of Latinx youth, 59; sociopolitical development of Latinx youth, 14, 93, 108, 118–122
birthright citizenship, 34–35, 151, 159
borderlands, 143; Gloria Anzaldúa, 199n34

Celine: belonging and citizenship rights, 38–39, 44, 56; Character Education values, 68–69; Civil Rights Movement, 158; Oakes Mural, 125–126; self-determination rights, 89–90; social identity development, 116, 118; voting rights, 152, 155
Change 4 Good: author's relationship to program, 21, 23; background of program, 1–2, 16; community organizing, 99–100, 104; demographics of Latinx youth participants, 187; discussions of citizenship, 31, 50, 56; discussions of Oakes Mural for community solidarity, 63–64, 99, 148; discussions of rights, 83, 89, 94, 149, 152, 155; emotional work, 130–131; fears of deportation, 38–40, 43; framework of youth empowerment, 19, 103; representing "The Pink Slips Story," 138–139; school elections, 140; sociopolitical citizenship, 173–175; students disciplining and reprimanding classmates, 72–73; students in trouble at school, 75–76; United Nations Convention on the Rights of the Child (UN-CRC), 80; youth-led action projects, 20, 173. *See also* Youth Participatory Action Research (YPAR)
Character Counts!, 41, 66
Character Education, 58; Celine, 68–70; Diego, 69–71; as hidden curriculum, 66–68, 77–78, 105, 179; Lina, 68–70
Child Protective Services (CPS), 42
childhood: in relation to adulthood, 2, 46, 55, 100, 192n41; Western Eurocentric frameworks of, 10, 24–25
Citizenship Education, 66

civic engagement, 14, 19, 60, 67, 172, 178; critical literacy as, 22; as collective action, 112, 115; as political engagement, 136, 150; civic duty as, 151; voting, 152

critical consciousness: belonging as an inalienable right, 161–162; defined as, 122–123; as foundation for sociopolitical citizenship, 112–113; Feliz, 134–135; as one of four domains, 15, 27, 90, 108, 115, 145–146, 171–172, 181; Lina, 144; Oakes Mural, 126–127, 139; and political engagement, 141–142; capacity for socioemotional awareness, 129–130, 133, 136; sociopolitical consciousness, 125, 128–129, 142–144; Roderick J. Watts, 13; Yesenia, 166

critical literacy: critical consciousness, 122, 125; development of, 59–61, 78, 87, 94, 99, 115; hidden curriculum, 69, 105; Lina, 92; mixed-status families, 113; Oakes Mural, 103; silence and marginality, 62, 66–67; sociopolitical development theory, 112

Cruz, Sophie, 98, 171–172

cultural citizenship: defined as, 162; Renato Rosaldo, 200n14

Daniela: citizenship in relation to socially acceptable behaviors, 70–71; emotional work, 131–132; Oakes Mural, 134; political engagement, 103, 164–165; rights, histories of struggle, and activism, 94–97; social identity development, 116

David: belonging and citizenship rights, 43–45; social identity development, 116

decolonial, 11, 128; feminisms, 141

Deferred Action for Childhood Arrivals (DACA), 48–49, 161

de-ideologization, 125, 128

deportability, 39–40, 42–43; Nicholas De Genova, 48, 144, 190n6

Diego: belonging and citizenship rights, 38–39, 44; Character Education, 69–71;

collective action, 114–115; critique of schooling structures, 60–62, 75, 77–78, 100; human rights, 168; immigrant workers' rights, 100; political engagement, 136; self-determination rights, 168; social identity development, 116, 118–119; voting rights, 150, 155–156

differential incorporation, 191n27

dissenting citizenship, 162; Sunaina Maira, 200n16

Estrada, Emir, 9

Feliz: analysis of ageism, 64; belonging and citizenship rights, 31, 38–39, 151–153, 157–159; critical consciousness 123–124, 134–135; critique of schooling structures, 77; discrimination against, 124, 166–167; importance of protesting, 103–104; Oakes Mural, 126, 134; *papeles*, 34–37, 53; silence and marginality, 62–64, 66–67; social identity development, 116, 118–119; socioemotional awareness, 133–134

flexible citizenship, 162; Aihwa Ong, 201n17

future citizens: as "good" students, 65, 67, 72; as noncitizens, 9–10, 12, 29; potential contributions to society, 12, 55, 74

hegemonic discourses: constructions of citizenship, 12–13, 28, 30; critical consciousness, 15, 125; de-ideologization, 128; reproducing deficit perspectives, 10, 24, 31–32, 72, 113, 173; hidden curriculum, 57, 65, 105; neoliberalism and, 86, 144; nurturance rights, 110; racist nativism, 3, 5, 7, 12–13, 27, 38, 177–178; resistance by Latinx youth, 14, 87, 142, 174–175, 181; self-determination rights, 165; status quo, 160. *See also* ageism; racist nativism

hegemony, 24, 57–58; defined as, 190n7; hidden curriculum and, 62, 67, 69; normalization of, 128; resistance to, 145 hidden curriculum, 61–62, 65; ageism, 64; Character Education, 66–69, 77–78, 105, 179; Regina D. Langhout and Cecily A. Mitchell, 58; as mechanism of hegemony, 57, 105; racist nativism, 64; Latinx youth subjectivities, 59–62; Latinx youth in trouble at school, 73–75

identification: with groups, 118; social, 120–121
immigrant status: access to education and jobs, 152, 160; discussions about citizenship with students, 31–32, 52; and notions of legality, 37, 190n2; parents and families of students, 2, 36, 38, 160; students' assumptions about each other, 44; voting rights, 151, 157
Immigration and Customs Enforcement (ICE), 4–5, 39, 42, 98, 178
inclusion, 8, 11, 22, 57, 67, 150, 170; activists, 96; conditional, 72; exclusionary, 7; Lina, 144; Sunaina Maira, 200n16; Oakes Mural, 139; Raymond Rocco, 191n27
intersections/intersectionality: critical consciousness, 122; Latinx youth, 3, 23, 112, 118; Kimberlé Crenshaw, 193n46; youth-centered framework, 12–13, 15, 28
Iris, 31, 44, 77; education as a right, 83–84; emotional work, 131; hidden curriculum, 61–62; rights, histories of struggle, and activism, 94–97; social identity development, 116, 118–119

Jackie: belonging and citizenship rights, 83–84, 155, 158, 160–162; perspective on education and learning, 77–78; immigrant workers' rights, 100; Oakes Mural, 126; social identity development, 116
Joaquín: belonging and citizenship rights, 43–45; emotional work, 130–132; importance of protesting, 104; mixed-status family, 149; *papeles*, 46–48, 52; political engagement, 136; rights, 148–149; self-determination rights, 89–90; social identity development, 116, 118–119; sociopolitical citizenship, 174; in trouble at school, 73–75; voting rights, 150, 156
ju soli citizens, 35, 38

Latinidad, 3; Felix Padilla, 191n12
Latinx: demographics of youth participants, 187; discussions with youth, 80, 87–88; overview of term, 189n1; racist nativism against, 3, 5, 7, 12–13, 27, 38, 177–178; recommendations for support, 28, 176; as second-class citizens, 74, 170, 179; sociocultural constructions of youth citizenship, 8, 113, 154, 173; sociopolitical development of youth, 14, 93, 108, 118–121; youth agency, 15, 28, 106, 112, 124, 136, 140; youth subjectivities, 39, 105, 111, 122, 124, 175
legal permanent resident (LPR), 35–36; deportation, 38; *papeles*, 37
legality: belonging and citizenship rights, 43–45, 50–52, 151; construction of, 23, 26; migrant "illegality," 190n6; *papeles*, 34–36, 46–48, 54; "tolerated illegality," 7, 191n28; voting rights, 153, 155, 158
Levine, Peter, 74. *See also* future citizens
Lina: analysis of ageism, 64, 147; Character Education values, 68–69; critical consciousness, 123, 142–144; critique of schooling structures, 62–63, 91–93, 101–102, 127, 137–138; gang-affiliated groups, 102; meaning of citizenship, 31; mixed-status family, 1–2, 53; Oakes Mural, 125–126; rights, 85–87, 148–149; school elections, 140; social identity development, 116, 118; in trouble at school, 91–92; socioemotional awareness, 144; voting rights, 153, 155, 158

Lucia: critique of schooling structures, 60–62; emotional work, 131–133; human rights, 165–166; right to freedom of speech, 164; school elections, 140; social identity development, 116, 118; voting rights, 153

Marshall, T. H., 29, 33, 55
mixed-status family/families, 4, 18–19, 23; defined as, 38, 189n2; Joaquín, 149; Lina, 1–2, 144, 149; sociocultural constructions of Latinx youth citizenship, 8, 113, 154, 173; stigmas, 122, 144; Luis H. Zayas, 40, 42–43

naturalization: author's positionality, 23; denaturalization, 128; legal permanent residence (LPR), 35, 159; Trump administration, 35–36
naturalized citizenship, 19, 33, 179; author's positionality, 23; Joaquín, 47; *papeles*, 34–36; Trump administration, 38; voting rights, 152; Yesenia, 50–51
neoliberalism, 86, 104, 197n6
nurturance rights: discussions with Latinx youth, 80, 87–88; self-determination rights and, 10, 26, 79–80, 83–84, 159

Oakes Mural, 125–127, 138–139, 178; Juana Alicia, 199n19
oppositional consciousness, 72

perpetual foreigners, 3, 7; alien citizens, 31; Raymond Rocco, 3, 191n13, 191n27; Iris Young, 191n13. *See also* belonging
"The Pink Slips Story," 138
pluralism, 33, 145
political engagement: agency, 141; Aída Hurtado, 120; Change 4 Good, 137, 174; collective action, 139; community experience, 98; enfranchisement, 136, 151–152; as one of four domains, 15, 27, 90, 108, 115, 145–146, 171–172, 181; youth leadership, 140; Oakes Mural, 139, 178; "The Pink Slips Story," 138–139; rights, 173; sociopolitical citizenship, 137, 140–141, 162, 165
present citizens, as a difference-centered approach, 10. *See also* future citizens
problematization, 128
punishment, 57, 60–61, 65, 120, 130, 139; Victor Rios, 92

racism, 6, 15, 30, 96–97, 124; institutionalized racism, 58
racist nativism: against Latinx communities, 3, 5, 7, 12–13, 27, 38, 177–178; Latinx youth subjectivities, 14, 39, 111, 173, 175; Lindsay Pérez Huber, 189n4; and President Trump, 49; Secure Communities and US government programs, 4, 36, 144, 172; student activism, 98, 142; students' heightened fears, 2, 72. *See also* ageism
rights. *See* nurturance rights; self-determination rights

Santiago: analysis of ageism, 88–89; critique of schooling and discipline, 59–60; emotional work, 130–131; social identity development, 116, 118; students disciplining and reprimanding classmates, 72–73; voting rights, 155–156
schooling: culture of discipline and punishment, 92; hidden curriculum, 57, 62, 65–66, 76–78; ageism, 64; as site of racist nativism, 64; Latinx youth as second-class citizens, 74, 170, 173, 179
Secure Communities, 4, 23
self-categorization, 120–121
self-determination rights: and critique of school structures, 93; nurturance rights and, 10, 26, 79–80, 83–84, 88, 159; as positive youth development, 82; social identities, 165; youth agency, 87, 89–90, 92, 100, 180

social comparison, 120–121
social identities: belonging as an inalienable right, 161–162; critical consciousness, 127; as one of four domains, 15, 27, 90, 108, 115, 145–146, 171–172, 181; Oakes Mural, 139; positionalities and most salient experiences, 117–120, 139, 142, 144; self-determination rights, 165; social comparison, 121; stigma, 121–122
socioemotional awareness: belonging as an inalienable right, 161–162; and critical consciousness, 129–133, 136, 141; Felix, 134–135; as one of four domains, 15, 27, 90, 108, 115, 145–146, 171–172, 181; Lina, 144; Oakes Mural, 139; sociopolitical development theory, 112–113
sociohistorical: analysis, 12, 15, 112, 128, 144, 155; defined as, 192n45
sociolegal: constructions of citizenship, 26, 36, 47, 80, 154; defined as, 194n73; and discussions about rights, 155, 159–160, 163, 168; and visa, 48
sociopolitical citizenship: challenging the limitations of US-based constructions, 9, 107, 114, 170, 181; Change 4 Good, 173–175; collective action, 115; critical consciousness, 125, 128–129, 142–144; and cultural citizenship, 162; defined as, 162; as youth resistance, 28, 111, 113, 141, 146–147, 161, 164; Latinx youth agency, 15, 28, 106, 108, 112, 124, 136, 140; Latinx youth subjectivities, 14–15, 105, 122; Oakes Mural, 139, 178; and pluralism, 145; present citizen framework, 10; youth rights, 104, 142–143, 165, 168, 171–172. *See also* cultural citizenship; socioemotional awareness
sociopolitical development: embodiments of citizenship, 12–14, 25–27, 72, 82; recommendations for how to support Latinx youth, 28, 176; reconceptualizing rights, 87, 95, 104, 106, 146; theory of, 112, 129, 142
solidarity, 63–64; collective action, 164; Oakes Mural, 127, 138; and political engagement, 98; United Nations Convention on the Rights of the Child (UN-CRC), 81
status quo: citizenship and, 23, 55, 77, 181; conforming to, 12–13, 57–58, 65; defined as, 192n44; discourses that uphold, 144, 149, 160, 165, 169; limitations faced by Latinx youth, 171, 175, 178; norms of schooling, 78, 122, 128, 141

temporary protected status (TPS), 7, 38
tolerated "illegality," 7; Genevieve Negrón-Gonzales, 191n28; Suzanne Oboler, 191n28
transmigrant, 2; defined as, 190n4
Treaty of Guadalupe Hidalgo, 6

United Nations Convention on the Rights of the Child (UN-CRC), 10, 26, 79–81, 83, 180, 192n41
UNICEF, 192n41

Yesenia: belonging and citizenship rights, 43–44, 50–52, 151; critique of schooling structures, 60–62, 75, 77–78, 101–102; gang-affiliated groups, 101–102; human rights, 165–166; Oakes Mural, 126; *papeles*, 46–48, 52; political engagement, 140; school elections, 140; self-determination rights, 89–90; social identity development, 116–120; understanding of civil rights history, 94
Youth Participatory Action Research (YPAR), 1, 19, 21–22, 24; students' engagement in, 174

ABOUT THE AUTHOR

JESICA SIHAM FERNÁNDEZ is Assistant Professor in the Ethnic Studies Department at Santa Clara University. Trained as a social-community psychologist, Fernández completed her PhD in social psychology with an emphasis in Latin American and Latino studies from the University of California, Santa Cruz. Her scholarship as a community-engaged researcher is grounded in a decolonial feminist praxis. Through a community-based participatory action research (PAR) paradigm, as well as LatCrit theory and methodologies, such as *testimonio*, Fernández engages with communities to identify social problems affecting their lives, determine actions to address them, and facilitate structural social change. Specifically, she collaborates with youth in education settings and community organizing spaces, as well as with Latinx immigrant families in the Greater Silicon Valley, to cultivate sociopolitical well-being and community thriving grounded in transformative justice and liberation. Together, these experiences form the foundation for her research on embodiments of citizenship, including sociopolitical development, youth activism, and community organizing. Her pedagogy is also interconnected with her activist-scholarship, which aims to challenge the coloniality of power in theory, knowledge, and practice.

www.ingramcontent.com/pod-product-compliance
Lightning Source LLC
Chambersburg PA
CBHW020405080526
44584CB00014B/1186